Alcohol Problems and Social Control

Earl Rubington
Northeastern University

Charles E. Merrill Publishing Company
A Bell & Howell Company
Columbus, Ohio

Merrill Social Problems Series

Under the editorship of

Edwin M. Lemert

University of California at Davis

Published by
Charles E. Merrill Publishing Co.
A Bell & Howell Company
Columbus, Ohio 43216

ISBN: 0-675-09046-6

Library of Congress Catalog Card Number: 72-86515

1 2 3 4 5 6 7 8 9 — 81 80 79 78 77 76 75 74 73

Printed in the United States of America

Preface

The use of alcoholic beverages is practically universal. It is hard to find a society that does not produce, distribute, and consume alcoholic beverages, although there probably are some. But what is truly universal is the fact that wherever alcoholic beverages exist, societies always regulate their use. No society leaves alcohol to chance. The particular forms that these regulations take vary with society and culture. Thus, if one society deems alcohol a sacred object, another sees it as a food. If a third society sees it as a facilitator of social intercourse, still a fourth views it as a tranquilizer. Where alcohol exists, its use is therefore regulated. And, if use follows regulations, so also do alcohol problems.

Drinking culture, a special collection of beliefs, values, and norms on the act of drinking, prescribes who will drink what, where, when, under what social conditions, in what containers, with what companions, according to what ritual, and for what kinds of social and individual effects. Societies regulate drinking because of the observed consequences of drinking situations. Drinking situations permit temporary release from social bonds. Whether or not there has been heavy intake, drinking situations reduce constraint and inhibition. Wherever constraints are relaxed, conduct becomes doubtful. For instance, the air of expectancy that surrounds a party of any kind may be rightfully attributed to the fact that one does not know exactly who will be there, what will happen, and whether or not a good time will be had at all. Given these volatile social conditions, the addition of alcohol is certain to compound anxiety as well as expectancy. Mild interpersonal disorder can, in time, spill over and become maximal social disorder. Given the threat along with the history of past actualities, societies make and enforce rules on drinking behavior.

Society, through the workings of its members, sets drinking norms. And, since practices rarely conform exactly with precepts, society, again through the workings of its members, sanctions those who violate the drinking norms. Making rules and enforcing them become then two sides of social control. If the rules are unclear, inconsistent, or in conflict with other rules, the chances of a social problem coming into being increase. Similarly, if the sanctions are unclear, inconsistent, or in conflict, the existence of a social problem is practically guaranteed.

The history of the use of alcoholic beverages in the United States suggests that conflicting norms together with erratic sanctions produced many if not most of our current alcohol problems. The effects of Prohibition alone supply ample evidence for this judgment. And because of the manner in which the issues of social control were joined, the social problems of alcohol are likely to be with us for some time to come. We can look forward to the resurrection of some old solutions, e.g., the return to prohibition, along with the suggestion of some new ones, e.g., courses in social drinking as part of the elementary school curriculum.

Besides the *social problems* of alcohol, there are also *sociological problems.* While they overlap in some instances, in others they may diverge considerably. The social problems of alcohol pertain to those drinking situations and their consequences which a significant number of people in society define as either threatening or troublesome and which they seek to alter in ways more conducive to the values they hold dear. Teen-age drinking, bootlegging, after-hours bottle clubs, drunken driving, and alcoholism in industry, to name but a few, may well be serious social problems without posing any problems at all for sociology as a scientific discipline. That is, the knowledge on how to solve or ameliorate all of these problems presently exists. Applications of this knowledge, in addition, do not wait upon the development of a new and as yet untried social technology.

When the social and sociological problems of alcohol overlap, as they sometimes do, then it is because some events that take place in connection with the act of drinking are also relevant for a particular sociological theory. A theory consists of an interrelated set of ideas or concepts from which it is possible to deduce a battery of propositions which are helpful in explaining events taking place in the real world. For instance, Robert Bales has formulated a tension-outlet theory which seems well suited to explaining why alcoholism is relatively rare among Jews and is relatively more frequent with the Irish. Utilitarian attitudes towards drinking, coupled with absence of other outlets for the relief of tension, accounts for the high rates of Irish alcoholism. According to Bales, while there is high rather than low consumption of alcohol among Jews, their drinking occurs more often in a sacred context which thereby insulates a person from experiencing alcohol effects as an isolated individual while guaranteeing that these effects are always experienced as part of a social and moral collectivity.[1] Bales' theory has the merit of dealing with the very serious social problem of alcoholism and of advancing a cogent explanation for cultural differences in rates of alcoholism.

Most of the chapters in this book deal with the public drunkenness offender. As such, they are relevant to contemporary sociological theories of deviance and control. While there are no rigorous tests of any specific proposition, taken together they constitute verification, albeit partial, of some postulates of Lemert's theory on deviant behavior.[2] These postulates are as follows:

1. There are modalities in human behavior and clusters of deviation from these modalities which can be identified and described for situations specified in time and space.
2. Behavioral deviations are a function of culture conflict expressed through social organization.
3. There are societal reactions to deviations ranging from strong approval through indifference to strong disapproval.
4. Sociopathic behavior is deviation which is effectively disapproved.
5. The deviant person is one whose role, status, function, and self-definition are importantly shaped by how much deviation he engages in, by the degree of its social visibility, by the particular exposure he has to the societal reaction and by the nature and strength of the societal reaction.
6. There are patterns of restriction and freedom in the social participation of deviants which are related directly to their status, role, and self-definitions. The biological strictures upon social participation of deviants are directly significant in comparatively few cases.
7. Deviants are individuated with respect to their vulnerability to the societal reaction because: (a) the person is a dynamic agent, (b) there is a structuring to each

---

1. Robert F. Bales, "Cultural Differences in Rates of Alcoholism," *Quarterly Journal of Studies on Alcohol* 6 (March 1946): 480-99.

2. Edwin M. Lemert, *Social Pathology* (New York: McGraw-Hill, 1951), pp. 22-23.

personality which acts as a set of limits within which the societal reaction operates.

While drunkenness is conventionally accepted as a social sign of alcoholism, many nonalcoholics do get drunk while a surprisingly large number of alcoholics do not get drunk. The frequency of drunkenness among the nonalcoholic and alcoholic alike is of little social consequence if it is not apparent. If, however, the act occurs in public and repeatedly, it is a visible violation of social and legal norms. Public drunkenness is not only a violation of municipal ordinances, it is also simultaneously the most frequent crime and the most frequently repeated crime in the streets. And there seems little doubt that chronic alcoholics are a significant minority in the public drunkenness statistics. For instance, in Portland, Oregon, in 1963 ". . . there were 11,000 law violations involving drunkenness or the effects of drinking, but only around 2,000 different persons accounted for these arrests."[3]

While conservative estimates of alcoholism in the United States place the number at around five and a half million, it seems that very few of that number commit the crime of public drunkenness. Consequently, an analysis of that minority who expose themselves to official sanctions frequently seems important if we are to assess the consequences of visibility, exposure, and severe societal reactions upon the role, status, function, and self-definition of the public drunkenness offender. For, in addition to illuminating propositions on the social response theory of deviant behavior, such study may also shed additional light on how the social problems of alcohol appear under conditions of low visibility, minimal exposure, and relatively mild societal reactions.

The chapters in this volume are organized around a simple, natural history framework. Part One is called "The Definition of the Problem." The first chapter sets forth the necessary conditions for considering alcohol use as problematic, the second documents how social movements arising to curtail a problem succeed more often in exaggerating it, while the third suggests that certain patterns of teaching norms lead more often to violation rather than to conformity.

In Part Two on "The Deviant Career," chapter four charts how societal reactions channel the vast number of alcoholics

3. David J. Pittman, ed. *Alcoholism* (New York: Harper & Row, 1967), p. 115.

into a career in secret deviance, chapter five suggests the conditions under which drunkenness offenders elect a particular criminal life style, while chapter six suggests that sifting and sorting devices which affect the deviant role and self-definition continue to occur in confinement.

In Part Three, "The Street," chapter seven describes the rules that are supposed to govern drinking on the street together with the conditions under which these rules are most apt to be broken. Chapter eight shows how changes in the larger society affect both public drunkenness offenders and those persons charged with either controlling or changing their behavior. Chapter nine briefly lists how changes in social definition from criminal to sick affect the responses of control agents.

In Part Four, "Personal Change," chapter ten calls attention to the fact that a new organization, such as the halfway house, can convert relapses to its own and its clients' advantage. Chapter eleven is a study of one alcoholic's relapse after a long sober career in and around a halfway house while chapter twelve documents some problems people have when they try to help alcoholics change.

Finally, in Part Five, "Organizational Change," chapter thirteen describes how halfway houses came into being as a new means of changing alcoholics while chapter fourteen lists some new ways for dealing with alcoholics in older health agencies such as hospitals and tuberculosis sanataria.

Contents

Part One

the Definition of the Problem

Chapter I

Survey of Alcohol Problems

In Webster's dictionary, one group of people see a problem as the basis for disputation or academic discussion. Some of them are described as historians. Yet another group of people see a problem as a difficulty to be settled. Webster does not say but clearly implies that men of affairs are in this second group.

A way to test the validity of a definition is to treat it simply as a recipe for social action. Webster, for instance, further implies that the way to create a problem which will neither get defined nor settled is to have these two groups come together. Dressing up Webster in contemporary language, the historians become "professionals"; the men of affairs, the "laymen." Frequently, these groups meet and lines are drawn between the "good guys" and the "bad guys." Meeting originally to define and settle a problem, they end in conflict among themselves.

There are times and places in which to think and dispute, just as there are times to form plans and take action. If it is clear that a school is a place for thinking and dispute according to stated rules, there need not be the confusion and conflict which Webster implies. A school of alcohol studies, for example, defines the problems of alcohol on the basis of study, theory, and research. Its students, on the other hand, take time off from everyday life to learn these findings, to digest and assimilate them, and to examine in their own mind their implications for the world of everyday life. The student role may be a little unfamiliar to them. But if they can shed their man-of-affairs stance during the school, they may suspend judgment until they have sorted out all the facts, values, and theories which they will hear, and even debate themselves. In school, then, there are neither "good guys" nor "bad guys," but only issues which need sharpening.

These issues can first be sharpened by the participants' assuming the student role and taking a new attitude toward the word "problem." A problem is not a troublesome difficulty to be gotten rid of as soon as possible. It is rather a challenge to the understanding. A problem becomes a piece in a puzzle which is itself part of a larger puzzle, with lots of questions attached, such as, why is this a puzzle in the first place, where does this piece go, and how do all the pieces fit together in the end. Getting correct names for the pieces, seeing their relation to each other, and knowing why the whole thing is a puzzle in the first place frequently help one solve this and other puzzles. Once a solution happens, the old cliche is proved that nothing is so practical as a good theory.

The issues here are simple. The task is to raise the questions, define them as simply as possible, and to suggest their interrelationships. The questions are (1) what is an alcohol problem, (2) what are the elements in alcohol problems, (3) what is the larger pattern in which alcohol problems fit as elements, and (4) what may be areas in which some solutions will be found to some of these problems.

Definition of Alcohol Problems

The main problem is what is the action of alcohol on people in society and what are the consequences of that action. Here we have implied a division of labor between those who find answers to this question and those who will apply the findings to problems of everyday life. While the definition just presented is broad (so broad as to be useless as it now stands), it is of course the definition of thousands, perhaps millions, of people. The trouble is that they do not stop with the definition, but rather go on to adduce or invent facts and interpret them in accordance with their preconceived solution.

Such people are not really concerned with understanding a problem so much as with applying their solution.[1] Such persons were and are the Drys who have defined the action of alcohol on people in society and its consequences as harmful, dangerous, and destructive. Their simple definition of a solution has made and probably continues to make it difficult to appreciate the complexity of alcohol problems. We may define a closed mind here as one which has a ready answer to a poorly-defined problem which does not exist. The difficulty, of course, is that social beliefs frequently become social realities. Closed minds, if they state their answer often enough, can send some open minds out to apply the solution. If the solution is applied diligently enough, the problem will finally be created.

The broad definition suffices for a beginning. But it immediately raises such questions as what is the action of alcohol, who are people, what is a society, and what are the consequences of alcohol. Each of these, in turn, raises its own questions for study. It is clear now that a formulation which defines the subject as *the problem of alcohol* is incorrect, narrow, and one-sided. Similarly, another formulation which reduces the subject to *the problem of alcoholism* is equally narrow, incorrect, and one-sided. This broad beginning is just a beginning, not an end. The next step, therefore, is to look at the elements of alcohol problems.

the Elements of Alcohol Problems

The elements of alcohol problems may be considered under four headings: (1) use, (2) individual effects, (3) social effects, and (4) controls. Each of these elements, in turn, suggests a number of sub-problems with their own definition. Each, in turn, is interdependent with all the other elements in the main alcohol problems. When, in time, all the sub-problems have been more sharply defined and solutions suggested, and when the problem of the interrelationships of the elements of all the alcohol problems has been more sharply defined, maybe all alcohol problems will be solved. This is rather unlikely, however, since scientific methods solve certain problems only to generate others.

1. *Use.* "Alcohol thus appears not as an original source of a problem but rather as a means for solving it and as a means out of which more and more problems arise."[2] This statement immediately raises the question of why alcohol exists in the first place and why men bother to

use it. The answer to the question will not be found in alcohol but rather in the relations among men in society. These relations generate the conditions for the use of alcohol. A comparison of primitive and complex societies will suggest why men drink.

Social life consists of constraints and bonds. All persons recognize the necessity for constraints if social order is to be at all possible. Similarly, all persons have ties to other people and other groups. At the same time, there still are all the problems of getting and making a living. Constraints and bonds are aspects of social organization while the struggle for existence is an aspect of economic and technical organization. Tensions and anxieties of one kind or another arise in both spheres of life.

Primitive societies have fewer constraints and tighter bonds, perhaps because there are more common interests. Such social anxieties as periodically arise can be abated in communal release rituals which are frequently religious in origin and include drinking and dancing, often to the point of excess. However, primitive societies seem less well equipped to cope with anxieties of technical organization or with such disorders as famines, storms, etc.

Complex societies, on the other hand, have a greater number of constraints with looser bonds among people. There is a greater divergence of interests at the same time that interdependence, particularly in the technical and economic organization, is much greater than with primitive societies. The restrictions upon the individual are almost in direct proportion to the emphasis upon freedom and individualism. As a result, there are more tensions arising from conflict and cooperation which demand relief. Since the world has become secularized, alcohol becomes profaned as an object.

Alcohol is now more abundant than formerly because of improvements in production and preservation. At the same time, a means has become an end. Formerly, the occasion of drinking was in tribal rituals, usually of a religious character, and alcohol's mystic properties symbolized the solidary relations of the tribe with its gods. In the secular society the individual follows his own calendar of release. The original motives for drinking in tribal ritual have now become transformed. Drinking has now become a folkway.

Most drinking in the modern world is for refreshment or prestige purposes. Occasionally, the average user resorts to alcohol for sedation. On the other hand, only a small percentage of users turn regularly to alcohol for relief. As they become intemperate, of course, they create one of the serious problems of alcohol. But all drinking starts with social drinking, and it becomes necessary to explain why alcohol is used in the first place. The second issue, an important though difficult one, is to establish what is moderate drinking (however defined) in the society. Then, and only then, does it make sense to consider the issue of intemperate drinkers.

2. *Individual effects.* The problem of effects on mind, body, and technical efficiency has stimulated most research and study and experimentation. Research continues unabated in this area. One reason for the disciplined search in the areas of physiology is the possibility of discovering how some persons use alcohol in the body in such a way as to launch them on an alcoholic drinking career from the very beginning. Another concern is working out with precision the effects of varying amounts of alcohol on technical performance.

It is clear (by way of an aside) that moderate drinking will not likely be fixed at a specified lower level of alcoholic intake. These standards will be set by customs. There is evidence that the United States over a hundred years has shifted from being a whiskey-drinking country to a beer-drinking country. As the need for precision in social as well as technical performance increases, the country may follow a two-drink norm when hard liquor is served. Whatever the facts turn out to be, their significance rests ultimately on the effects of alcohol on the individual.

Alcohol depresses cortical activity, decreases judgment, and gives some mild surcease from the strains of social life. Given increasing tension and need for more relief, an interesting question is why some people drink more than others, drink to excess, and continue on to become alcoholics. As already suggested, for many people this is *the problem of alcohol.* Considering the serious nature of alcoholism and its consequences (it is the nation's fourth most serious health problem), it is understandable how people might arrive at this incorrect deduction. Nevertheless, considerable research effort and theorizing on the etiology of alcoholism continue. And this is primarily because there is hope that a knowledge of causes will lead some day to workable treatments.

3. *Social effects.* Analysis and discussion of social effects have always taken place more or less in an atmosphere of controversy. Hence the problem of social effects has more often gotten an inconclusive, vague, and disputatious discussion rather than a clear and precise definition. There are, however, four alternate outcomes of alcohol use in society, and each deserves consideration as a problem in its own right. These are positive, negative, neutral, and ambivalent effects.

Alcohol is found in many societies, is used by a majority of them, and is found to be a substance of some value. In the main, its effects have been positive, offering mild relaxing of tensions and facilitating social intercourse. Though its originating motives have, over time, lost their religious sanction, the social sanctions for use are persuasive, though not powerful. On the other hand, like eating and sleeping, drinking alcoholic beverages is a source of well-being, but transitory, and of no lasting importance.

Negative effects occur when some persons seem to turn this system of values on its head. Persons who make this kind of transvaluation ostensibly find alcohol the main source of well-being, seek it out above all else, and make it the pivotal interest in their lives. Fortunately, the sample of pleasure-seeking topers who fit this category is small and perhaps dwindling. It is even possible that such a category never existed. Nevertheless, this is the stereotype of the "drunk," who prefers the bottle to all else. Superimposed upon the alcoholic is the picture of the compulsive drinker who may and very frequently does hate the taste of alcohol, who very frequently hates himself for his drinking and for its effects on himself and others, but who cannot stop drinking no matter how hard he tries. Other people view him and assume that since people generally seek comfort and well-being, he must be a pleasure-seeker of the worst sort. That he may be really avoiding a greater pain by drinking is probably more to the point. It is in the consequences of that mentality as much as in the results of excessive drinking that negative effects are seen most clearly.

There are persons and groups who become high, tight, or drunk in the course of drinking episodes. Sometimes these are sought effects; sometimes they are unintended. An occasional accompaniment of intoxication, mild or acute, is, or course, violence. Unfortunately, many people, like most nations today, still settle disputes by violence. The greater the severity of the violence, however, the more apt the participants are to be intimately involved with one another and in conflict. Frequently, people take a drink to mend their quarrel; but alcohol has a way of making internal conflicts explicit.

Using "neutral" in the sense of zero effects, it is clear that abstinence "neutralizes" alcohol. It is not surprising that the temperance movement, pleading for moderate use or for total abstinence, argues for this kind of neutralization. Moderate use of alcohol as a food, like drinking wine while eating, should also be considered here as neutralization, since there is no effect on social behavior following such use of alcohol.

The ambivalent effects of alcohol follow, in part, from the cultural attitude of ambivalence.[3] Vacillation between hedonic and ascetic attitudes produces ambivalence. If the focus stays on effects on social behavior, then it seems clear that ambivalence comes from a failure to predict how people (or one's self) will act once drinking has begun.

Moods can shift with increased intake. A hail-fellow-well-met one night seeks on the next night to fight everyone in the house. Sebastian Franck, in 1531, made observations on individual reactions to alcoholic intoxication. They reveal why both drinkers and onlookers should feel ambivalent:

> This man sings, that man weeps. One man wants to fight and the other one wishes to count the money he does not even have. One man becomes abusive, the other one meticulously polite. One man boasts and another one belittles himself. One man falls asleep, another one vomits. If these men are not fools, I do not know what a fool is.[4]

REASON 4

4. *Controls.* It is understandable that any object which can produce the variety of pleasant as well as unpleasant effects as does alcohol will be subject to controls—both personal and social. A key problem in the consideration of alcohol is what kinds of controls, upon whom, in what situations, and for what purposes.

Here it may be well to make an important set of distinctions. First, drinking is a custom. Second, drunkenness is a transitory ego-state. Third, alcoholism is a complex social and psychological process. Control measures, past and present, frequently fail to distinguish the three. This same error in control continues and must be reckoned as one of the current and severe alcohol problems.

Controls imposed on drinking have been both self-imposed and put on by others. When imposed by others, such as friends and family, they have been informal. When imposed by social agencies, such as police, courts, and jails, they have been formal. Certain controls have worked on some people but not on others. One crucial problem for students of alcohol problems is working out what kinds of controls will work with whom and under what conditions. It is safe to say at this moment that the controls imposed on teenage drinking by both parents and the law seem to produce the very opposite of what they intend. This, in turn, indicates that alcohol education as a means of gaining control is here either ineffective or actually superfluous.

Formal controls imposed on public drunkenness have been as unpredictable as the effects of large amounts of alcohol. There is little rhyme or reason to who gets arrested for public drunkenness where or when, or to the kinds of sentences passed out. And since, frequently, arrests are made for drunkenness when the suspect is actually sober, it is hard to see how any control is at work here unless these may be called "preventive arrests."

Controls imposed upon alcoholism seem in some areas to be making very real progress. The failure to coordinate treatment and educational controls is an organizational issue of major importance for those who wish to solve a major alcohol problem. Another issue has to do with a lack of facilities and a tendency to call all inebriates alcoholics. If all municipal court judges tomorrow morning sent all persons charged with public drunkenness to treatment centers rather than to jail, they would dramatize both the confusion in definitions and the appalling shortages in alcoholic treatment facilities.

the Pattern of Problems and Solutions

This chapter has tried to define and to list the elements of alcohol problems, and to suggest how some issues may be interrelated in a larger pattern. How some solutions may arise from that pattern becomes its last task.

Alcohol is one fairly workable solution to the problem of gaining some relief from periodic social tensions. As tensions mount, more persons may resort to increased relief drinking. As tensions abate, so may relief drinking. On the other hand, another formulation might be as follows. Though constraints mount in complex society, social bonds may grow tighter rather than looser. As this happens, more groups may begin to define a clear and precise moderate drinking norm, one that removes the ambivalence from drinking. In addition, if these same groups eliminate mildly contemptuous, amused, and half-hearted sanctions against drunkenness, and replace them with consistent and strong social disapproval, then more and more people will use alcoholic beverages moderately with resulting mild but positive effects. Similarly, drunkenness, and possibly alcoholism, will decline. This urbane solution to a major social problem of urban society does not seem too unlikely at this juncture.

Notes

[1] Howard W. Haggard and E. M. Jellinek, *Alcohol Explored* (New York: Doubleday, 1942), p. 27.

[2] E. M. Jellinek, "The Problems of Alcohol," in *Alcohol, Science, and Society* (New Haven, Conn.: Journal of Studies on Alcohol, 1945), p. 27. The discussion here on use relies heavily on Jellinek's seminal paper.

[3] Abraham Myerson, "Alcohol: A Study of Social Ambivalence," *Quarterly Journal of Studies on Alcohol* 1 (June 1940): 13-20.

[4] E. M. Jellinek, "A Document of the Reformation Period on Inebriety: Sebastian Franck's 'On the Horrible Vice of Drunkenness, etc.'" *Quarterly Journal of Studies on Alcohol* 2 (September 1941): 395.

Chapter II

the Nature of Social Problems

Drinking, drunkenness, and alcoholism are contemporary social facts. Some 90 million adults use alcoholic beverages and perhaps 6 million of them are said to be alcoholics. The prevalence of drunkenness among the drinking population for any given year is, of course, unknown. It is known, however, that in 1965 there were 1,535,040 arrests for public drunkenness, and 241,511 arrests for driving under the influence. It is estimated that one-third of all admissions to mental hospitals stem from some variety of problem drinking, that one-third of all crimes (exclusive of the two just cited) involve alcohol use, and that one-third of all persons on public welfare use alcohol excessively.

These statistics would satisfy some groups that drinking, drunkenness, and alcoholism all are social problems. Many groups, hearing these statistics, would be willing to define some of these facts or some of the situations which produced them as true social problems. Few groups would deny that these statistics indicate the existence of some kind of a social problem. Yet none of these groups would really agree on the definition of what a social problem is, in general, nor, in particular, would they agree that drinking, drunkenness, and alcoholism, whether taken separately or together, are social problems.

Reprinted from the *British Journal of Addictions* 64 (May 1969): 31-46 by permission of the publisher.

American society, from its inception to this very moment, has not agreed on *(a)* what is drinking, drunkenness, and alcoholism; *(b)* what kinds of problems, if any, these three phenomena entail; and *(c)* what their solutions might be (granted there was agreement that one or all of them were social problems). Frequently, drinking, drunkenness, and alcoholism arise out of conflict. But, more often, drinking, drunkenness, and alcoholism create conflict. There are, of course, signs of a gradual though grudging consensus on these three issues. But this growth is painful, slow, and not without its own problems. For social change is painful. And its pace is too fast for one minority, too slow for yet another, and usually both for the majority.

These facts limit the purposes of this chapter while supplying it with a strategy. This chapter will not set forth *the* definition of drinking, drunkenness, and alcoholism. Nor will it present *the* taxonomy of alcohol-related social problems. Nor will it offer *the* solution to any or all social problems of alcohol. It remains for students of alcohol studies to give definitions of drinking, drunkenness, and alcoholism, to present taxonomies of alcohol-related problems, and to offer solutions to some of the social problems of alcohol.

What this chapter will do is suggest a sociology of social problems. As such, it will discuss (1) the definition of social problems, their types and social movements which arise in response to them; (2) the temperance movement; (3) the alcoholism movement; and, finally (4) social problems which both movements have begotten.

Some social problems beget social movements. Of these, some go on to solve the original problems while others do not. Of those which solve the original problem, some produce additional, though different social problems. And, of those which fail to solve the original social problems, some of them manage to survive as social movements simply because they feed the problem they seek to resolve. Both the temperance movement and the alcoholism movement supply examples of all these possible relations between social problems and social movements. A detailed examination of these points follows. But first, a definition of social problems.

Social Problems

Social life has order and regularity simply because people have some ideas on how to live and an organization for putting those ideas into practice. This stock of ideas, consisting of beliefs, values, and norms, is their culture. Culture gives them symbols for understanding social life. Social organization consists of patterned actions they take in pursuit of values.

Any discrepancy between culture and social organization may well give rise to a social problem. If, for example, rules do not exist for certain situations or conflict with other rules, the normative breakdown may cause social problems. Or, if rules exist while social organization frustrates the pursuit of or attainment of values, problems may well develop. Situations of the kinds just described are called *social disorganization.*

Social problems may arise when there is conflict within or between cultures. When different groups in the society hold to opposing values, a social problem can arise. These situations are called *value-conflict.*

Finally, if people violate rules in pursuit of values, a social problem may develop. Drunkenness, for instance, is a violation of abstinence rules in some cultures. In others, it is a violation of moderate drinking norms. However, in still other cultures, it stands for the successful pursuit of the high value set on intoxication. Violation of social rules is called *personal deviation.*

All social problems consist of some parts value-conflict, some parts social disorganization, and some parts personal deviation. But social disorganization, value-conflict, or personal deviation, by themselves, do not define a social problem. Any or all three may be causes, conditions or effects of social problems. Any or all three may be present in situations which are not customarily treated as social problems. Because of the contingent character of social life, a certain amount of social disorganization, value-conflict, and personal deviation is inevitable. The presence of any of these factors does not make a social problem. Organized reactions of people to situations they label as disorganization, conflict, or deviation does.

Problems are defined, then, by the solutions which people propose and the consequences of their solutions. A working definition of social problems is as follows:

> A social problem arises when there is an *awareness* among a given people that a particular *social situation* is a threat to certain *group values* which they cherish and that this situation can be removed or corrected only by *collective action.*[1]

But obviously some social situations are more threatening than others, some problems according to this definition will implicate more values than others, some problems will induce less awareness than others, and finally collective action of whatever type may prove more workable for some rather than other problems. There are, then, different orders of magnitude here which make it possible to distinguish *primary* from *secondary* social problems.

Most social problems persist. But secondary social problems are more persistent than primary problems. In part, this tenacity comes from the original threat to values. But more important, the secondary social problem persists because of the actions taken to ameliorate it.

The analogy here with the alcoholic's response to his personal problems is obvious. The alcoholic faces severe problems of adjustment. He chances upon excessive drinking as an escape from or solution to his personal problems. As a short-run solution, drinking does take care of his immediate problems. In the long run, however, the number of problems he faces adds up, then only multiplies because of his stylized drinking. Excessive drinking, given present culture and social organization, usually creates more problems than it solves.

By the same token, certain secondary social problems beget a mode of collective action called the social movement. The social movement organizes an awareness of the problem situation, defines the values at stake and the nature of the threat, and then embarks upon a course of social action to change the situation. Just as an excess use of alcohol generates additional problems for the alcoholic, so does the social movement beget social problems in its attempt to secure or protect values it holds dear.

Now this is precisely what social movements do, particularly if people outside the movement disapprove of the proposed remedy. This social disapproval frequently occasions counter-movements and the establishment of conflict groups. In the meantime, the original situation which provoked an awareness of a situation which seemed in need of change persists, very much like a bone over which two dogs quarrel.

Not all social problems, as suggested, necessarily give rise to movements of social reform. Those which are deeply embedded in culture and social organization, as drinking, drunkenness, and alcoholism so obviously are, are much more conducive to the formation of social movements. And it is just because they are so deeply embedded in the social texture that persons or movements advocating change in the situation are labelled "trouble-makers."

A frequent side effect of good intentions, therefore, is the creation of a situation which some people regard as troublesome. The medical profession, for example, gives a public label to a set of disorders as iatrogenic which it, quite obviously discusses, if at all, only in private.

Iatrogenic disorders come in two sizes. In the small size, a patient, seemingly ill but really well, seeks the help of a physician. The physician looks hard for an ailment and finally succeeds in giving the patient what he wants, namely, an illness. In the large size, the physician's diagnosis and treatment of a minor illness results in a major illness. Laymen in public discussions of iatrogenic situations typically say the cure was worse than the disease or the operation was a success but the patient died.

Social movements which set out to cure certain socially defined ills create a number of iatrogenic problems very much as the physician does. What ailments did the temperance movement create in its attempt to control drinking? What disorders has the alcoholism movement created, if any? What side effects has each movement, in its pursuit of values, produced for the other? And what does an analysis of these side effects suggest about social problems, in general, and the future prospects of the alcoholism movement, in particular? First, the temperance movement; second, the alcoholism movement; and, finally, the analysis of side effects and prospects for the future.

the Temperance Movement

A listing of some of the groups which existed or continue to exist and to labor on behalf of temperance values will give some idea of the scope, nature, and activities of the movement. Groups involved directly or indirectly include the following: American Temperance Society, International Order of Good Templars, Woman's Christian Temperance Union, Prohibition Party, Knights of Labor, Anti-Saloon League, Scientific Temperance Society, Social Gospel, National Temperance Union, National Temperance Society, Sons of Temperance, Washingtonian Movement, Permanent Committee on Temperance and Prohibition of the Methodist Episcopal Church, International Congress Against Alcoholism, Catholic Total Abstinence Union of America, Connecticut Temperance Society, Catholic Prohibition League of America, Christian Temperance Alliance of Pennsylvania, Catholic Clergy Prohibition League of America, etc.

Mention of some groups in temperance work gives a fair idea of its spread in time, place and circumstances. Clearly, the temperance movement extends widely over time and many people come under its umbrella. This extension strongly supports its classification as a social movement in accordance with the following definition. A social movement is

> . . . a group venture extending beyond a local community or a single event and involving a systematic effort to inaugurate changes in thought, behavior, and social relationships.[2]

Social movements, then, generally consist of a loose confederation of groups which seek to change a situation. As movements, they concern themselves with norms or values. They seek to restore an old norm or to impose a new one on the situation. Or they wish to return to an earlier set of values or to establish an entirely new set of values. Socialism, for example, is a movement which seeks to impose a new set of values on society as a whole. By contrast, the labor movement, or, for that matter, the civil rights movement, are both conservative. Each simply asks that certain well-established norms apply to their constituents as well as to people outside the movement.

The assorted groups that made up and continue to make up the temperance movement are concerned with values. They have sought and continue to work for the restoration of traditional values regarding the use of alcoholic beverages. The alcoholism movement, by contrast, seeks to impose a new norm for handling alcoholics.

Social movements oppose other groups. They are in conflict with other groups and are usually a congeries of conflict groups in their own right. Their stance towards the majority makes it rather easy to classify them as being either radical, moderate, or conservative. Internally, however, the movements experience conflict on their own terms. All social movements have their conservative, moderate, and social wings. The rise, oscillation, and decline of many social movements parallels factional fights in the struggle for internal power, success or failure in the achievement of the movement's goals, changes in the social targets of the movement, and, finally, changes in the internal social composition of the movements themselves. These remarks fit all aspects of the temperance movement. The extent to which they fit the alcoholism movement remains to be seen.

That loose array of formidable persons called the temperance movement experienced its own phases of conservatism, moderation, and radicalism over a period of some 250 years. Similarly, each of these groups went through its own internal phases of conservatism, moderation, and radicalism. A number were torn apart by factional fights over the definitions of drinking, drunkenness, and alcoholism and the success and failure of responses the movement made on behalf of its goals. And for some portions of the movement, social targets, goals, and internal composition changed with the failure to achieve values. The WCTU is the best known example of this last phenomenon.[3]

In general, it is clear that the movement went from persuasion to force as its fortunes changed. And, in so doing, the history of the temperance movement suggests the general proposition that strong medicine begets equally powerful side effects.

Passage of the Maine Law in 1851 prohibiting the manufacture, sale, and importation of alcoholic beverages in that state marks a turning-point in temperance strategy. From its inception in the early eighteenth century until the passage of Neal Dow's Maine Law, the temperance movement subscribed to a policy of moral suasion. Suasion simply required that persons of some influence, primarily clergymen, point out the consequences of drinking, show how they implied or threatened traditional values, and suggest that conformity with religiously sanctioned norms would perpetuate sacred values.

After passage of the Maine Law, the movement turned to legal coercion.[4] In this policy, the proponents affirmed the negative consequences of drinking without discussion, declared that traditional values were at stake, and sought to compel conformity with religiously sanctioned norms by means of restrictive legislation. Ultimate victory of this strategy came, of course, with the passage of the 18th Amendment. Its legal defeat, similarly, came with repeal and the passage of the 21st Amendment.

Pursuit of one value to the exclusion of all others blinds persons and groups to consequences at the same time that it speeds them into action. Had latter-day temperance enthusiasts studied early Georgian history, they might have paused in their hasty pursuit of rectitude. For all the cycles, conflicts, and subterfuges which came with Prohibition were plainly seen in Georgia in the 7 years between 1735 and 1742.[5]

During that 7-year period, the crown colony of Georgia experimented with prohibition. As a result, the settlers spent a little more time getting liquor, a little less on doing their work. The first moonshine stills in the country were set up, rum runners from South Carolina supplied Georgia bootleggers with rum and brandy, and speakeasies sprang up. There was even an occasional hijacking. Few of the Georgia colonists believed that there was anything illegal in selling or drinking ardent spirits. If caught for violations of liquor laws, they demanded, and got, jury trials, and usually went home scot-free. Vigorous efforts to enforce the law brought on a riot in Savannah. And some officials began to dabble in the illegal trade while British merchants began to put pressure on for repeal.

Finally, in 1742, Georgia gave up prohibition, and switched to a licensing system.

> The rum runners, bootleggers, and speakeasies soon vanished, and the colony began to prosper under the stimulus of the rum trade.

> A report to the Trustees a few years later said that drunkenness had greatly decreased.[6]

Ironically, however, the failure of early prohibition in Georgia and the massive national failure some 200 years later actually constitute a dramatic victory for the radical wing of the temperance movement.

Early temperance reformers, for the most part clergymen, focused on intemperance, or excess use of alcoholic beverages as defined by their notions of what colonial drinking norms ought to have been. The local distillation of spirits, the importation of rum, and widespread use of intoxicants by the clergy themselves raised important questions for these early temperance reformers. But their attack was not upon alcoholic beverages *per se.* Actually, they espoused a policy of moderate drinking, favouring the use of beer and wines, and extreme caution in the use of ardent spirits.

In time, more and more clergymen began to renounce the use of distilled spirits. And, as Benjamin Rush's writings on the effects of alcohol on mind and body became more widely known, the temperance movement rallied around a cry for abstinence in the use of distilled spirits, moderation in the use of beer and wines. The first great factional fights within the movement took place between drys and dry-wets. Several writers argued that alcohol was the factor common to beer, wines, and spirits, and therefore it alone was the common enemy. The victory of Neal Dow in 1851 sealed the fate of the moderates. In the process, a strange linguistic transformation indicated the radical return to early, stringent values. Now temperance meant total abstinence.

The turn towards extremism signaled the failure of moral suasion to gain temperance ends. The new strategy of legal coercion rose on the backs of suasion and produced factionalism. For the second great internal conflict in the Temperance Movement was over means. Many adherents left the movement because they could not subscribe to a position of moral legislation. They preferred to persuade men on temperance virtues rather than to compel their compliance with them. They lost, they left, and the movement underwent changes.

Single-mindedness and a strain towards moral indignation, if not outright vindictiveness, developed. And, in turn, an end-justifies-the-means philosophy began to emerge. The following comments of Senator Hall made on behalf of prohibition legislation in the Washington State Senate around 1917 are representative:

> Our opponents seem to think that a prohibitionist must be fair; that isn't the definition of a prohibitionist. He is a man who always hits whisky a blow, whether above the belt or below the belt. He

> isn't expected to be fair. In the past year we didn't get fair treatment. Now we've got the votes, don't ask us to be fair for we are not built that way. . . .[7]

By means of a Jesuitical morality, temperance values would prevail.

What were the values the Temperance Movement sought to preserve by legislating morality? They were those of the rural middle-class, those which had grown out of small-town evangelical Protestantism and had been re-tailored for use by the growing numbers of persons who entered or rose into the middle classes in the burgeoning urban, industrial society. And, of course, these values were sobriety, thrift, industry, self-control, and respectability. Early Protestant clergymen had found it necessary to police their own ranks before they could carry the reformist message to constituents. That millions aspired to these values cannot be doubted. And these values, needless to say, were shared by enough city folk so that the 18th Amendment carried many, though not all, urban districts in addition to most rural areas.[8]

And what, then, were the consequences of their vigorous collective actions on behalf of these values after some 200 years of struggle? The cultural consequences outweigh the organizational ones. Temperance organizations continue to exist in the United States and may well become again a sizeable social, moral, and political force. But, at least of this moment, the movement as an organized social movement cannot be counted as the formidable power it once was. Its current organizational weakness, however, is more than matched by the cultural victory it gained, despite the ostensible defeat of Prohibition in 1932. And this victory may be seen in the simple fact that millions of Americans define drinking, drunkenness, and alcoholism as social problems and in exactly the terms of the temperance movement.[9] Unwittingly, these Americans continue to define *alcohol* as *the problem.* And for them the solution to the problem remains constant. Simply eliminate alcohol; then, drinking, drunkenness, and alcoholism will disappear immediately.

the Alcoholism Movement

In December 1942, Dwight Anderson concluded a paper on alcohol and public opinion with these four ideas:

(1) That the problem drinker is a sick man, exceptionally reactive to alcohol.
(2) That he can be helped.

(3) That he is worth helping.
(4) That the problem is therefore a responsibility of the healing professions, as well as of the established health authorities.[10]

And in 1944, the National Council on Alcoholism was formed, to disseminate these four ideas to the public. These ideas, of course, constitute the norms of the alcoholism movement. The various state programs on alcoholism, the National Council on Alcoholism and all of its affiliates, the various schools of alcohol studies, the Rutgers Center of Alcohol Studies, the Alcoholism and Drug Abuse Section of the U.S. Department of Health, Education, and Welfare, the American Medical Association, Alcoholics Anonymous, Al-Anon, Al-A-Teen, are only some of the groups and agencies which express these norms.

What threat formed this movement, what collective actions did it take, and what effect did they have? Answers to these questions only make sense against the background of the temperance movement. For the hand of the temperance movement lies heavily on anything the alcoholism movement touches.

For instance, the notion that alcoholism is an illness is, like many another seminal idea, not really very new. Dr. Thomas Trotter in England in the early 19th century, and Dr. Benjamin Rush here in the 18th century as already noted, had begun to advance this view. The issue here, however, is not so much the presence of an illness concept but rather the absence of any organized social action on its behalf.

The amount of organized social action on behalf of this conception is markedly scant in comparison with temperance activity over the same period of time. As Jellinek notes:

> . . . some physicians in the 1830's, notably Dr. Samuel Woodward, the first superintendent of the Worcester State Hospital, and Dr. Eli Todd of Hartford, as well as the Connecticut Medical Society, suggested special institutions for inebriates.[11]

And between 1857 and 1874 at least 11 non-profit hospitals and homes for inebriates came into existence in the United States. Finally a journal of inebriety came out in 1876 and ran, not without some difficulty, for some 38 years. In that time, it published at least 100 papers which partly, if not entirely, derived from the idea of alcoholism as an illness.[12] Needless to say, the temperance movement did not look with favor on the journal or the idea that alcoholism might be considered an illness. This notion conflicted with their views, views which prevailed up to, through, and beyond Prohibition.

There had already been some scientific study of alcohol, particularly on whether it was a food, a poison, a stimulant, and whether it caused poverty, vice, crime, and disease. The climate of opinion at that time, of course, favored studies whose conclusions agreed with temperance ideology. As a result, many researchers chose other fields in which to work or were actually happy if the temperance movement put their findings to its own uses. For instance, when the famous European psychiatrist Emil Kraepelin discovered that alcohol was actually a depressant, rather than a stimulant, he himself became a strong advocate of total abstinence.[13] And many doctors wrote articles describing alcohol as a poison.

It is clear that the temperance movement had no interest in the drunkard. Its main concern was in focusing attention on him as the obvious, irreversible and inevitable outcome of drinking alcoholic beverages. The movement needed him as a negative symbol of the failure of will-power and middle-class nerve. Therefore, it was not until the end of Prohibition that interest in scientific study of alcohol and in the very real problems of alcoholism came to life perhaps for the very first time.

Then the cultural log jam broke. The organization later to become the Yale Center of Alcohol Studies embarked on its extensive studies of alcohol in 1932. Just 3 years later in 1935, Alcoholics Anonymous, the world-renowned self-help movement came into being. In 1943 the first state alcoholism programs, in Oregon and Utah, were started. And in 1957 the North American Association of Alcoholism Programs formed to co-ordinate activities and to deal with problems state programs faced in helping alcoholics.

The alcoholism movement, unlike the temperance movement, did not reduce all problems of alcohol to one, namely drinking. Nor did it come out with any specific statements for or against drunkenness. For the alcoholism movement, like the temperance movement, also centers on the middle-class values of sobriety, industry, respectability, and self-control. It adds to this complex of values, however, a specific concern with the normative problems of dealing with persons afflicted with a condition it describes as an illness, rather than as a moral vice.

the Side Effects of Both Social Movements

What general lessons do these movements teach about *(a)* problems of drinking, drunkenness, and alcoholism; and *(b)* about the relationships between social problems and social movements generally? The conclusions come under four main headings: namely (1) the legacy of temperance; (2) the alcoholic as a client; (3) experts who deal with alcoholics; and (4) the world of alcoholic rehabilitation.

(1) The Legacy of Temperance

The temperance movement polarized attitudes towards drinking. People had four options on drinking. They could be for it, against it, undecided, or indifferent. These four options yielded four social types—Wets, Drys, Mixers and Passers.

(a) Wets

Wets as a group require little comment save to point out that for many of them, their values on the question of drinking had been distinctly clarified through Dry pressure against drinking.

(b) Drys

Drys constituted, for the most part, persons who were militant reformers. They had banded together to ask if society should tolerate alcoholic beverages. To raise the question was to answer it. They planned that others should be lifted up morally. This moral ascent was to be managed more rapidly by renunciation of alcohol.

(c) Mixers

Mixers include an assortment of principled moderates. Their prototype in the 18th and 19th century were those who thought abstinence from distilled spirits alone would suffice to attain temperance values. They felt no need to give up beer or wine. In the 20th century, many Mixers voted for Prohibition not because they were against beer, wine or spirits, but because they were against the saloon. Put simply, Mixers voted Dry on certain questions while on others they voted Wet.

(d) Passers

Those indifferent to questions raised by temperance advocates, whether they were moderate drinkers or abstainers, stepped out of the Wet—Dry cross-fire. Apathy always works in urban society. Passers used that adaptation whenever someone tried to make drinking an issue.

Because it had stated the issue so sharply, the temperance movement polarized drinking attitudes. In the long run, this brought Prohibition down. And this obvious legacy of polarized attitudes continues today. Other legacies with graver consequences for drunkenness and alcoholism are not so obvious. Prevalent attitudes on drunkenness and alcoholism are some of the hidden legacies of the temperance movement.

The majority of adults drink and so they hold Wet attitudes more or less. There is still a sizeable number of abstainers and they cling to Dry attitudes. And since American drinking norms are neither clear, consistent, nor predictable, there is still room for people to be Mixers or Passers on questions of drinking.

On the other hand, not too many people become intoxicated (at least, not in the relative proportions that forebears are said to have done). And only a small number of those continue inebriety until they become full-blown alcoholics. These last two minorities are less apt to share current consensus on drunkenness and alcoholism. But most of them agree that drunkenness ought to be avoided at all costs and that alcoholism whether or not it is an illness, is still quite obviously a distinct failure of will and nerve. Alcoholism, popular logic says, comes from self-indulgence. Despite widespread efforts to gain acceptance for the proposition that the alcoholic is a sick person, many persons, including millions of alcoholics still refuse to define the situation in these terms. Sick, no. Indulgent, yes. Given the persistence of these attitudes, one may well ask if the temperance movement lost a battle, only to win a war.

(2) The Alcoholic as a Client

These general attitudes have specific applications when alcoholics come into treatment or custodial settings. Obviously, it is to the alcoholic's advantage to define himself as a sick person, particularly when he is in treatment. For at least, on the surface, in making that self-definition he is saying that he will take the patient role. In so doing, of course, he becomes more amenable to taking treatment directives and perhaps even acting on them.

Despite obvious advantages, however, there were and still are corresponding disadvantages. Ironically, temperance, a middle-class movement of moral reform, blocked recovery for middle-class alcoholics. To begin with, communication, as is true in all reform movements, goes downhill. That is, the message of uplift traveled down from those with much virtue to those with less or no virtue. The best candidates, of course, were those with a few rather than many vices. Yet, at the same time, the joy of reforming derelict topers was inversely proportional to their frequency.

Since the temperance movement demands if not actually requires a number of derelicts in order to dramatize the moral symbolism of its position, the middle-class alcoholic is able for years to keep up the pretense that he has not lost control of his drinking and that he is not a full-blown alcoholic. How can this be true? He still manages to hold wife, family, and job in a social juggling act. And so long as this is true and he stays off Skid Row, he cannot see himself as an alcoholic. He literally refuses to put himself in that category because of the stigma temperance put on the drunkard.

This is undergoing change, of course, particularly since Alcoholics Anonymous came into being. Unaccepted in the sick role when they tried it or unwilling to play it when offered the part, the middle-class alcoholics were thrust back into private suffering until Bill W. and Dr. Bob took recovery into their own hands. Yet the need for "surrender" still makes temperance the victor, even in Alcoholics Anonymous. And those alcoholics of all classes who believe that eating "humble pie" is a necessary condition of their recovery frequently prefer to go hungry.

(3) The Expert Who Deals With Alcoholics

Experts who deal with alcoholics in various agencies of social control are also creatures of American culture. They too have an inheritance from the temperance movement. Unaware that they were also mentioned in the will, they draw unwittingly on temperance ideas of drinking, drunkenness and alcoholism. The slogan, "once a drunk, always a drunk," competes on very successful terms with the newer slogan, "the alcoholic is a sick person," particularly as these experts make more rather than less contact with alcoholics.

Doctors in private medical practice, for instance, are still unlikely to view alcoholics as sick although the American Medical Association said only a few years ago that alcoholism is an illness. Those who have tried to treat alcoholics report them as intractable, unpredictable, and unresponsive to treatment; in a word, alcoholics have the reputation of being "difficult patients." The doctor who has tried to treat them is apt to stop taking alcoholics especially if they should "make a scene" in his office in front of other patients.

The physician will then deny that alcoholics are sick because they do not behave as other patients or will agree that they are sick but mentally so and therefore need the ministrations of a psychiatrist rather than his own. In either case, he is now well rid of the alcoholic as a patient in his own practice. But try as he may to rationalize this position on clinical or professional grounds, the moral judgment he has made here on the alcoholic is no different than a similar one when made by the most rabid temperance advocate.

(4) The World of Alcoholic Rehabilitation

In the world of alcoholic rehabilitation, social disorganization, value-conflict, and personal deviation are all at work. This can be seen in *(a)* ideas; *(b)* facilities; and *(c)* co-ordination.

(a) Ideas

The alcoholism movement says the alcoholic is a sick person. The behavior of the alcoholic as a patient in the hospital, however, is frequently as baffling to the staff as their behavior is to him. All are most willing to concede that a person who comes into a hospital suffering acute intoxication or delirium tremens is "sick," in lay as well as professional medical terms. But 5 or 6 days later when the same patient, now over the acute effects sneaks bottles into the ward, he is no longer acting like a sick person, but rather like an adolescent rebel according to ward staff.

And though alcoholism is a chronic illness, relapses are forbidden. For example, one New England state hospital had an alcoholic ward. To prevent a "revolving door," it admitted alcoholics who relapsed to the ward for the criminally insane. Needless to say, this form of therapeutic punishment or punitive therapy did not cut traffic down. Yet when the same patients later served jail sentences for public drunkenness and found guards dispensing tender loving care, they became only more baffled. Obviously, though alcoholics may be sick, they are criminals first, patients second. If the organization cannot make up its mind on whether alcoholics are sick, criminal, both, or neither, there is little reason for alcoholics to be clear about what they are themselves. Any confusion they reveal here stems from social disorganization rather than uncontrolled drinking.

(b) Facilities

Scarcity aside, the alcoholism movement faces two kinds of problems over facilities. If the first problem is a left-over from temperance attitudes, the second is a direct consequence of successful alcoholism movement propaganda.

In the first instance, many persons on hospital staffs claim they would actually accept alcoholics as patients but the shortage of facilities prevents them from so doing. As two different studies of hospital policies have shown, there is frequently little relation between stated hospital policy on accepting alcoholics and actual rate of admissions.[14] That some hospitals claim they deny admission to alcoholics as a matter of policy while they actually treat them, while others claim they treat alcoholics as a matter of policy while they in fact deny them admission only attests to the amount of social disorganization in the world of alcoholic rehabilitation.

The lack of facilities outcry smacks of temperance attitudes towards the drunkard. Temperance advocates always told the drunkard when he said he was unable to stop drinking that "can't means won't." Since several hospitals with fewer facilities, as reported in one study (i) admitted more alcoholics than hospitals with superior facilities, and (ii) actually reported more success with their treatment, it may be true that for hospitals with better facilities, not treating alcoholics may be just another case of "can't means won't." [15]

In the second instance, when a staff that accepts the illness concept deplores lack of facilities, it becomes clear how successful adoption of alcoholism movement ideology may produce several kinds of failures, particularly in extension of treatment services. Too early, too easy, or too hasty an acceptance of this ideology entails side effects of frustration. The movement each year indoctrinates thousands of persons with the illness concept only to send them back to a treatment world they never made and one without the necessary facilities. Unless the movement also schools its pupils to expect temperance relapses from the world of alcoholic rehabilitation, it may experience a boomerang effect. Some pupils, when their extremism in adopting the illness concept exposes them to increased frustration in the face of persistent treatment shortages of one kind or another may turn against the ideas which are making so much personal trouble for them. For example, lip-service to alcoholism movement norms without action on those norms is one sensible adjustment when there are no facilities.

(c) Co-ordination

The alcoholism movement faces two kinds of factional fights, those taking place within its ranks, and those taking place between some of its members and personnel in co-ordinate health agencies.

(i) *Factionalism within the ranks.* While most adherents of the alcoholism movement support its basic norms, many differ on how to act in support of those norms. A number of cleavages exist, perhaps the most important being the conflict between laymen and professionals.[16] Of necessity, many workers in the movement's ranks are recovered alcoholics themselves. Those who are not members of Alcoholics Anonymous place great stress on "theory" as opposed to experience. Those who are members of Alcoholics Anonymous have a strong though private faith in its works which they sometimes feel they must conceal behind lip-service to the concept of the professional approach to alcoholic rehabilitation. Less diplomatic AA workers engage in open conflict, opposing their views to the professionals. This kind of internal strife, which tore apart several temperance organizations, has jeopardized the effectiveness of agencies working with alcoholics. In addition to discord, high turnover and even relapses among the recovered alcoholics on the staff may be attributed in part to this variety of extreme factionalism.

(ii) *Factionalism between the ranks.* Many agencies in the world of alcoholic rehabilitation feel or are made to feel like second-class citizens. Ostensibly, members of an on-going treatment unit (as for example when a state alcoholism program is integrated in the department of public or mental health), they find many decisions or referrals are made without their knowledge, that other agencies in the system do not even know of their existence, or believe they should be used as a "dumping ground" for treatment rejects who are labeled "repeaters." This style of relations makes a mockery of both team and illness concepts. The upshot, of course, is antagonism followed by mutual withdrawal. And not infrequently, the alcoholic patient may well find himself caught in the agency cross-fire.

From what has been said thus far, it is clear that reactions to the temperance movement have been a source of discomfort to the growing alcoholism movement. But, at the same time, the alcoholism movement itself has generated its own reactions which, similarly, are sources of discomfort. Is it possible from the analyses of both movements given here to say what may be some additional strains for the alcoholism movement and to suggest some possible means of coping with these troubles? On the basis of knowledge about social problems and social movements in general and the world of alcoholic rehabilitation in particular, the following suggestions seem in order.

Coping with Movement-Induced Disorder

Social movements, as already noted, polarize attitudes. The temperance movement reduced the problems of drinking, drunkenness, and alcoholism to elimination of alcoholic beverages. Similarly, the alcoholism movement, where it has succeeded, has polarized attitudes on alcoholism. Hence there are now people who reduce all drinking and all drunkenness to alcoholism and all alcoholism to illness. The first suggestion to the movement, therefore, is to de-polarize.

A readiness to be polarized on the part of the target public, of course, accounts for the process and the success of any social movement. Another consequence of polarization, however, is the institutionalization of social movements. These movements as already suggested have their own natural history. As a degree of inner stability is realized, the movement experiences organizational success after some precarious years. This stability now makes it possible to relax while repeating the old rallying cries but now as tired and stale formulas. There are generational changes going on to be sure. But internal polarization usually means that the movement has begun to run behind the problem. Then criticisms are sometimes heard that the leaders are out of touch with the harsh realities of what is still happening at the grass-roots level.

Institutionalization, however, raises even more severe questions. For instance, many people after a stay in a hospital, write articles or books all dealing with the question: "Does the hospital exist for the staff or for the patients?" And, with this question goes the question of results. With institutionalization, the movement runs better while it achieves less. As it gets set in its ways, the goals are frequently lost sight of. For example, the temperance movement, in settling on legal coercion, forgot its original goals. The second suggestion is therefore that the alcoholism movement examine (a) extent of institutionalization and (b) current effectiveness.

Next comes the question of facilities. For instance, in 1948 some 473 patients were seen by state alcoholism programs. In 1961, the number of patients seen had climbed to 177,000.[17] This growth is partly explained by increase in number of state programs. The term "patients seen" is ambiguous, of course. But making the Utopian assumption that to date 200,000 patients have not only been seen but have improved and that another 300,000 are currently members of Alcoholics Anonymous in good standing, there still remains more than 5,000,000 alcoholics who are outside of treatment. In part, this is because of some factors already noted, such as the slow pace at which the illness concept is accepted in some quarters (including alcoholics, themselves). But in the main, it may simply be due to the lack of facilities. If that is true, then the movement has to soft-pedal the illness message or work harder at obtaining facilities and entree to them for staff and alcoholics.

And that brings to mind three other simple suggestions. There needs to be less talk about alcoholism as an illness and more action on that proposition. Fewer people need to be lectured on the notion but more and more of them need training on what to do when something the movement labels alcoholism appears. Many persons of good will, over-committed to the illness concept, reach for the phone and make a referral as soon as they find out that the persons they are talking to have a drinking problem. Soon, for example, municipal courts all over the country will be "making referrals" to non-existent or ineffective facilities rather than to the county jail as usual.

Finally, it is time to stop arguing about whether alcoholism is or is not some kind of illness and if so what kind.[18] It is time to take those steps that all people can agree are necessary whether or not they believe alcoholism is an illness. Otherwise the alcoholism movement may get into a factional fight with the general public. Should that happen, the alcoholic will be caught in the cross-fire again.

Notes

[1] Richard C. Fuller, "Social Problems," in *An Outline of the Principles of Sociology*, ed. Robert E. Park (New York: Barnes and Noble, 1943), p. 7.

[2] C. Wendell King, *Social Movements* (New York: Random House, 1956), p. 27.

[3] Joseph R. Gusfield, "Social Structure and Moral Reform: A Study of the Woman's Christian Temperance Union," *American Journal of Sociology* 61 (November 1955): 221-32.

[4] John Allen Krout, *The Origins of Prohibition* (New York: Alfred A. Knopf, 1925).

[5] Herbert Asbury, *The Great Illusion. An Informal History of Prohibition* (New York: Doubleday, 1950), pp. 21-23.

[6] Ibid., p. 23.

[7] Norman H. Clark, *The Dry Years. Prohibition and Social Change in Washington* (Seattle: University of Washington Press, 1965), p. 67.

[8] James H. Timberlake, *Prohibition and the Progressive Movement* (Cambridge: Harvard University Press, 1963), p. 99.

[9] Selden D. Bacon, "The Classic Temperance Movement of the U. S. A.: Impact Today on Attitudes, Action and Research" (Paper presented at the Twelfth International Institute on the Prevention and Treatment of Alcoholism, Prague, Czechoslovakia, June 20, 1966).

[10] Dwight Anderson, "Alcohol and Public Opinion," *Quarterly Journal of Studies on Alcohol* 3 (December 1942): 392.

[11] E. M. Jellinek, *The Disease Concept of Alcoholism* (New Haven, Conn.: Hillhouse Press, 1960), p. 1.

[12] Ibid., p. 2.

[13] Timberlake, *Prohibition and the Progressive Movement*, pp. 41, 46.

[14] Ralph G. Connor, Richard Flowers, Joan K. Jackson, and H. Wallace Lane, *The Washington Hospital Survey. A Study of the Policies and Practices of General Hospitals in the Admission and Management of Alcoholic Patients* (Washington State Department of Health, n. d.); David J. Pittman and Muriel W. Sterne, "The Carousel: Hospitals, Social Agencies, and the Alcoholic" (Mimeographed report presented to the Missouri Division of Health, 1962).

[15] Connor et al., *The Washington Hospital Survey*, pp. 12-18.

[16] Milton A. Maxwell, "An Exploratory Study: Alcoholics Anonymous and Professional Relations," in *Selected Papers*, Fifteenth Annual NAAAP Meeting, Washington, D. C., North American Association of Alcoholism Programs, 1965, pp. 115-30.

[17] Morris E. Chafetz and Harold W. Demone, Jr., *Alcoholism and Society* (New York: Oxford University Press, 1962), p. 114.

[18] David Mechanic and Barbara Sewell, "Community Action and Alcohol Rehabilitation," *Mental Hygiene* 49 (April 1965): 288-95.

Chapter III
Alcohol and Social Responsibility

Somebody made up the rules which govern the presence or absence of teenage drinking. Other persons state the rules to adolescents. They obey or break those rules as they see fit. Other people interpret rules on alcohol education and teenage drinking. In a complex society, family, church, school and mass media all define drinking. The school has a special responsibility in defining these rules.

Here we examine briefly (1) official statements about drinking made to students in elementary and secondary schools, (2) student definitions and actions on these rules, (3) recent research findings on alcohol education from both textbook analyses and student attitudes, and (4) some suggestions on how to reduce discrepancy between official definitions and student responses.

Official Statement on the Rules

Statements about what people may or may not say or do together with penalties for violations are called laws. A good deal of what teenagers, school officials and teachers, and other

Reprinted from the *Bulletin of the Association for the Advancement of Instruction about Alcohol and Narcotics* 12 (May 1966): 13-23 by permission of the publisher.

persons say and do about alcohol depends on laws. For example, New Jersey statutes on alcohol education, and teenage drinking read as follows:

> *Alcohol Education.* "The nature of alcoholic drinks and narcotics and their effect upon the human system shall be taught in all schools supported wholly or in part by public moneys in such manner as may be adapted to the age and understanding of the pupils and shall be emphasized in appropriate places of the curriculum sufficiently for a full and adequate treatment of the subject. The failure or refusal of any district to comply with the provisions of their section shall be sufficient cause for withholding from such district the State appropriation."
>
> *Teenage Drinking.* "It shall be unlawful for a minor (in New Jersey a person under 21) to consume any alcoholic beverage on premises licensed for the retail sale of alcoholic beverages, or to purchase, attempt to purchase or have another purchase for him or her any alcoholic beverage." The statute goes on to say that people who violate this rule shall be designated as disorderly persons and shall be fined not more than fifty dollars.)

A look at appropriate legal sources shows no court actions involving violation of the alcohol education statute by either teachers or school districts.[1] Violations may or may not have occurred. Violations may not exist because (a) no agency exists for the enforcement of the statute; or (b) because no one broke any rules. Conformity with the statute has probably been more with the letter rather than the spirit of the law. Certainly, conformity here is an unknown quantity, awaiting systematic study.

Many teenagers have broken the second law and some of them have been caught and punished. The general opinion of the public probably would be that teachers obey alcohol education statutes and teenagers break drinking rules.

Another interpretation of these rules is that only adults have legal rights to drink. One's legal majority includes voting and drinking (though never at the same time—on Election Day). Public drinking places are closed when the polls are open because adults are supposed to act in a moderate, restrained, and discreet fashion. Public drinking places are sealed off from adolescents for much the same reasons. Until adolescents come of age, the law presumes them incapable of drinking moderately and of practicing restraint in social relations. To this end, schools teach alcohol facts and support adult rules. Reaching adulthood, students can then make up their own minds on whether to drink, what to drink, where, when, with whom, under what circumstances, and with what effects.

This definition of the situation asks only that young people bide their time. They may well have both motivation and capacity for drinking. But their elders counsel restraint and restrict legitimate opportunities for drinking in public. To get the teenagers to support the official timetable [2] on drinking, adults teach self-control and then employ various social controls on those who fail to exercise restraint.

Teenage Drinking: Definitions, Actions, Interpretations

The school in the plural society is the Great Homogenizer. Families, social classes, ethnic and religious bodies all hold assorted views on drinking. Some churches accept moderation but call drunkenness a sin. Still others impose a strict abstinence code on their congregations. The law restricts alcohol use to specific times and places and enjoins drinking on certain jobs. Families may well disagree among themselves on drinking, only agreeing when it comes to condemning the drinking practices of other families. Schools assume responsibility for presenting objective facts about drinking in some "neutral" manner. Absence of a single set of American drinking customs only makes the school's task that much harder.

The schools state the rules on drinking. What do young people do with this information? Do teenagers drink and if so, how much, what, where, when, with whom, under what circumstances, and with what effects?

Results of Teenage Drinking Surveys

Surveys of teenage drinking attitudes and practices have developed only within the last twenty years. These studies, carried out in assorted communities, agree on certain uniformities. Uniformities reported in these studies on which there is most agreement can be summarized as follows: [3]

1. first use begins between ages 13 and 14
2. most adolescents will have had at least one drink before they graduate from high school

3. there are marked variations in proportions of users
4. first use begins at home with parents present
5. teenagers, whether abstaining or drinking, tend to follow parental usage
6. parental approval is greatest for those who drink at home
7. chances of becoming a user increase with age; use varies with age, sex, ethnic, religious, class, urban or rural backgrounds
8. young people see drinking as legitimate adult activity
9. chances of use increase with proximity of adult roles
10. alcohol, for youth, is a social beverage, not a drug
11. legal prohibitions against teenage drinking are rather ineffective
12. only a minority, even if abstinent, see drinking as morally wrong for adults or teenagers
13. problem drinking and use of beverages of high alcohol content are both infrequent

a Comparison with Current Knowledge of Adult Drinking

These findings make more sense when compared with cumulative evidence on adult drinking in the United States. Here again are findings from a battery of surveys:[4]

1. somewhere between 60 and 70 percent of the adult population drink alcoholic beverages. Perhaps three-fourths of the men drink, as over against a little more than half of the women
2. men, of course, report themselves more often as regular drinkers than women, three times more often. Women are more often occasional drinkers
3. frequency of drinking tends to increase with education and income
4. the longer the native background, the less frequent the drinking
5. Protestants abstain more frequently than Catholics who in turn abstain more frequently than Jews; at the other end of the spectrum, Irish Catholics have the highest rates of alcoholism, Jews the lowest
6. since World War II, more persons have become users of alcoholic beverages; at the same time, there has been some decrease in per capita consumption
7. more women drink now than a generation ago
8. drinking increases with urbanization
9. beer is currently the favorite alcoholic beverage; a hundred years ago whiskey was the favorite

10. moderate social drinking appears to be the national norm
11. off-premises sales have increased, on-premises sales have decreased
12. most adults drink just to be sociable
13. only a small minority become problem drinkers; currently there are an estimated 5,500,000 alcoholics in a drinking population in excess of 90,000,000

These findings on adult drinking accord well with the uniformities in teenage drinking. They show that adolescents support the timetable norms which adults have defined for them. That is, with advancing maturity, teenagers imbibe with somewhat more regularity and ease. As they are trying out new roles and responsibilities, drinking becomes a symbol of adult activity. Under certain conditions, it clearly stands for emancipation from adult supervision.

The development and acquisition of teenage drinking norms also fits in rather well with recent social changes.[5] Age at onset of puberty is lowering while age at leaving school is rising. Soon virtually everyone will have had at least a high school education. And soon a little more than half the people who go on to college will actually graduate. At the same time, demands on people have risen. Youth are kept in a dependent situation much longer, yet are simultaneously being trained for independence in a society which has institutionalized and emphasized individualism. Once they come of age, they will be asked to assume even more responsibilities than their parents, and correspondingly, will be expected to be even more autonomous. All this is in keeping with the revolution of rising expectations now sweeping the whole world.

The modern urban industrial society has no clearly marked route out of adolescence into adulthood. Primitive societies signalize this transition in and through special ceremonies. But American society has no rituals marking these important changes in status and role. And laws only increase the confusion—young men at 18 are subject to military conscription, but must wait until 21 for voting and drinking rights. Coming of age in this sense widens the gulf between adults and teenagers.

the Necessary Emergence of "Youth Culture"

To ease transition, the "youth culture" emerges.[6] Frequently misunderstood as a revolt against adults, actually the youth culture serves to help reduce the special "storm and stress" of adolescence. The youth culture sets down rules for governing one's self in making the switch from teenager to adult. When students drink to excess, for example, their peers do not report them to the elders. A conspiracy of silence develops.[7] They remain silent, protecting insiders from outsiders. Amongst themselves, however, they censure drinking deviants and also mark well how swiftly adults punish the transgression of drinking norms. In effect, the youth culture, left to itself, aids and abets growing up. Data from teenage and adult drinking surveys support this conclusion.

Youth culture defines conduct for persons between generations. Such persons sometimes act like children, sometimes like adolescents, and sometimes like adults. Most of the time, the youth culture is alive and sensitive to adult norms. Currently, it points towards being "hip" and "cool," both useful postures for future moderate, restrained and discreet adults in city life.

Many junior and senior high school teachers are alarmed at these trends toward use of alcohol. So are many parents, police officers, and legislators. Use of alcohol always includes risks of mistakes in social interaction. With apparent increases in drinking excesses, significant adults resort to repressive legal measures to regain social control over teenage drinking. Just as these controls go into action, available evidence suggest that today, although more teenagers use alcoholic beverages than teenagers a generation or two ago, fewer of them are getting into trouble through drinking. Per capita consumption may be up, but per capita "troubles," however defined, are down and declining steadily. This shift stems from the changing functions of youth culture.

Drinking More— but Resultant Troubles Are Less

A generation or two ago youth were more defiant of their elders and less subtle in defiance. Similarly, dependence on parents was less than today. A generation or two ago, youth culture specified infrequent but excessive use of alcohol. Hence, fewer teenagers actually drank, but when they did they drank in greater quantities, and troubles they experienced or made were in direct proportion to amounts drunk. Today's youth culture performs more integrative functions and provides more discreet modes of periodic revolt. Today's teenagers, aping parents, begin to drink at a much earlier age, take alcohol in milder forms, at more and varied kinds of social functions, use much less and on the whole get into less rather than more trouble. In effect, more of them are drinking today than a generation ago, they are learning the custom earlier and in a wider assortment of social contexts, and, in general are more responsive to drinking controls, both internal and external.

Given these stabilizing functions of the youth culture, what will increased legal prohibitions and surveillance cause? Discrepant liquor laws in Connecticut and New York prompted more stringent controls, both public and private, on teenage drinking. A Connecticut law passed in July makes it an offense to possess alcoholic beverages in a car if the driver and/or passengers are under 21. In a little more than three months, Connecticut highway patrolmen have made 201 arrests under this new law. Obviously, legal fiat here, like Prohibition, manufactures interest in drinking, and makes possible some new ways of playing "hide and seek."

Teenage drinking already is illicit. Such laws as the one just passed in Connecticut only accentuate the "forbidden game" atmosphere which now surrounds drinking among teenagers. This atmosphere invites persons to take premature risks before they understand consequences. But breaking rules frequently invites people simply on that account alone. A sense of adventure and daring always develops when participating in a "forbidden game." Outwitting police, liquor-sellers, parents and teachers are their own rewards. For others, outfoxing the elders becomes fun only if an audience of peers is present to applaud "beating the system." And, for a small number, those already enmeshed in personal problems, drinking is its own reward. These unfortunate young people have begun to assume a problem drinker's role as a means of solving acute problems of transition. To date, however, only incipient alcoholics drink for relief, and significantly, most young people who drink this way are *out of touch with the youth culture.* They are as much estranged from that culture as they are from parents and teachers and other significant adults.[8]

Predictably, then, zeal in writing new laws and enforcing old ones will only encourage more teenage violations. And, importantly, zeal which has become intemperate alters youth controls on drinking situations. As it is, teenagers in Mississippi now get their whiskey from bootleggers, a circumstance not likely to surround the act of drinking with that air of relaxed sociability characteristic of most adult gatherings where alcoholic beverages are used. Obtaining a source of supply puts many teenagers in the role of an alcoholic seeking to stave off withdrawal distress on the one hand, or of a rum runner on the other. Neither role has a contribution to make to the developing American consensus on moderate social drinking.

Youth Culture Could Be Worse

The very real danger is that zeal in stating and enforcing rules on teenage drinking can only push the youth culture into increased defiance. Should this happen, that youth culture will change rapidly from a "loyal opposition" to a tightly-knit group of young rebels now armed with a "wet" cause. Clandestine haste in drinking and a con man's mentality could well supplant current role-models of sophisticated and relaxed social drinkers.

Rules ought to be few in number, simply stated. Penalties should be fair, precise, and punishment should fall swiftly and openly on the violators. Any sociological analysis of Prohibition supports these conclusions and, in turn, makes the remedy to some of the present difficulties self-evident.

Alcohol Education: Textbook Analyses and Student Attitudes

Many persons take the view that alcohol education in the schools is necessary. They list recipes of what a text ought to contain, how materials should fit curricula, what kinds of teaching aids ought to be used, and what strategies to use in different grades. Now, as with the field of education generally, there is little hard data on which to make or revise policies. Schools, textbooks, and teachers all have their own styles and traditions. Until harsh facts show them to be wrong (and sometimes not even then) their interests in teaching their own way will remain strong. Changing teachers, schools, curricula and textbooks may be as hard as (or harder than) teaching and changing students. Probably it will be harder—if only because there is less sanction for changing teachers than for teaching students.

Currently, all education is supposed to fit young students for a complex, urban world. Alcohol use is one demand that the world will attempt to make of them, even before they come of age. The evidence already discussed supports that conclusion. To what extent does current alcohol education meet that demand? How well, if at all, does it prepare students, both at the elementary levels and again in secondary schools, to understand alcoholic beverages, their place in society, their uses and misuses, their effects on mind and body, reasons for drinking, alcoholism, intoxication, etc.?

There are three ways of testing alcohol education, and a complete test, of course, would include all three: (1) content analysis of texts or other materials, (2) survey of student attitudes, and (3) comparative study of how pupils exposed to two different kinds of alcohol education perform on certain attitude tests or actually respond in diverse drinking situations. At present, there exists no study which includes all three of these methods. There are, however, two textbook analyses and one study of student attitudes.[9] The most recent of these two studies makes these criticisms of textbook coverage in elementary and secondary schools.

1. texts do not distinguish sharply enough between alcohol and narcotics
2. use of related source materials is inadequate
3. emphasis on alcohol education is slight
4. reasons why people drink gets meager coverage
5. a "negative attitude" and an overemphasis on "problems" pervades discussion on drinking
6. most texts cover effects on mind and body adequately
7. alcoholism gets much too much stress

The author goes on to make these recommendations:

1. there ought to be more teaching about alcohol in as wide a variety of subjects and classroom contexts as possible
2. controversial facts require a neutral manner and extensive coverage
3. ethical neutrality dictates more precise, less evaluative terminology
4. more educational effort is necessary

Paul's recent survey of student attitudes finds much room for improvement.[10] He surveyed eighth graders in five junior high schools and 11th graders in three senior high schools in Michigan, and asked for their comments on alcohol education. A total of 973 students responded to his questionnaire. For both junior high and senior high students, interest centered in three major areas: (a) effects of drinking, (b) reasons for drinking, and (c) alcoholism. Almost three-quarters of the students in both grades sampled raised questions on these points. A slightly larger percentage of junior high school students were more interested in effects of drinking, very probably because of their lesser acquaintance with drinking. Similarly, 11th graders asked somewhat more questions about alcoholism for much the same reasons. That is, more of them probably had either the experience of drinking to excess on one or more occasions, had been exposed to other peoples' reaction to their own and others' excesses, and may well have begun, in consequence, to harbor doubts or feel anxiety about their drinking.

Paul makes these recommendations. Students in senior high need more factual interpretation on laws regarding alcohol use and more information on alcoholism and problems of alcoholism. Students in junior high school require more factual information, particularly on effects of drinking. And both grades need to know in much greater detail the many reasons for drinking.

Reduction of Discrepancy Between Statements and Actions

One price of coming of age in a complex society is a high exposure to choices and ambiguous grounds for distinguishing between them. The youth culture tries to solve this problem when teenage drinking is defined as both illegal and deviant. There are ways in which the discrepancy between statements and actions, both those of officials, parents, liquor sellers, and teenagers themselves may be reduced. The point here is not to eliminate ambiguity in modern social life. No one could possibly do so even if he wished to. The point is to leave ambiguity in those areas where matters cannot be settled by fiat.

For instance, making 18 the year of legal majority in all 50 states would not guarantee that all persons at age 18 would act as moderate, restrained and discreet adults.[11] But this is one area in which reduction of ambiguity would remove drinking as a way of achieving adult status by illicit presumption.

Enforcement of liquor laws, moreover, has always proven difficult. As far back as colonial times, stringent regulations on times and places of sales and characteristics of buyers had to be relaxed in the face of commercial class pressures and consumer demands.[12] All these ingredients were present on a massive scale during Prohibition, and they bid fair to return again in the teenage drinking case. Here an 18 year-old majority would solve most of the law enforcement problems—as some have already begun to advocate.[13] One should not be surprised if a youth movement centers on these and related issues. During wartime, the issue fades. There are fewer mentions of the teenage drinking and driving problem in New Jersey in the newspapers now than there were three years ago.

An alternative (one ambiguous in its own right) is the policy of lax and shifting enforcement of liquor laws. For instance, during World War II, inspectors of the New Jersey Alcoholic Beverage Control board found themselves in bars where persons under 21 were drinking alcoholic beverages. Eighteen year-old Rutgers students were often sacrificed to the law, though eighteen year-old soldiers were drinking in the very same bars. Selective perception in the matter of law enforcement is always wrong. Just lowering the drinking age would reduce the area in which agents of law enforcement would be forced to violate the rules of their own organizations.

Two different studies on interviewer effects, in turn, have their implications for alcohol education in the classroom. Mulford found that abstainers interviewed more abstainers in Iowa than could be expected by chance distribution alone, while, in the same study, moderate social drinkers interviewed more moderate drinkers than could be expected if distributed randomly in the adult drinking population.[14] This and the evidence from other studies suggests that respondents "read" their interviewers rather accurately and give them what they want. Additional supporting evidence comes from Coleman's study of the adolescent society. He cites a study of drinking in a Baltimore high school. In this study, the interviewers were teenagers themselves, and they found a much greater number of drinkers than Coleman's own interviewers, all of whom were adults.[15]

Students "Read" Teacher Attitudes

The point is that students will have no difficulty in "reading" their own teachers' messages on alcoholic beverages when the subject arises for discussion in school classrooms. It becomes easy here to respond in the words teachers want to hear, only to act differently once school is out. To correct for this (for to eliminate it is, or course, impossible), a wide variety of teachers need to cover much the same ground in different ways and in different courses. In time, students come to see that the same messages can be sent by adults of different ages, sexes, interests, prejudices, personality types. The solution to the ambiguity problem is then not rigidity, a rapid decision, a blacking out of the whites (or a whiting out of the blacks) but rather only more of the same, now approaching the richly colored and ambiguous texture of real life.

And yet another point arises when the focus shifts to real life. A deficiency of much alcohol education seems to be that it is unreal, based heavily on biology which no one can really see, taste, feel, or hear. And, in too many instances, a prurient view characterizes or, more narrowly, and probably more frequently, a psychology of fear surrounds the subject. The solution to this point is to discuss and reveal and examine teenage drinking *as a part of social life,* drawing on the findings of social scientists. Schools have fired sufficient proscriptions at students in the past. What is needed now are rich and complete descriptions of adult drinking and teenage drinking. Students will come to evaluate these descriptions and, in time, will arrive at sound moral evaluations for themselves. These in time will become the prescriptive language which they themselves will put into action while drinking, as the youth culture supplies a now more well-informed sanction.

a Somewhat Radical Conclusion

A word, in conclusion. No teacher need fear making his or her own position on alcoholic beverages clear. What he or she needs to do is to lay out in clear and precise detail the operations he or she went through to arrive at that position. The students can take it from there. It is better for them to be exposed to a reasoned position than to none at all. And, if it is a reasoned position, they are more apt to take it than leave it.

Notes

[1] Thomas D. Moore, "Alcohol Education in the Somerville and Bridgewater-Raritan Public Schools" (Unpublished paper, Center of Alcohol Studies, Rutgers University, 1964), p. 10.

[2] The notion that passage of time obtains moral and social definition is the main theme of Julius A. Roth, *Timetables* (Indianapolis: Bobbs-Merrill, 1963).

[3] This summary is a paraphrase of George L. Maddox, "Adolescence and Alcohol," in *Alcohol Education for Classroom and Community,* ed. Raymond G. McCarthy (New York: McGraw-Hill, 1964), pp. 35-37.

[4] The most recent survey is Harold A. Mulford, "Drinking and Deviant Drinking, U. S. A.," *Quarterly Journal of Studies on Alcohol* 25 (December 1964): 634-50. Additional surveys are reported in Raymond G. McCarthy, ed., *Drinking and Intoxication* (Glencoe, Ill.: The Free Press, 1959), pp. 179-245.

[5] The discussion here on social changes and "youth culture" follows very closely the argument in Talcott Parsons' essay "Youth in the Context of American Society," pp. 155-82 in his *Social Structure and Personality* (New York: The Free Press of Glencoe, 1964).

[6] For an excellent discussion of "youth culture," see Bennett M. Berger, "Adolescence and Beyond: An Essay Review of Three Books on the Problems of Growing Up," *Social Problems* 10 (Spring 1963): 394-408.

[7] See August B. Hollingshead, *Elmtown's Youth* (New York: John Wiley, 1949), pp. 319-25.

[8] For an analysis which shows that alcoholics follow no social rules when they drink, see Selden D. Bacon, "Alcoholics Don't Drink," *The Annals* 315 (January 1958): 55-64.

[9] Daniel L. Paul, *An Evaluation of Alcohol Education Materials in Elementary, Junior High School, and Senior High School Textbooks as Related to Student Needs* (Kalamazoo, Mich.: Western Michigan University, 1964); and Anne Roe, *A Survey of Alcohol Education in Elementary and High Schools in the United States* (New Haven, Conn.: Journal of Studies on Alcohol, 1943).

[10] Paul, *Evaluation of Alcohol Education Materials,* pp. 101-12.

[11] Norbert L. Kelly, "Social and Legal Programs of Control in the United States," in *Alcohol Education for Classroom and Community,* ed. Raymond G. McCarthy (New York: McGraw-Hill, 1964), p. 25.

[12] John Allen Krout, *The Origins of Prohibition* (New York: Alfred A. Knopf, 1925), p. 5.

[13] Muriel W. Sterne, David J. Pittman, and Thomas Coe, "Teenagers, Drinking, and the Law," *Crime and Delinquency* 11 (January 1965): 78-85.

[14] See Harold A. Mulford and Donald E. Miller, "Drinking in Iowa. 1. Sociocultural Distribution of Drinkers. With a Methodological Model for Sampling Evaluation and Interpretation of Findings," *Quarterly Journal of Studies on Alcohol* 20 (December 1959): 704-26. The discussion of interviewer effects is on pp. 710-12.

[15] James S. Coleman, *The Adolescent Society* (New York: The Free Press of Glencoe, 1961), pp. 16-17.

Part Two

the Deviant Career

Chapter IV

the Hidden Alcoholic

Common discourse is filled with terms for alcoholism. Definition of and enforcement of social rule on alcoholism changes constantly, and new terms rise up to meet the demand for understanding, prediction and control. One such frequently heard expression is "the hidden alcoholic." A sociological analysis of that expression is long overdue. It is the purpose of this chapter to explore this commonly used idea, examining what it points to, the conditions under which it is used, the consequences of its uses, and some recommendations for improving its usage.

Accordingly, the chapter first a) makes some very brief and introductory remarks about the idea of hiding, b) discusses the social definition of alcoholism, c) examines the facts on prevalence. Next it examines briefly some codes on drinking and responses to its violation (the relationship between culture as a set of symbolic definitions and social organization as a set of actions on those definitions is explored), the factors that define an alcoholic's social situation (labeling, disapproval, exposure, and sanctions) some general propositions on types of hidden alcoholics and their world, and finally, a set of prescriptions which might be useful in playing this game of hide-and-seek.

Hiding as an Interactional Process

Hiding is an interactional process as the game of hide-and-seek implies. In its simplest form it takes two, the hider and the seeker. Nevertheless, in most discussions of the hidden alcoholic, the tendency is to focus upon the person in the game who has been tagged "it" (defined by the others as the "alcoholic"). In this use of the term, the person decides that he has attributes about himself that ought to be concealed from the eyes of others. To make use of the term "hidden alcoholic" broader and capable of wider understanding, prediction and control, it is necessary to include seekers as well as hiders, their numbers, and dimensions of activity and passivity.

Seekers would then include persons who want to apply the term alcoholic to at least one other person and then to take some kind of action on that term. Obviously, there can be several varieties of seekers who take alternate kinds of actions to, for, with, or against alcoholics. In addition, they can be further classified in the action sphere as either active or passive. And, of course, seekers can reach out aggressively to tag alcoholics as such and take some kind of controlling action on them, or they can rest quietly, waiting passively for people to come to them for social redefinition as alcoholics.

In turn, those who play the role of hider can go about this actively, with great skill, finesse, and determination, making a career in social and self-deception, as it were. There are also their counterparts, those who hide rather passively. These latter types do not so much seek concealment as have it thrust upon them if they are lucky.

The relations between the two in the simple game of hide-and-seek are simple when the rules are clear and when active and passive dimensions are equally distributed and adhered to. These relations, however, become quite complex when the numbers of hiders and seekers multiply, when people choose sides and form teams, and when activity and passivity are found in the same players on the same teams. When these complexities arise, it becomes clear that focus on attributes of persons said to be alcoholics is insufficient to account for variations in the hiding process. To extend the analysis and to explain better what is happening, the language of social relationships needs to be included in any models of explanation that seriously try to account for what seems to be happening.

Alcoholism: the Attribute for Hiding

Hiding, as a social relationship, however, does require some attribute which seems to require concealment. It is useful to remember that social relationships have histories and dynamics of their own. This means that attributes may give rise to the form of relationship in the first instance. But, in the second instance, the relationship itself, in time, assumes command over attributes. In time, attributes may even take second place; on occasion, they may even be lost sight of.

In the beginning, nevertheless, an attribute, an indication of something about the person who bears the attribute, is necessary. As a general rule, any sign which increases the chances that one person will be reduced in the eyes of another person similarly increases the chances that the person so tagged will seek by some means to conceal the sign. For the sign, should it gain wide enough currency, will itself come to work as a symbol of low status. Other things equal, men seek, wherever possible, high rather than low status in the eyes of other men. Alcoholism, however defined, cannot raise a man's status in the eyes of others. No matter how it is called, it is bound to lower him. Consequently, a need to hide the signs of alcoholism exists given its stigmatizing role in society (1).

A good common-sense working definition of alcoholism is damage to health, family, work, and social life brought on by uncontrolled drinking (2). Anybody who becomes involved in this sequence of events is bound, at least at the outset, to avoid by whatever means, usually denial, being labeled alcoholic. To accept the designation, as already noted, is to accept a reduction in social status.

The term alcoholic when applied to another human being makes the person the equivalent of his acts. The person is redefined morally and other people are now free to enforce the redefined person in accordance with the terms and implications of the definition as alcoholic. And seekers as well as hiders, simply by being members of society, have some awareness, of one kind or another, of the moral typing of persons labeled as alcoholics. A combination of negative images sustains alcoholism as a stigmatizing attribute and engenders hiding.

Traces of drinking behavior that directly or indirectly injure the even tenor of social relationships eventually become known though in different ways, times, places, and by different persons. For persons who ultimately become assigned the alcoholic role by others (and/or by themselves as agents of society) impinge on others at different points in their own life cycle. And, in turn, their own drinking behavior impinges on that life cycle in different ways, and with different degrees of intensity and consequences. Considering alcoholism as a set of damages which are inflicted on persons (including the drinker himself) and on social relationships, three general kinds can be distinguished, *sudden, erratic,* and *delayed.* Sudden damages are gross, immediate and follow soon after the person is introduced to drinking. Erratic damages are sustained in unpredictable, less patterned ways and though they slowly tend to cumulate in intensity and costs, there is no steady line. Delayed damages take place years after the introduction to drinking and take two forms, one in which damages are gross, the other in which damages grow gradually, almost in fixed stages over the years. Gross damages become obvious as when a person turns to repeated drinking as an adjustment to an extreme personal crisis such as loss of a loved one, job or business. Essential alcoholics (3) more often inflict sudden and gross damages on themselves, their intimates, and their system of social relationships. Delayed though gross damages are sustained by reactive alcoholics (3).

Drinking behavior is but one aspect of any person's unique biography or career through time. This means quite simply that any changes in career, notably marital and occupational, influence changes in drinking behavior (4). And, similarly, changes in drinking behavior exert strong influences upon marital and occupational careers. Since all people move through time into and out of several kinds of social networks and experience rises, stabilities, and falls in status, and, in turn, come into contact with changing numbers and types of persons, the kinds of impact their drinking behavior can have on social circles similarly varies with all of these important aspects of their social lives. The impact of these damages is counted up in a number of ways by a variety of seekers after alcoholics. Systematic counts by students of alcohol use give rise to estimates of the prevalence of alcoholism. These estimates, in turn, lead to speculation about "hidden alcoholics."

the Prevalence of "Hidden Alcoholics"

The Jellinek formula for estimating the prevalence of alcoholics relies on morbidity data (5). A certain percentage of deaths from cirrhosis of the liver are attributed to chronic alcoholism. Here the primary indicator of damage is massive and final damage inflicted on the self by uncontrolled drinking resulting in death. This formula yields currently the oft-cited estimate that in a population in excess of 90 million drinkers there are 5,500,000 alcoholics. Of this number, 500,000 are women. This formula has, of course, been criticized (6). To date, however, it is the best there is.

It is on the basis of these estimates that additional informed guesses on the prevalence of "hidden alcoholics" can be made. This estimate comes from subtracting the number of alcoholics who are known to treatment agencies, who are known to correctional agencies, who are thought to be living on Skid Row, and comparing their characteristics. The usual result of such a discussion is that the great bulk of the alcoholics, anywhere from 70 to 85 percent of them are "hidden." Of course, the term "hidden" here begs all of the questions raised already. They will be answered in a moment.

According to the best estimates to date, some 500,000 alcoholics are known to the variety of official treatment agencies such as mental hospitals, alcoholism clinics (both in-patient and out-patient), and the like. No accurate count of the number of persons who are currently in Alcoholics Anonymous exists; a very liberal estimate might be that right now another 500,000 persons belong to this famous self-help movement.

Estimates of the number of Skid Row alcoholics in the country pose a number of problems, all of them crucial for an understanding of the significance and importance of the concept of the "hidden alcoholic." Two figures are frequently cited: either experts say no more than 8 percent (or 440,000) of all alcoholics are on Skid Row (7), or they say no more than 3 percent (or 165,000) of all alcoholics are on Skid Row (8). But three different surveys of metropolitan Skid Rows (Chicago, Minneapolis, and Philadelphia) reveal that only a third of the residents in the homeless man's quarter are chronic alcoholics (9,10,11). And Bogue's study of Skid Row in 44 American cities estimates only 100,000 homeless men (and his estimates of Skid Row necessarily overlapped with census tracts with different population characteristics) only 35,000 of whom according to his own projections could conceivably be chronic alcoholics (9).

The chronic drunkenness offender population, in turn, poses additional problems for estimating the prevalence of alcoholism, "hidden" as well as unhidden. Last year there were close to 2,500,000 arrests for alcohol-related offenses (e.g., public intoxication, vagrancy, simple assault, driving under the influence, family offenses, etc.) (12). The number of offenders is not the same as arrests; in turn some small yet significant percentage of these offenders are probably alcoholics. And, of course to some extent, there is some overlap here with so-called Skid Row alcoholics. Combining these so-called Skid Row alcoholics with the true chronic drunkenness offenders, it might be fair to say, as a liberal estimate, that of the most visible, overt alcoholics (in both of these two latter categories) there are probably 500,000.

These estimates lead to these inferences about the prevalence of alcoholism.

1. Most alcoholism in the U. S. is "hidden."

2. One million alcoholics are known to treatment agencies, a half-million to correctional agencies. Allowing for some overlap between these two known populations, more than 75 percent of the estimated alcoholics are *officially* hidden.

3. Of the 1 million known to treatment agencies, most are partially hidden in various degrees (outside of being known to family, agency, and some employers).

4. The most visible of all are the Skid Row alcoholics and the chronic drunkenness offenders.

5. Though definitions are undergoing rapid change, conflict continues and older conceptions still have considerable influence. Since a vast number of people still view derelicts as the simple equivalent of alcoholism, obvious damages to health and social relationships from unrestrained drinking are still not called alcoholism.

Studies of hospital and clinic populations reveal the old stereotypes to be a) wrong but b) still influential. Several of these studies show that more than 75 percent of the patients in treatment for alcoholism are still married and still holding jobs, contrary to what the traditional moral typology on alcoholism holds. The standard set of ideas on the subject holds that alcoholics are disorganized socially and personally, socially isolated, lacking in any ties to organized primary and secondary groups. The facts show the reverse to be the case. There is here as in so many other areas a gap between ideas and actions. How is it possible for a behavior pattern such as repeated and prolonged drinking to simultaneously produce damages in so many spheres of life, yet go so unnoticed as to be not socially defined as the public problem it has been made out to be by so many experts? An examination of the relation of rules on drinking to action taken against violation of those rules may provide an understanding of how this is at all possible and, at the same time, reveal several varieties of hiding relationships.

Some Types of Drinking Codes

Groups, whatever the basis and forms of their association and the particular life-style they subscribe to, set forth a code on drinking (13). This code defines how alcoholic beverages are to be understood, the style and meaning of use, and the distinction (if any) between user and abuser. The code must assign meaning to the act of drinking, the state of intoxication, and the process of alcoholism. All parts of this code, taken together, constitute a group's definition of moral rule on drinking. Set against definition of moral rule, itself a collection of ideas, is enforcement of that rule, or organized actions on its behalf. Thus, for instance, an abstinence code bans drinking, thereby reducing the chances that many adherents of the code will experience intoxication let alone alcoholism. The use of alcoholic beverages is prohibited, usually on religious grounds.

Set over against proscription on all use, are a set of drinking codes which both within and between themselves make distinctions on drinking, intoxication, and alcoholism and in turn prescribe differential enforcements on infractions of rules pertaining to drinking, to intoxication, and to alcoholism.

Restricting the discussion to the U.S., a number of religious groups like Baptists, Christian Scientists, Methodists, and Mormons proscribe drinking in accordance with an abstinence code (14). Orthodox Jews, for example prescribe drinking on religious grounds and in moderation, proscribe intoxication and alcohol (15,16). Italian-Americans prescribe drinking in moderate to fairly large quantities on commensal grounds, proscribe intoxication, and denounce alcoholism (17). White American non-ascetic middle-class Protestants permit drinking on convivial grounds, permit intoxication, yet proscribe alcoholism (18). Irish-Americans prescribe drinking on utilitarian grounds, permit intoxication, and proscribe alcoholism (13,16). And black Americans prescribe drinking on convivial grounds, prescribe or permit intoxication, and tolerate alcoholism (19).

These brief examples lead to two simple conclusions noted over and over again by students of alcoholism. First, drinking codes as a special instance of culture vary in how clearly and consistently they are defined with respect to the wider culture of the group (20). And, second, the codes also vary in both the severity and certainty of enforcement (18). This relation between culture and social organization defines the situation and conditions under which abusers or alcoholics come into being, are defined, and dealt with, if at all. In turn, the prevalence of hidden alcoholics depends upon the interaction between culture and social organization.

Persons who abuse alcoholic beverages violate the drinking codes of their respective groups. As the abuse mounts and damages become more clearly connected to that abuse, as difficulties in simple living begin to cumulate, the person who begins to show the signs and attributes of alcoholism risks moral redefinition. Should he continue in violating drinking codes, he runs the risk of being assigned the alcoholic role as that behavior pattern is understood and constituted in his respective groups. This role is one of the more general classes of roles classed as deviant. Four principal risks any deviant runs are *labeling, disapproval, exposure,* and *sanctions* (21).

Labeling refers to the chance that other people will call him an alcoholic; disapproval to the chances that persons important to him will express their displeasure at his actions; exposure to chances that his actions or his reputation will become known to a wider number of people; and sanctions refers to the chances that other persons will take action against his alcoholism. Sanctions usually refer to behavior of others in response to behavior that violates drinking codes, and these sanctions are generally correctional (legal or criminal) or treatment (and sometimes as in the case of civil commitment they are medico-legal).

Societal Reactions to Deviant Drinking Behavior

As effects of unrestrained drinking cumulate, the probability that the signs of alcoholism will also appear increases proportionately. Because of the characteristics of drinking codes, the frequency and kind of infractions, the ratio of violators to non-violators, and the rank of violators, three kinds of events occur in producing figures in counts of prevalence. And all three may be explained as three different societal reactions to deviant drinking behavior.

First, some persons are defined almost as suddenly as the damages appear and become subjected to immediate enforcement. Often in cases of this kind overreactions take place and some persons are falsely assigned the alcoholic role though they accept it dutifully. Second, the process of redefinition and enforcement is both cyclical and vacillating resulting in the great bulk of what is known as the "hidden alcoholics." And, third, application of the label is made in due and appropriate course, almost a steady progression as it were, approximating Jellinek's analysis of the alcoholic progression (14). Here, sanctions are either regular, doled out in stereotyped fashion, or, less frequently, out of proportion to the characteristics of the infraction itself.

There is then a small category of persons who are tagged rapidly though incorrectly as alcoholics and responded to uniformly as such, another small category of persons who are tagged gradually and correctly as alcoholics and responded to erratically as such, and a vast assemblage of persons, the great bulk of "hidden alcoholics," who experience inconsistent definition and enforcement as alcoholics. Some examples of these differences and a set of propositions which may account for these selfsame differences follows.

1. *Characteristics of drinking codes.* Violation of an abstinence code, by definition, is an extreme reaction to a strong and powerful prohibition. Consequently, persons who violate abstinence codes not only do so in an extremely rapid fashion, but they also do so in a situation where their actions are much more likely to come to the attention of other persons since most of these latter subscribe to the no drinking rule. Given the probabilities of an extreme sanction, usually the case when codes are formed prohibitively, the frequency of infractions of the rules are relatively rare, but extreme in their own right. Several studies have already suggested that the number of persons from abstinent traditions who drink is extremely low. But, in turn, most of these seem to develop rather rapidly the signs of alcoholism (22,23). In consequence, it is fair to formulate the proposition that persons who are members of groups that sustain a no drinking rule and who drink will be labeled as alcoholics almost as rapidly as the damages they produce for themselves and others, will experience strong and immediate disapproval from significant others, will be exposed to a wider number of persons, and will invite and receive rapid and severe punitive sanctions. It is rather likely that here sociology and psychiatry may well join hands, in that more of these persons may be the essential alcoholics of whom Knight wrote (3). The underlying psychic disturbance or degree of stress is so great that strong remedies, such as for example explosive relief drinking, seem required. But this in turn, should it all take place in abstinence terrain, only quickens and confirms (possibly in some instances quite erroneously) a social diagnosis of alcoholism.

2. *Frequency and kind of infractions.* Reciprocity holds in the relations between persons coming to be defined as deviants and their significant others. Strong, severe, sudden, and violent infractions are quite obviously unpredictable and not routine matters and, in turn, they induce reactions of almost equal strength. As a consequence, some studies of relations between wives and their alcoholic husbands indicate that at the first signs of violence, wives label husbands as alcoholics, show strong displeasure immediately (frequently attacking or defending with equal power), exposing the husband to a range of other people, and imposing the strongest negative sanction they have at their command, that is suing for divorce, soon after this breach of marital norms (24).

By the same token, alcoholic behavior on the job invites all of these social reactions in the same swift bundle when the violations are of such massive character, when the damages inflicted are widespread and costly. The tolerance for deviant behavior always depends upon the gravity of the violations; beyond a certain vague point, retaliation is rapid, extreme, unrelenting. Consequently, the more frequent (and predictable) and grave the infractions of drinking codes, the swifter and more certain the labeling, the stronger the personal displeasure, the broader the exposure to the eyes of others, and the stronger the negative sanctions that are brought against the alcoholic. Given these circumstances, the possibilities of hiding or alternatively being hidden drop appreciably.

3. *Ratio of violators to non-violators.* Again here as elsewhere, the part-whole relationship affects the responses to the deviant behavior. It may also be thought of as an aspect of the figure-ground relationship in Gestalt psychology. For instance, it is one kind of situation if one or two Mormon college students, reared in an abstinence tradition, suddenly turn to drinking alcoholic beverages regularly. It is another kind of situation if a group of persons decides to do some serious bar-hopping in a Skid Row or honky-tonk district. Or, for another example, if soldiers, sailors, and merchant marine personnel go off on a protracted week-end drunk. In the first case, the number of violators to non-violators is so low as to call down extreme penalties, as noted above. In the second case, however, there is actually a widespread tolerance of deviant behavior in the kinds of settings noted (all-male societies celebrating relief from institutionally-induced tensions). The same argument holds when wives of alcoholics delay labeling their husbands as alcoholics when they learn of the drunken behavior of all of their neighbors' husbands (25).

When, then, the ratio of violators of drinking codes to non-violators is relatively high, labeling, exposure, disapproval, and sanctions are, in sequence, late if not non-existent, narrow in scope, and mild. In these circumstances, the chances of hiding one's alcoholism from one's self and others is optimal. And insofar as damages are done to other people, relationships, or property, all again can either be written off or reduced in the eyes of others by virtue of the sheer numbers of other persons implicated in the infractions of drinking codes.

4. *Rank of violators.* High or low tolerance for the infraction of drinking codes varies inversely with the damages produced and the rank of the violator. What this means in actual practice is that persons of relatively high social status are expected to be alcoholics in private rather than in public. Otherwise, awareness of their behavior and its consequences for others, real or imagined, would evoke very strong societal reactions paralleling the costly damages such high-ranking alcoholics might well inflict upon others.

A number of studies in alcoholism in industry all point to this inverse relationship between identification as alcoholic and tolerance of this variety of social deviance (26, 27). Unskilled workers become more rapidly identified as alcoholics by supervisors and fellow-workers than do higher white-collar supervisory workers. On the other hand, the on-the-job sanctions for alcoholic behavior visited against relatively low-ranking workers are mild compared to both sentiments against and actions taken against supervisors when their alcoholism becomes known and its damages clearly seen. The tolerance of alcoholic behavior here parallels the attitudes towards black criminality as shown in studies of adjudications in southern courts (28). Violence against blacks by other Negroes is expected if not tacitly encouraged while the legal penalties inflicted are extremely mild. By way of extreme contrast, black violence of any kind against whites is simply not expected, is explicitly discouraged, while the penalties are extremely severe.

Given these relationships, it seems quite clear that the social status of the violator of drinking codes, the alcoholic, markedly affects the social response of others. Other things equal, these propositions would seem to hold. The higher the social status of the alcoholic, the slower the label alcoholic will be affixed to the person (and correlatively, the later the assignment to the alcoholic role). In addition, the stronger the displeasure of intimate others. Also, the higher the social status of the alcoholic, the less exposed he is *qua* alcoholic to the eyes of others. And, finally, the less severe the public sanctions brought against him (in contrast to the severity of the private sanctions).

In part, these propositions derive almost directly from the effects of mistakes on social status. For, in general, the higher a person's social status, the more he stands to lose should he err in social interaction. Status commits a person to a stake in the social order, and the higher the status, the higher the stakes (29). Given this, it stands to reason that persons of high status would strive for low visibility.

the Social Conditions of Hiding

Labeling, disapproval, exposure, and sanctions constitute risks for all persons who exhibit the signs of alcoholism. As noted already, high status conduces to evasive maneuvers. Yet all persons on general principles strive to gain, then maintain status in the eyes of others. Given the fact that all persons seek status, it need not follow that others will necessarily collaborate with them in that understandable human quest or support them in that regular venture. There are a number of equally intriguing possibilities here and all of them condition the presence or absence of hiding as a social relationship as well as the success attending concealment practices.

Here it becomes a little clearer as to how teams may or may not form, on the one hand, and, on the other, the extent to which they will play well or poorly. Similarly, the object of the game they play is not unaffected by the circumstances in which they play hide-and-seek. There are several kinds of examples of factors that affect the social conditions and outcomes of hiding of alcoholics. Three sites in which hiding may or may not take place as a collaborative venture are the home, the job, and the street.

1. *At home.* Once again, status acts as a powerful intervening variable in determining who will attempt to hide an alcoholic in what circumstances and with what success. Considering the salience of status, it is perhaps fairly well-known that in the instance of drunken violence at home as when an alcoholic husband abuses wife and children, the police are often called in to quell the outbreaks when these damaging outbursts occur in low-status homes. It is less well-known, perhaps, that despite the violence of a similar intensity and in a similar situation, the police are less frequently called in when it happens in a home of much higher social status. In the second case, assailant and victim are more apt to collaborate in hiding the incident which is not the case when such violence happens in the low-status home.

2. *At work.* In industry, the status of the worker who is an alcoholic once again shapes hiding as a social relationship and team effort. To begin with, the lower the status of the worker the more likely that many more people in the plant know of his alcoholism (27). But at the same time, and paradoxically, the more often a greater number of persons will assist in cover-up operations. And this includes, on the one hand, lower level supervisors covering up for the worker, and, on the other, other workers actually performing his work for him. The supervisor may help hide a man to cement their personal relationship, or to bind him for future good work. Fellow-workers, in addition to repaying old favors, may also assist an alcoholic worker who is under the weather, not so much out of loyalty to him as out of antagonism towards management. The results of the cover-up may well be the same and equally successful; the motives in both instances are markedly different.

When persons of high status, as for example executives, are involved, the size of the team assisting in the hiding process is considerably smaller. In part, this is because executives have greater job control determining which people can or cannot have access to them, a degree of freedom and control not open to men in the ranks. In part, however, it is also due to the high costs of exposure. As a result, some executives of large corporations are full-blown alcoholics, yet their drinking behavior is known to the small circle of corporate others, usually no more than four at the most. In addition, the size of the team is directly related to the number of people who could conceivably know of the executive's alcoholism. Finally, the person is probably in more advanced stages of alcoholism, thus necessitating more clandestine social support.

The stakes for which the collaborative hiders are playing in the case of the alcoholic executive are much higher than in the instance of the low-ranking unskilled blue-collar worker. Survival of the firm, protection of one's own high income, a sense of hidden but great power all seem to be involved in varying degrees and amounts.

In either of these cases, however, it makes a real difference if the alcoholic actively consents to hiding or whether he accepts hiding efforts made on his behalf passively. In turn, it makes even a greater difference particularly so far as success of the effort goes, if he actively resists hiding on his behalf or whether he only passively resists these efforts. In the first situation, the team is united, thus more apt to succeed. In the second situation, the team is at odds with the person who has the attributes to be hidden. And, given that discord, success in hiding as a joint venture seems far less likely.

3. *On the street.* Police officers in certain sections of the city make frequent contact with inebriates. And, other things equal, the more frequent their contact with certain inebriates, the more likely these persons (usually men) are alcoholics. Once again the matter of the status of the violator of drinking codes enters to determine if hiding efforts will be made on his behalf with or without his cooperation.

At an AA meeting, a police sergeant, himself an alcoholic, recounted an intriguing instance of unsolicited street hiding (30). A certain judge in an affluent suburb, also an alcoholic, parked his car in the middle of a busy street and committed a nuisance while quite obviously violating the statute against public intoxication. Three police officers appeared on the scene almost immediately. One quickly removed the judge's car from its illegal parking place while the other two, against the judge's most violent and vituperative objections, placed the judge in a patrol car and took him home speedily. Against his own will, and despite strenuous opposition, a team of strangers formed to protect the judge's reputation and remove him from public view, thus ensuring that labeling, exposure, disapproval, and sanction would not all rapidly come down about the judge's head.

This infrequent event, of course, can be set against its much more frequent opposite number. Frequently, men of low status (judging by their clothing and habitat) yet as desirous if not more so of status in the eyes of others may plead against arrest on charges of public intoxication. On many occasions, they are sober enough to argue their case cogently; to no avail, usually, as the police officers refuse to form a team on their behalf in those circumstances (31). Perhaps, more often, they no longer seek or are in a position to seek status in the eyes of others, and the police, seeing them in an acutely intoxicated condition, only validate their seeming lack of concern of status by locking them up. In this last and most frequent instance, of course, the police act only as the arm of the wider society. For in locking up chronic alcoholics in jail, the police only abide by a collective policy of hiding. In locking up public drunkards, particularly if they are chronic alcoholics, the police succeed in hiding intermittently at least a vast alcohol problem that the society seeks to deny by averting its gaze.

Hide-and-seek takes two persons or two sides when more become involved. The converse of this interaction can be called show and deny. In this second instance, which seems to be increasing as awareness and understanding of alcoholism spreads, while more and more people are calling attention to their own or others' alcoholism, substantial numbers of people deny or look away.

Prescriptions on Hiding Alcoholics

From what has been said thus far, it seems axiomatic that status has a set of reverse effects upon the possibilities of hiding alcoholics. To summarize, the higher an alcoholic's social status, the later he will be identified (if at all) as an alcoholic. In part this is because of a narrower field of exposure and that more protective efforts are made by himself and others to conceal his alcoholism from other persons, if for no other reasons than the high stakes that are involved. On the other hand, private disapproval (subject to variations according to drinking codes) will be much stronger as will be the ultimate private sanctions (by contrast public disapproval and public sanctions are less infrequent, can be guarded against, and, other things equal, considerably milder than in the case of a low status alcoholic person placed in similar circumstances).

These effects reverse in the condition of low social status. Then identification comes much more rapidly, the person being labeled (if not by himself, then by significant others at work and at home) as an alcoholic. However, private displeasure is not at all commensurate with the wide exposure and severe treatment as well as punitive sanctions that are brought. The net effect of these social facts is that high public tolerance for alcoholism among persons of low social status only guarantees that its prevalence, in hidden as well as overt forms, is bound to remain at its present high levels. Meanwhile, high private intolerance among hidden alcoholics of high rank works to both sustain its current high levels also; but more important, given high stakes, greater and stronger informal, hidden pressures can also be brought to bear to coerce successfully high status alcoholics to take treatment for their condition and reduce its spreading damages.

The conclusions by way of prescriptions on hiding by now should be obvious. There is no necessary call here for complete openness for everybody on the prevalence of alcoholism in all of its stages and forms. There is no call here to necessarily reduce the amount of hidden alcoholism. Rather, the call here is for raising the stakes so that persons now identified, sometimes all too soon, will want to not only keep their alcoholism hidden but to recover from it and the sooner the better. So much for the prescriptions for low status alcoholics—improving their lot in life in whatever ways possible and increasing their awareness of alcoholism and its predictable, almost certain damages are two ways that immediately come to mind to achieve this end.

The prescriptions on high-status hidden alcoholism are a little different. Here the call would be to increase the public penalties wherever there is exposure and, at the same time, to reduce the stake that team-players might have in helping high status persons to conceal their alcoholism. This second is perhaps a more difficult task. One possible remedy, of course, is the same one that can and ultimately will cure all forms of blackmail. And that of course is by taking the profit out of it. But so long as some men can gain status simply by pointing to men who have less status than themselves, which means for this paper as long as alcoholism is still a stigmatized attribute, to that degree will there be, perhaps inevitably, hidden alcoholism among persons of high status.

References

1. Goffman, Erving. *Stigma.* New York: Prentice-Hall, 1963.
2. Keller, Mark. "The Definition of Alcoholism and the Estimation of of its Prevalence." In *Society, Culture, and Drinking Patterns,* edited by David J. Pittman and Charles R. Snyder. New York: John Wiley, 1962, pp. 310-29.
3. Knight, Robert P. "The Psychodynamics of Chronic Alcoholism." *Journal of Nervous and Mental Disease* 86 (November 1937): 538-48.

4. Jellinek, E. M. "Phases of Alcohol Addiction." *Quarterly Journal of Studies on Alcohol* 13 (December 1952): 673-84.

5. Jellinek, E. M. "Estimating the Prevalence of Alcoholism: Modified Values in the Jellinek Formula and an Alternative Approach." *Quarterly Journal of Studies on Alcohol* 20 (June 1959): 261-69.

6. Seeley, John R. "Estimating the Prevalence of Alcoholism: A Critical Analysis of the Jellinek Formula." *Quarterly Journal of Studies on Alcohol* 20 (June 1959): 245-54.

7. Wellman, Wayne M.; Maxwell, Milton A.; and O'Hollaren, Paul. "Private Hospital Alcoholic Patients and the Changing Conception of the 'Typical' Alcoholic." *Quarterly Journal of Studies on Alcohol* 18 (September 1957): 388-404.

8. National Council on Alcoholism. "The Committee on the Homeless and Institutional Alcoholic." New York, 1958, pp. 9-10.

9. Bogue, Donald R. *Skid Row in American Cities.* Chicago: The University of Chicago Press, 1963.

10. Caplow, Theodore; Lovald, Keith A.; and Wallace, Samuel E. *A General Report on the Problem of Relocating the Population of the Lower Loop Redevelopment Area.* Minneapolis, Minn.: Minneapolis Redevelopment Authority, 1958.

11. *The Men on Skid Row. A Study of Philadelphia's Homeless Man Population.* Philadelphia, Pa.: Temple University, Department of Psychiatry, 1960.

12. *Uniform Crime Reports.* Washington, D.C.: Department of Justice, 1966, p. 109.

13. Bales, Robert F. "Cultural Differences in Rates of Alcoholism." *Quarterly Journal of Studies on Alcohol* 6 (March 1946): 480-99.

14. Pittman, David J. "International Overview: Social and Cultural Factors in Drinking Patterns, Pathological and Nonpathological." In *Alcoholism,* edited by David J. Pittman. New York: Harper and Row, 1967, pp. 3-20.

15. Snyder, Charles R. *Alcohol and the Jews.* New Haven, Conn.: Yale Center of Alcohol Studies, 1958.

16. Knupfer, Genevieve, and Room, Robin. "Drinking Patterns and Attitudes of Irish, Jewish and White Protestant American Men." *Quarterly Journal of Studies on Alcohol* 28 (December 1967): 676-99.

17. Lolli, Giorgio; Serianni, Emidio; Golder, Grace M.; and Luzzatto-Fegiz, P. *Alcohol in Italian Culture.* New Haven, Conn.: Yale Center of Alcohol Studies, 1958.

18. Bacon, Selden D. "Social Settings Conducive to Alcoholism." *Journal of the American Medical Association* 164 (May 11, 1957): 177-81.

19. Sterne, Muriel W. "Drinking Patterns and Alcoholism among American Negroes." In *Alcoholism,* edited by David J. Pittman. New York: Harper and Row, 1967, pp. 66-99.

20. Ullman, Albert D. "Socio-cultural Backgrounds of Alcoholism." *The Annals* 315 (January 1958): 48-54.

21. Rubington, Earl. "Two Types of Drug Use." *International Journal of the Addictions* 3 (Fall 1968): 301-18.

22. Straus, Robert, and Bacon, Selden D. *Drinking in College.* New Haven, Conn.: Yale University Press, 1954.

23. Mizruchi, Ephraim H., and Perruci, Robert. "Norm Qualities and Differential Effects of Deviant Behavior: An Exploratory Analysis." *American Sociological Review* 27 (June 1962): 391-99.

24. Jackson, Joan K., and Kogan, Kate L. "The Search for Solutions: Help-Seeking Patterns of Families of Active and Inactive Alcoholics." *Quarterly Journal of Studies on Alcohol* 24 (September 1963): 449-72.

25. Jackson, Joan K. "The Adjustment of the Family to the Crisis of Alcoholism." *Quarterly Journal of Studies on Alcohol* 15 (December 1954): 562-85.

26. Trice, Harrison M. "The Job Behavior of Problem Drinkers." In *Society, Culture, and Drinking Patterns,* edited by David J. Pittman and Charles R. Snyder. New York: John Wiley, 1962, pp. 493-510.

27. Warkov, Seymour; Bacon, Selden; and Hawkins, Arthur. "Social Correlates of Industrial Problem Drinking." *Quarterly Journal of Studies on Alcohol* 26 (March 1965): 58-71.

28. Davis, Alison; Gardner, Burleigh; and Gardner, Mary R. *Deep South: A Social Anthropological Study of Caste and Class.* Chicago: The University of Chicago Press, 1941.

29. Briar, Scott, and Piliavin, Irving. "Delinquency, Situational Inducements, and Commitment to Conformity." *Social Problems* 13 (Summer 1965): 35-45.

30. A police officer and member of Alcoholics Anonymous reported this incident while telling his "story" to a meeting of the Orange Street AA Group, New Haven, Connecticut, July 1958.

31. Bittner, Egon. "The Police on Skid-Row: A Study of Peace Keeping." *American Sociological Review* 32 (October 1967): 699-715.

Chapter V

Types of Alcoholic Offenders

When ideas and actions clash, social problems may develop. Clashes assume three forms. Men may seek contradictory values. Seeking both war and peace exemplifies *value-conflict.* Men may obey rules, yet fail to achieve desired values. When conformity brings no rewards, *social disorganization* exists. Men, finally, may violate rules, yet achieve desired values; stealing is one example. When violations bring rewards, *personal deviance* results.

When society seems relatively stable, clashes of great magnitude often go unnoticed by interested groups. As society undergoes change, some clashes become more apparent and then groups become alarmed. If enough groups find clashes troublesome and seek changes, then and only then does a social problem exist.

In alcoholism and the law, there are several good examples of the three kinds of clashes between ideas and actions. When, for instance, agents of law enforcement seek simultaneously to both treat and punish alcoholic offenders, value-conflict exists. When, for another example, locking up public drunkards fails to lower arrests for public intoxication, social disorganization exists. And, for a final instance, if judges punish alcoholic offenders in the name of treatment, then violation of rules exists.

Reprinted from *Federal Probation* 33 (March 1969): 28-35 by permission of the publisher.

These three kinds of clashes have existed for many years in the legal handling of alcoholic offenders. Now, however, in a period of rapid change, these clashes between ideas and actions will probably generate some disturbing social problems. At present, many changes are taking place in alcoholism and the law. For example, community mental health centers have been suggested as a response to problems of alcoholism.[1] And, for another example, higher courts have ruled that chronic alcoholism is a defense against public intoxication.[2] Unless, then, ideas are brought in line with actions, some very severe problems are bound to distress all persons concerned with alcoholism and the law.

For years, there has been a curious similarity between the alcoholic's actions and legal responses to those selfsame actions. Faced with mounting problems, the alcoholic takes immediate action—he tries to drink his problems away. His action, a fixed response to a changing set of problems, guarantees an increase rather than a decrease in those problems. The result is predictable; unless he finds another set of responses to his problems, he will continue to drink.

Faced with his fixed response, agents of criminal justice formulated an equally simple set of ideas on which they took repeated action—lock him up. The result, of course, is that arrests for public intoxication have kept pace with the rising prevalence of drunkenness in public view. For years now, alcoholics and all kinds of law enforcement agents have been engaged in a fixed and unchanging social relationship. Because of the simplicity of this relationship, there had been little reason to change, despite the fact that clashes between ideas and actions have always surrounded the legal reaction to alcoholic offenders.

Now, however, with legal and medical groups pressing for change, social problems of great magnitude very likely will come into being. Legal ideas on alcoholics and legal actions on those ideas have become both objects of study and targets for change. In the recent past, simple combination of the notions that alcoholics are immoral, sick, and criminal shaped law enforcement. Little attempt was made to define the kinds of immorality, the nature of the illness, and the degree and scope of criminality. Presently, the pressure is to make such an attempt, to formulate ideas, and to take action on them. Unless, however, the system of law enforcement responds to these pressures for changes in handling alcoholic offenders, value-conflict, social disorganization, and personal deviance in law enforcement will rise rather than fall.

Once a coherent system of ideas for sorting out alcoholic offenders develops, the problem of what kinds of actions to take on these ideas can be solved more efficiently than in the past. This chapter outlines one way for developing such a system of ideas. First, it shows how observed divergence from prevailing drinking practices defines the alcoholic. Second, it shows that current styles in managing problems of alcoholism yield two social types. Third, it examines three types of alcoholic offenders. And finally, it suggests how to apply these ideas in law enforcement.

Drinking Culture and Drinking Practices

Drinking culture, the set of ideas on how to drink, is either sacred or secular.[3] In sacred drinking, alcoholic beverages become religious symbols. Sacred beliefs require that drinking mark an event in tribal life and symbolize communion with tribal gods. And religious specialists prescribe drinking norms and control drinking situations.

In secular drinking, drinkers believe drinking alcoholic beverages helps to pass time; they value drinking for its intrinsic effects and make up their own rules on how to drink. An individualistic drinker, a species of the secular, believes that alcoholic beverages will make him feel good, values drinking to the extent that it produces desired effects, and makes his own rules on drinking.

Drinking culture also includes abstinence, or how not to drink. There are three kinds of abstinence orientations—one is clearly sacred while the other two, whether collective or individualistic, are secular. For instance many persons belong to religious groups which forbid drinking. But some groups may prescribe periodic or situational abstinence (as, for example, when they agree not to drink while performing work). Some individuals abstain on secular grounds (for reasons of health). Finally, alcoholics, who at one time drank for personal reasons, later abstain on religious grounds. Many conversions in rescue missions as well as affiliations with Alcoholics Anonymous have these characteristics.

Individualistic attitudes toward drinking increase the chances of becoming an alcoholic.[4] In general, alcoholics have personal reasons for drinking. As their drinking careers develop, the object of drinking shifts from feeling good to escaping pain. Secular drinking encourages feeling good while in groups. But persons who need to feel good more often or for a longer time soon bypass the group for drinking itself. Once drinking facilitates feeling, groups can be dispensed with, particularly if members of the group try to control one's drinking behavior. Secular drinking, under appropriate conditions, is more likely to foster alcoholic drinking than sacred drinking.

The United States as a multigroup society contains not one but several drinking cultures. Despite diversity of drinking cultures and regional variations, drinking practices have become somewhat more uniform in recent years. Evidence from surveys[5] permits the following generalizations on drinking in the United States.

1. Somewhere between 60 and 70 percent of the adult population drink alcoholic beverages. Perhaps three-fourths of the men drink as over against a little more than half of the women.
2. Men drink more regularly than women, three times more often. Women, more often, are occasional drinkers.
3. Drinking goes up with education and income.
4. The longer the native background, the less frequent the drinking.
5. Protestants abstain more frequently than Catholics who, in turn, abstain more frequently than Jews; on the other hand, Irish Catholics have the highest rates of alcoholism, Jews the lowest.
6. Since World War II, more persons have become users of alcoholic beverages; at the same time, there has been a marked decrease in per capita consumption.
7. More women drink now than a generation ago.
8. Drinking increases with urbanization.
9. Americans currently favor beer; a hundred years ago, whiskey was their favorite.
10. Moderate social drinking is rapidly becoming the national norm.
11. Off-premise sales have risen, on-premise sales have fallen.
12. Most adults drink to be sociable.
13. A minority develops drinking problems; currently, there are an estimated 5½ million alcoholics in a drinking population of 90 million people.

These findings show increasing uniformities in American drinking practices. The Nation has begun to adopt a moderate drinking style. Two-fisted whiskey drinkers were more common on the frontier than they now are in the bars, cocktail lounges, restaurants, and night clubs throughout the country. Several varieties of "hard" drinkers still remain; some of them, under specified conditions, go on to become alcoholics.

the Social Definition of Alcoholism

Alcoholism can only be defined by the degree and type of divergence between drinking culture and drinking practices among certain groups.

A marked and repeated discrepancy between ideas on drinking in those groups, on the one hand, and how some members of those groups actually drink, on the other, sets the stage for redefinition as an alcoholic. The divergence calls attention to the person, creates a labeling crisis, and ultimately produces changes in actions and attitudes toward the person so singled out because of his drinking. Because of diversity in drinking cultures, minor and major divergences are often lumped together and called alcoholism. However, anybody who persistently damages his health (mental and physical), his work, and his relations with other people by repeated drinking, is probably an alcoholic.[6]

There is great variety among alcoholics and changes constantly take place in their careers. Still, it is possible to distinguish *addictive* from *symptomatic* alcoholics. Addictive alcoholics are either *pure addicts* or *habitues.* Pure addicts can abstain from drinking for long periods at a time. Once they begin to drink, however, they cannot control how much or how long they will drink. They usually cannot stop until acute intoxication or stupor. Habitues or inveterate alcoholics reverse the start-stop pattern. They can regulate how much they are drinking but they cannot go without drinking. Abstinence produces withdrawal symptoms for them (though not as severely as it sometimes does for pure addicts).

Symptomatic alcoholics are either *essential* or *reactive.* Essential alcoholics behave differently from other people almost immediately after their first taste of alcoholic beverages. An underlying personality disturbance gets relief from prolonged and frequently explosive drinking. Damage to health, self-image, work, and social relations cumulates rapidly for essential alcoholics. Yet they are able to control their drinking and can abstain when they wish. Reactive alcoholics, in contrast to essential alcoholics, appear much later in life. They respond to sudden and major changes, such as a wife's or mother's death or the loss of an important job or business, by drinking heavily.

People often classify alcoholics by causes, styles and consequences of drinking. But unless these are carefully distinguished at the outset, drinkers will get sorted into the wrong categories. Additionally, because of tolerance, habituation, and dependence, alcoholics who start for different reasons, drink differently and suffer different consequences, all end up looking alike years later. Distinctions between cause and effects are required. Personality disturbance usually comes after but not necessarily before addiction. In turn, personality disturbance, which produces symptomatic alcoholics, may also lead in time to true addiction, whether of the pure or inveterate variety.

Alcoholics as Social Types

Once a person is labeled an "alcoholic," he faces social redefinition. Usually he has only three ways of handling his problem. First, he can stop drinking. A few persons probably do just that rather than suffer more damages from alcoholism. Most alcoholics, however, continue to drink and deal with their problems in one of two ways. Either they reduce their membership in conventional groups and drink privately or they sever all ties with conventional groups and seek the company of people who drink the way they do.[7]

Both kinds of alcoholics must face those social and psychological problems that heavy drinking produces. In the group case, the alcoholic joins with others who try to solve alcoholic problems collectively. In the individualistic case, the alcoholic tries to manage these problems on his own. The alcoholic who shares ideas and actions on problems of alcoholism with others participates in an alcoholic culture. The alcoholic who lacks or shuns that access is a nonparticipant in that culture. Nevertheless, because of the progressive character of alcoholic drinking, a large though unknown number of alcoholics seems headed for entry into alcoholic culture. To type alcoholics socially, then, it is necessary to know how they cope with problems of alcoholism at different stages of their careers.

The table below and the discussion that follows it indicate the differences between two social types of alcoholics. The table is based on how they manage the social problems of alcoholism. As the table shows,

Participation in Alcoholic Culture

	HIGH	LOW
1. Drinking behavior	predictable, fixed, and simple	unpredictable, changing and complex
2. Self-image as alcoholic	accepts	rejects
3. Number of group memberships	few, mainly on drinking role	many, few on drinking role
4. Characteristics of ideology	antisocial	social
5. Degree of social visibility	relatively high	relatively low
6. Exposure to criminal sanctions	relatively high	relatively low
7. Exposure to treatment sanctions	relatively low	relatively high

participants in alcoholic culture deal with their problems somewhat differently than nonparticipants.

1. *Drinking behavior.*—Participants in alcoholic culture show more uniformity in drinking behavior than nonparticipants. Reasons for drinking, amounts, occasions, beverages, companions, places, and consequences are more likely to be the same for participants than for nonparticipants.

2. *Self-image as alcoholics.*—Participants in alcoholic culture are much more likely to accept the self-definition of alcoholic. Nonparticipants are more likely to deny their alcoholism.

3. *Number of group memberships.*—Participants in alcoholic culture belong to fewer groups. And many of these groups center on drinking. Nonparticipants belong to a greater variety of groups, few of which focus on drinking.

4. *Characteristics of the ideology.*—Participants in alcoholic culture defend drinking. In general, they share antisocial attitudes. By contrast, nonparticipants make no claims on behalf of drinking. In general, they have either prosocial or asocial attitudes.

5. *Degree of social visibility.*—Heavy drinking brings participants in alcoholic culture to other people's attention. Social support for heavy drinking and small concern for appearances increase their visibility. Nonparticipants are seen less often in public as heavy drinkers; this is because they have much less social support for drinking and because they are more concerned with appearances.

6. *Exposure to criminal sanctions.*—Participants in alcoholic culture are much more likely to get caught for their offenses than are nonparticipants. Regardless of the true prevalence of offenses among both categories, arrest rates are much higher for participants than for nonparticipants.

7. *Exposure to treatment sanctions.*—Participants in alcoholic culture are less likely to view alcoholism as an illness. Their experience with treatment will be meager, for the most part confined mainly to "drying out." Nonparticipants by contrast more often subscribe to the view that alcoholism is an illness and consequently have more experience with various treatments for alcoholism.

Types of Alcoholic Offenders

The discussion just concluded has suggested a way of typing alcoholics socially. Two questions that come to mind immediately are (1) what is the relationship of alcoholism to crime and (2) how can the suggested typology clarify that relationship? This chapter now turns to a consideration of these issues. First, it provides a survey of research findings on alcoholism and crime. Second, it discusses three types of alcoholic offenders. Third, it examines these offenders in the light of the foregoing social typology. And then, in the final section, it suggests how this typology may be used to improve correctional practice with alcoholic offenders.

A recent survey of studies on alcoholism and crime lists the following findings:

> 1. More alcoholics and excessive drinkers are arrested than are moderate drinkers and, individually, they are arrested more often. Across the country, the police spend approximately 75 percent of their time handling people who have been drinking excessively. As a general rule, being drunk itself is the offense with which these persons are charged. A sizeable proportion of those who are arrested for being drunk have frequently been arrested for being drunk, often several times in the same year.
>
> 2. Alcoholics are more likely to be arrested for misdemeanors than for felonies.
>
> 3. In prison populations composed of those committed for felonies, between 24 and 40 percent had histories of excessive drinking and between 8 and 24 percent were inebriated at the time they were apprehended. Eighty to 90 percent of the inmates blamed their incarceration on alcohol.
>
> 4. Alcoholics and inebriated persons are more likely to be involved in crimes against individuals than against property. They are more likely to act as individuals than as members of organized criminal groups. The crime is more likely to be impulsive than planned.
>
> 5. The crimes of women alcoholics are different from those of women nonalcoholics only in that there is a preponderance of illegal sexual behavior. There has been no study of the relationship between crime and drinking of a nonalcoholic type among women.
>
> 6. Imprisoned alcoholics tend to be older than imprisoned nonalcoholics.
>
> 7. Between 30 and 40 percent of persons chronically arrested for drunkenness have histories of earlier criminal careers.[8]

Four elements are required to designate any event a crime.[9] Crime exists if, and only if, a government through its officially designated agents applies legitimate force against any person who engages in a specifically proscribed act. Without *politicality, specificity, uniformity,* and *penal sanctions,* there is no crime. The law specifies three broad classes of crimes: crimes, against persons, crimes against property, and crimes against public order.

This chapter turns, then, in sequence, to alcoholic offenders who commit crimes against persons, alcoholic offenders who commit crimes against property, and alcoholic offenders who commit crimes against public order.

1. *Alcoholic offenders who commit crimes against persons.*—Roebuck and Johnson compared a sample of 40 Negro offenders, composed mainly of simultaneous "drunk and assault" charges, with 360 Negro offenders who had one or more of a large number of other arrest patterns.[10] In 24 of 34 comparisons, the drunk-and-assault group differed significantly. The assaultive drunks more often came from patriarchal homes where the father supervised in a harsh, but erratic manner. These men had considerable conflict at home, yet maintained close primary ties with their families, through adolescence and early adulthood, 35 not leaving home until they were 21. They were more often disciplinary school problems but less often truants or runaways from home. They were less often reared in slums, less often employed in street trades, and had few police contacts before 18, less often adjudicated as juvenile delinquents, less often with delinquent companions or members of delinquent gangs. And all had more positive attitudes toward work, were more often married, and had closer family ties. No one was addicted to drugs. But all were more frequently gamblers and problem drinkers.

All were concerned about not being "pushed around." And all were concerned with physical courage and with the necessity for violence and fighting as a means of resolving conflict and of self-preservation. These 40 offenders faced a dilemma where rigid home controls coupled with close attachments made it impossible to discharge frustrations there. Aggressions, contained at home, sought discharge outside. But this came about in part because of the successful socialization process of teaching discipline, inculcating religious scruples, and developing conscience. Thus, alcohol use reduced inhibitions on explosive aggression, the consequences of strong internal controls. Then, these young men all overreacted to their rigid family background.

"These 40 offenders," the authors write, "had the usual frustrations of the Northern urban Negro, but because of a strict fundamentalist upbringing were unable to express hostilities, except when inhibitions were weakened by alcohol. Drinking and crimes of violence (as opposed to crimes against property) may be a result of the interactive effects of continued frustration and of parental and societal success in building up inhibitions to aggression." [11]

This study brings to mind the stereotype of lower class behavior (drinking, fighting, fornicating, and gambling). These men, however, are participants in the "respectable" segment of Negro subculture.[12] The evidence for their respectability comes from their close family ties, marital status, and attitudes toward work. It becomes clear, then, that socialization exacts different costs in different social settings. One obvious cost, of course, is the propensity to drink away deeply seated conflicts.

There are some striking similarities in this study with some of Bales' theories on Irish drinking, itself a cultural response to high socialization costs.[13] A fundamentalist attitude on certain issues, a harsh yet erratic father, close attachment to home coupled with high conflict establish ambivalence, so crucial for the genesis of alcoholism. Much like the Irish, these "lace curtain" Negroes seem on their way toward alcoholism. The form their alcoholism takes, however, derives from contingencies of socialization into Negro subculture. And their incipient alcoholism makes them a special type of alcoholic offender who commits drunken assaults. (Each man averaged 15 arrests for such assaults.)

2. *Alcoholic offenders who commit crimes against property.*—A 1959 California prison study compared 675 problem drinkers with 1,582 nonproblem drinkers.[14] Inmates were called problem drinkers if they answered "Yes" to the question: "In general, has the use of alcoholic beverages been a problem in your life in any way?" If they answered "No" to the question, they were called nonproblem drinkers. The results of the comparison yielded some significant differences.

The most frequent offenses of the problem drinking group were forgery-and-check offenses. Indeed, the rate of these offenses was significantly higher among the problem drinking group. And, in addition, there were significant differences between problem and nonproblem drinkers in two less frequently committed offenses. In this prison population, auto theft was rather infrequent. Yet problem drinkers committed this offense much more frequently than did the nonproblem drinkers.

For the problem drinkers in this prison population some intriguing changes in offense patterns took place in their criminal careers. For example, robbery was associated with younger offenders while forgery-and-check offenses were more often associated with older offenders. Finally, homicide and sex offenses also increased with age, though the association was less obvious.

These data invite speculation. Offenders may all be classified by whether they experienced a heavy, moderate, or low degree of stress during childhood and adolescent socialization. In addition, they may be further classified by the number and type of skills in their personal response kits for dealing with the stress of social life. It seems possible that fairly well-equipped offenders switched from robbery to forgery as they got older and as their drinking became more of a problem for them. To a certain extent, this might be called a relatively successful adaptation to the usually unsuccessful criminal career of most alcoholic offenders. And, in both instances, the offenders probably had a couple of drinks before committing the crimes; alcohol in small doses improves certain performances.

By contrast, the less well-equipped offenders may well manifest another kind of switch as they get older which suggests that the high degree of stress experienced during early socialization was not offset by a large enough repertory of skills for coping with life. In consequence, as drinking increased, more violent rather than less violent kinds of criminal activities took place.

3. *Alcoholic offenders who commit crimes against public order.*—In 1958 Pittman and Gordon reported on their study of 187 chronic drunkenness offenders.[15] These offenders, for the most part, specialize in public disorder. The number of alcoholics in this country who are also chronic drunkenness offenders is decidedly small. Nevertheless, because of their high visibility they have a significance and influence far in excess of their numbers. In general, they form the image of the alcoholic derelict in the public mind. These are only some of the reasons why the Pittman and Gordon study is important.

Their study, among other things, reveals that specialization in crimes against public order is true for approximately one-third of the sample they studied. Fifty-eight men (31 percent) had a "pure" arrest record of public intoxication only; these men might be conceived as true specialists in breaching the peace. Another 59 men (32 percent), however, in addition to arrests for public intoxication had also been arrested for vagrancy, disorderly conduct, driving while intoxicated, gambling, violation of liquor laws, family offenses, etc. Finally, 69 men (37 percent) had histories of more serious offenses in addition to their long record of public intoxication. In addition to public intoxication, these men had "been charged with criminal homicide, rape, robbery, burglary, larceny, automobile theft, forgery, counterfeiting, embezzlement, fraud, narcotics law violations." [16]

Pittman and Gordon advance the notion of "double failure" to account for this last category of chronic drunkenness offender. Arrests for drunkenness, for all offenders, tend to rise with age. And for the specialists this was true. For those offenders with mixed offense patterns (intoxication + other misdemeanor group and intoxication + felony group) arrests for other offenses, particularly felonies, varied inversely with age. Thus, as men got older, they got arrested more often for drunkenness and little else. These same men in their youth, however, had been arrested for serious offenses. Hence, the notion of "double failure." For, according to the authors, chronic drunkenness offenders use alcohol as an adaptation to social failure in general. And the intoxication + felony offenders are the most clear-cut case of "double failure." First, they were ill-equipped to succeed in the legitimate world, and second, they failed in their attempts to launch a successful criminal career. Having failed twice, they turned more frequently to alcohol for relief. This switch in offense patterns marks a downwardly mobile career in crime which parallels closely their increasing involvement in alcoholic drinking.

The same categories used to type alcoholics can, of course, be used to type criminals.[17] Role, self-image, group memberships, ideology, visibility and social support, and exposure to social controls similarly vary with extent and degree of participation in a criminal subculture. Role includes what police generally call the *modus operandi* or offense style. Self-image refers to whether the person does or does not define himself as a criminal; group membership points to the presence or absence of affiliations with other criminals; ideology refers to whether the individual holds prosocial, antisocial, or asocial beliefs; visibility and social support refer to the numbers of other people who are aware of the role and whether they support it or not, and exposure to social controls refers to the number and type of sanctions the individual may have experienced.

A simple illustration follows comparing pickpockets[18] who belong to a criminal culture with embezzlers[19] who do not. Pickpockets perform a highly skilled role as part of a group; embezzlers also perform a highly skilled role but alone. Pickpockets see themselves as criminals; embezzlers define themselves as law-abiding citizens. Pickpockets belong to a few other groups, many of which are composed of criminals; embezzlers belong to a greater number of groups, none of which are criminal. Pickpockets are highly visible (to law enforcement agents) and enjoy little social support; embezzlers are practically invisible and enjoy high support. Finally, pickpockets, as professionals, experience both high and regular exposure to criminal sanctions; embezzlers, as amateurs, experience low and irregular exposure to sanctions.

The use of alcohol usually begins in adolescence; heavy use starts in early adulthood. A person may begin heavy use for inner reasons, in response to external circumstances, or a combination of the two. Changes in his life situation alter his drinking pattern. In turn, changes in drinking alter his situation. Similarly, persons may first become socialized to the legitimate world, only later to try their hands at crime. They may also start out relatively early as one or another kind of professional criminal and remain so the rest of their lives. In effect, then, legitimate, alcoholic, and criminal careers contain their own contingencies and their own critical stages.

With this discussion in mind, it is now possible to fit the three types of alcoholic offenders to the foregoing social typology of alcoholics and criminals. The young assaultive drunk offenders are neither alcoholics nor criminals from their point of view despite their already extensive police records. Their drinking behavior makes them personae non gratae to alcoholics while their self-conceptions and ideology keep them apart from criminal culture. However, should they persist in problem drinking, they will very likely become alcoholics. And later on, some, though not all of them, will gain entry into alcoholic culture.

The problem drinkers studied in the California prison participate in criminal culture in varying degrees; few at the moment share in alcoholic culture. Were they asked if they see themselves as criminals, most of them would answer yes. Were they asked *in a nonprison setting,* if they were alcoholics, most of them would deny it. In later years, however, should they continue unsuccessfully as criminals, increased heavy drinking will no doubt cause them to switch from criminality to alcoholism. At that point, a substantial number of them will seek and gain entry into alcoholic culture.

Finally, the chronic drunkenness offenders studied by Pittman and Gordon are neither legitimate persons nor criminals. All are alcoholics by the definition presented earlier in this paper, though all need not necessarily agree with that designation. Yet most of them participate intensively in alcoholic culture. More advanced in years than the previous two types of offenders, their involvement in that alcoholic culture is almost complete.

Social Typology and Law Enforcement

Currently, drastic changes are taking place in the world of alcoholism and the law. Up until fairly recently, a modus vivendi had been worked out between agents of law enforcement and various kinds of alcoholic offenders. While no one needed necessarily to like the situation, it was the accepted situation and fairly well understood by all persons involved in it. Now changes are coming into that situation with more to follow. The first change is in the definition of the alcoholic who enters the system of criminal justice. If he is now to be defined as a sick person, then law enforcement agents have to see him in those terms and act towards him on the basis of that idea.

The ideas set forth in this chapter may help both alcoholics and law enforcement agents get through the difficult period of readjustment ahead. Social typology may be of some use in developing a set of ideas on alcoholic offenders, responding to them in terms of these ideas, and then noting the difference it makes, if any. It has the merit of being simple and understandable, of suggesting the kinds of actions to be taken, and of lending itself to evaluative research.

Once they enter the system of criminal justice, alcoholic offenders can be fitted to the typology during a brief interview. Once they have been typed, the kind of correctional experience from which they may profit can be derived from their location in the typology. The final step, of course, is to assign them to just that kind of experience and then to study the extent to which and the ways in which they profit from that experience.

The usefulness of this typology is that it can be employed in the ways suggested at any stage in the correctional cycle. For example, it can be put to use by the probation officer when he prepares his presentence report, in the conditions of probation, while the defendant is serving his sentence, and finally, while he is on parole.

The major inference for correctional responses is that nonparticipants (or marginal participants) in alcoholic culture are most likely to respond positively to some form of two-person treatment group (probation, social casework, psychotherapy, correctional, and alcoholism counseling). By contrast, participants in alcoholic culture are more likely to profit from a larger treatment group in which they take at various points staff as well as patient roles (group therapy, guided group interaction, Alcoholics Anonymous, the halfway house). It should be pointed out that these are inferences from the theory. Until correctional research on them has been done they will remain inferences.

The system of criminal justice, however, needs a set of systematic inferences on which to guide its work, particularly in correction. Pressure for such inferences is bound to increase rather than decrease given the rapidly changing definitions of alcoholic offenders and the call for rehabilitative action. This chapter has offered one set of inferences for answering that call.

Notes

[1] *Alcohol Problems,* A Report to the Nation by the Cooperative Commission on the Study of Alcoholism. Prepared by Thomas F. A. Plaut (New York: Oxford University Press, 1967), pp. 93-94.

[2] Peter Barton Hutt, "The Legal Control of Alcoholism: Towards a Public Health Concept," *Alcoholism,* ed. David J. Pittman (New York: Harper and Row, 1967), pp. 124-28.

[3] Robert F. Bales, "Cultural Differences in Rates of Alcoholism," *Quarterly Journal of Studies on Alcohol* 6 (March 1946): 482-98.

[4] Robert F. Bales, "The 'Fixation Factor' in Alcohol Addiction: An Hypothesis Derived From a Comparative Study of Irish and Jewish Social Norms" (Ph. D. diss., Harvard University, 1944).

[5] A recent survey is Harold A. Mulford, "Drinking and Deviant Drinking, U. S. A.," *Quarterly Journal of Studies on Alcohol* 25 (December 1964): 634-50. Additional surveys are reported in *Drinking and Intoxication,* ed. Raymond G. McCarthy (Glencoe, Ill.: The Free Press, 1959), pp. 179-245.

[6] E. M. Jellinek, *The Disease Concept of Alcoholism* (New Haven, Conn.: Hillhouse Press, 1960), p. 35.

[7] Harrison M. Trice, *Alcoholism in America* (New York: McGraw-Hill, 1966), pp. 55-58.

[8] Joan K. Jackson, "Alcohol and Crime," *Alcohol Education for Classroom and Community,* ed. Raymond G. McCarthy (New York: McGraw-Hill, 1964), p. 169.

[9] Donald R. Cressey, "Crime," *Contemporary Social Problems,* ed. Robert K. Merton and Robert A. Nisbet (New York: Harcourt, Brace and World, 1966), p. 140.

[10] Julian Roebuck and Ronald Johnson, "The Negro Drinker and Assaulter as a Criminal Type," *Crime and Delinquency* 8 (January 1962): 21-33.

[11] Ibid., pp. 32-33.

[12] Hylan Lewis, *Blackways of Kent* (Chapel Hill: University of North Carolina Press, 1955).

[13] Bales, "Cultural Differences in Rates of Alcoholism."

[14] Division of Alcoholic Rehabilitation, *Alcoholism and California, Criminal Offenders and Drinking Involvement,* part 2, February 1964. Publication No. 10. (Berkeley, Calif.: California Department of Mental Health, 1964).

[15] David J. Pittman and C. Wayne Gordon, *The Revolving Door* (New Haven, Conn: Yale Center of Alcohol Studies, 1958).

[16] Ibid., p. 47.

[17] For an extended discussion of the application of criminal typology to correctional treatment, see Don C. Gibbons, *Changing the Lawbreaker* (New York: Prentice-Hall, 1965).

[18] David W. Maurer, *Whiz Mob* (New Haven, Conn.: College and University Press, 1964).

[19] Donald R. Cressey, *Other People's Money* (Glencoe, Ill.: The Free Press, 1953).

Chapter VI

the Alcoholic and the Jail

Behavior is always in response to some definition of the situation. Alcoholic inmates behave as they do because of their definitions of the jail situation. If we want to know why they act as they do, we have to ask them for their definitions. If we want to change their actions, we have to change their definitions. Sometimes this can be done best by changing the situation.

Another way of putting the questions is to ask: What is the jail supposed to do, what does it actually do, and what can it do with the alcoholic inmate? And if the questions are put in terms of the main actors, then we may ask what do correctional officers and alcoholic inmates do when they come in contact with each other, and what do alcoholic inmates do when they come in contact with each other?

There are many opinions in this field and very few well-established facts. To offer some tentative answers to these questions, I shall sketch in some background before comparing opinions with facts. So we must first talk about some basic crime statistics before we compare opinions on the effects of jail with facts established by research.

There has been much recent talk about crime in the streets. And TV screens continue to ooze blood! This is all just so much big talk. For basically, we are a nation of misdemeanants, specialists in nuisances, petty offenders.

Reprinted from *Federal Probation* 29 (June 1965): 30-33 by permission of the publisher.

FBI Uniform Crime Reports last year recorded over 1½ million arrests for public drunkenness. If we add breach of peace, vagrancy, panhandling, and a few other minor alcohol-related offenses, we get a grand total of over 2 million arrests in which drinking played an important part. This is not counting drunken driving nor all the police departments which do not report arrests to the FBI.

Probably 20 percent of all persons arrested for drunkenness account for between 60 and 80 percent of the total arrests. This means a very high rate of recidivism. It also suggests that some of the repeaters as well as the occasional offenders are alcoholics.

For our purposes here we will call a person an alcoholic if his life centers on drinking, if once he starts he can't stop, and if his personal troubles multiply with his intake. Now not all of the people who get arrested for drunkenness go to jail; the lower the income and the higher the offender's age, the more likely he is to do time. But from all these statistics one fact stands out: At this very moment in any of the 3,000 jails in this country, between 40 and 60 percent of the inmates there right now are doing time for drunkenness. And they'll be back; that's why someone spoke of our "revolving door" jails when talking about the correctional response to alcohol problems.

What Is the Jail Supposed To Do?

Organizations usually have specific goals they seek. What does the jail seek for its alcoholic inmates? What is it supposed to do with them? What effect is it supposed to have upon them after they have served their sentences?

The jail's stated goals are fairly clear and well-known. Jail is supposed to protect the community, to punish the offender, to deter him from future wrong-doing, and, to resocialize him, if possible.

Because of recent ambiguities in the definition of the alcohol offender, it is not yet clear whether he is sick but not a criminal, sick but also a criminal, not sick but a criminal, or none of them. So to add to the confusion, perhaps jails are also expected to protect the alcoholic inmate from himself as well as other members of the community who seek to do him harm.

Effects of Jail Socialization

We have heard what jails are supposed to do to, for, and with alcoholic inmates. Now what is expert opinion on the matter? Here is a sampling of what authorities regard as the effects of jail socialization for alcoholic inmates: "does not reform," "does nothing besides affording a temporary service to the community," "prepares alcoholics for Skid Row," "if the first arrest shocks, after the sentence the alcoholic only wants to get drunk," "lack of psychotherapy defeats the alcoholic."

Experts seem satisfied that jail does not accomplish its stated goals with alcoholic inmates. They all agree that the jail degrades by thrusting alcoholics in with other kinds of offenders, and that correctional officers hold conventional attitudes toward alcoholics—thus, officers are more often punitive than therapeutic.

The indictment is rather clearly summed up in the words of one expert who says "jail is no place for the alcoholic." And while one or two experts see where correctional officers can be of some help in preventing these essentially negative outcomes of jail socialization, the view, in general, is that so long as officers treat the alcoholic inmate in terms of his offense, they are satisfied to see him as an offender who needs to be punished rather than treated. And those who have given any thought to the matter at all agree that the alcoholic inmate makes a very good prisoner, presumably a person who abides by jail norms. Thus, in expert opinion the bleak picture is that the jail houses repeaters over and over again without positive effect, that correctional officers as surrogates of society are impersonal, indifferent if not harsh, and that contact with other inmates only serves to further degrade the alcoholic inmate and confirm him in dependency on alcohol and the jail itself.

Recent Research Findings

To what extent do recent research findings agree with these expert opinions? To begin with, there have been no studies of jail as a social system. There has been one study [1] of a sample of chronic drunkenness offenders in jail and one survey[2] of an institution for drunkenness offenders. These and a handful of data here and there on observed behavior of alcoholic offenders in jail support some of these opinions, while challenging others. We are led, then, back to an ancient piece of scientific wisdom which says that one must specify the conditions under which the generalization holds good.

Sidlofsky studied chronic drunkenness offenders in Toronto's Don Jail. In all, he interviewed some 29 men from 1 to 3 hours apiece. His conclusions, he notes, are mainly from the perspective of the old-timers. Even so, they suggest that the lot of the chronic drunkenness offender is not as hard as many may surmise. More to the point, his study is yet another which shows that organizations frequently, if not always, serve functions other than those intended by their designers.

Firstly, jail is not quite as punitive as it was intended. In addition, it neither deters nor resocializes. Secondly, most of its harshest aspects are mitigated, at least for the men Sidlofsky studied. Loss of freedom was only minimal, physical hardships were rare (some men actually gained weight), little sex deprivation was felt by a group of relatively inactive men sexually, and given their meager affective relationships "on the outside," there was little here for the jail to disrupt.

Conversely, the jail offered these three sets of rewards: a stable environment, a substitute social system, and a quasi-familial setting. On the street men had to make decisions about uncertain moments, not to say about their future. On the street, their positions with regard to others was amorphous if not highly disesteemed. On the street, there were few who would care or show an interest in them. All this, the jail reverses.

Sidlofsky goes on to show that both inmate criteria and imposed differences from the setting give rise to a differentiated social structure. Status and mobility are possible, primarily through jobs. In short, the jail system is a mirror-image of the outside community. Those workers with the highest status get the most.

Strangely, a man's irregularity from the point of view of the conventional world is what gives him status in the Don Jail. Only the regular repeaters, the ones the crew chiefs can count on to be back within 5 days to serve another sentence, are the ones who get the best jobs in the jail and have the highest status among their fellow chronic drunkenness offenders. This only indicates, of course, that the most stable supply of jail labor comes from the ranks of the chronic drunkenness offenders. But Sidlofsky's findings are important for other reasons.

The experts, in talking about the effects of jail socialization, refer exclusively to the alcoholic inmate. Sidlofsky and two other studies speak of the chronic drunkenness offender. If, as we noted earlier, men respond in terms of their definition of the situation, then chronic drunkenness offenders respond differently to the jail situation than the alcoholic inmate. And, similarly, correction officers act differently, depending on whether they regard their charges as chronic drunkenness offenders or as alcoholics. In an earlier day, one sought to distinguish the two types by the term "alcoholic" and "drunk." But to show you some more ambiguities, consider this comment an alcoholic made in talking about his first imprisonment for drunkenness:

> The first time you get here, it is a shock. What's wrong with the place? I'll tell you. It is too much a prison. It's a workhorse. ... There is no incentive to do anything about your drinking problem and you are made to feel low. This is bad for the drunk. Even if he is a hopeless case anyway, this place just confirms for him that there is nothing else but drinking for him.[3]

Social Psychology of Confinement

Prisoners in most institutions, whether long-term or short-term, subscribe to a code which says "do your own time." All have an equal interest in a peaceful and orderly institution. But if some alcoholic inmates "do easy time," "on the ear" or "on one leg," others "do hard time." These differences stem largely from how they define themselves and the jail situation. If we make a distinction between the "hidden alcoholic" and the "overt alcoholic," we may be able to find yet other differences.

Hidden alcoholics do "hard time," while "overt alcoholics" do "easy time." Hidden alcoholics, to begin with, are fewer in number in jail. In addition, they have some rather special antecedents as well as ways of being alcoholics. Being an alcoholic nets one social punishments as well as self-punishments. Hidden alcoholics managed for a longer period of time to break drinking rules in private, thus being better able to conceal their alcoholism from most other people. A majority of them were also solitary drinkers; lacking a group, however, they were free to torture themselves about their drinking problem, which only triggered more drinking and more self-punishment. When such men are finally arrested and jailed for drunkenness, social punishment and self-punishments combine. In addition, they look around at the motley crew in jail and see how low they have fallen and experience profound remorse.

Occasionally, this has amounted to "hitting bottom." The man in this situation then surrenders and joins Alcoholics Anonymous on his release, never to drink again. But just as often if not more often, he cannot wait to finish his sentence so he can get drunk and dispose of his guilt in the usual manner.

Overt alcoholics, by contrast, experience much more social punishment than self-punishment because of their heavy drinking. But being more often social drinkers, they have group supports for their actions. It is most unlikely that their heavy drinking can be an illness if so many of them drink the same way. But sharing common punishments, of course, only binds them closer together at the same time that it differentiates them from other people. It seems that most of the men in the Don Jail were in this category; interestingly enough, they had no unkind feelings toward their guards, whom they felt were just doing their jobs. And the high-status inmates were on rather excellent if not friendly terms with the guards. However, they were most antagonistic toward the police and the courts. A feasible hypothesis is that hidden alcoholics reverse these feelings. They feel neutral toward police and courts who also only were doing their jobs while feeling most antagonistic toward the jail guards whose behavior toward them symbolizes only too well their status loss.

Someone will say, no doubt, it's all relative. And he will be quite right. For the overt alcoholic, who has been "on the street," going to jail is not so bad, as Sidlofsky's study shows. By contrast, for the hidden alcoholic, more often of middle class background if not pretensions, coming to jail is a loss, not a gain.

Jail's Future as a Resocializing Agency

What, then, is the jail's future as an agency of resocialization? And, what can it do now to be more helpful in dealing with the alcoholic inmate? And how can what has been said here be of some use in this quest for improvement?

First, the matter of distinctions. Just as expert opinions on jail socialization have been wide of the mark, mainly because they failed to specify the conditions under which their generalizations held, so too have other experts, like correction officers, been off the mark, mainly because they either believed all persons arrested for drunkenness were alcoholics or that they were just "common drunks." The first category invites some sympathy and some urges to offer treatment; the second one frequently arouses indifference, if not outright annoyance. To confuse one with the other, however, is to nullify the possibilities of achieving some of the jail's stated goals. By paying attention to "modus operandi," by observing how drunkenness offenders "do time" in the broadest sense, officers may yet be in a position to speed the day when these same offenders will do less time in penal institutions.

Secondly, a point which follows from this is that there would seem to be too many "good prisoners" or "model prisoners" among the ranks of the drunkenness offenders. If officers might be able to figure out ways and means of making them or helping them to become "bad prisoners," these offenders might end up by eventually taking their trade and their time elsewhere.

And finally, a third point. The story is told of a correctional center where the guards announce publicly in the evening that there will be an A.A. meeting by yelling out: "All right, all 'winoes,' fall out for A.A." One can imagine the hidden alcoholics in the group, anxious to find solace for their drinking problem, but fearful of exposure in this setting. Given the stigma and ridicule the guard attaches to their condition, they conceal their problem, thus hoping to save face. By contrast, some brazen overt alcoholics and some non-alcoholics laughingly fall in line to go to the meeting because it means more free time away from their cells, coffee and doughnuts, and a chance to hear some funny stories. Our point here is that correctional officers do need to be on guard lest they diminish respect for themselves as they maintain distance from inmates.

Notes

[1] Samuel Sidlofsky, *The Role of the Prison Community in the Behaviour of the Chronic Drunkenness Offender* (Master's thesis, University of Toronto, 1961).

[2] David Kantor and Edward Blacker, *A Survey of Bridgewater. An Institution for the Chronic Drunkenness Offender* (Boston, Mass.: Office of the Commissioner on Alcoholism, 1958).

[3] Ibid., p. 38.

Part Three
the Street

Chapter VII

the Bottle Gang

Those who practice deviance openly in groups face internal and external problems of social control. Overt deviants, in addition to managing their own deviant careers, have to screen their activities from conformists and regulate both their own conduct and that of other similar deviants. Theoretically the solution to these problems comes from a deviant subculture.[1] Such a subculture teaches skills, supplies a more favorable self-image, sets rules for dealing with others, deviant or conformist, and justifies deviant behavior by a special ideology.

Deviant subcultures supply ideas on social actions; they do not, however, guarantee that prescribed actions will take place. And since discrepancy between ideas and actions is a fact of social life, it becomes necessary to ask how well deviant beliefs, values and norms are honored in practice, the extent to which conformity to deviant norms produces rewards, and exactly how deviants control one another.

This chapter examines the case of social control in deviant groups. The group considered, the "bottle gang," is relevant since it meets three conditions: bottle gangs are public, not private; members have more contacts with persons like themselves than with conformists; and members participate in the Skid Row subculture. Rules and sanctions are the major concerns here. The central question is: How well does the

Reprinted from the *Quarterly Journal of Studies on Alcohol* 29 (December 1968): 943-55 by permission of the publisher.

bottle gang regulate interaction and activity, and screen both from outsiders?

To answer the question I shall describe a typical East Coast bottle gang, abstract its rules and functions, discuss typical breaches and their sanctions, and posit a set of conditions which may account for differences in social controls in East and West Coast bottle gangs.

Control in the deviant group rests in part on the number of overt deviants visible and known to one another, in part on whether they have a territory and sufficient resources for engaging in deviant activities and interaction, and in part on the nature of their "deviance contract" with authorities. Thus, if public deviants are allowed to control their own activities, the amount of their public deviance will be within tolerable limits. But, if they are not permitted to control these activities, there will be high visibility of deviance, frequent attempts at legitimate control coupled with ineffective deviant-group controls, and a low tolerance of deviant behavior generally.

"Bottle gang" refers to the typical form of street drinking in which indigent unattached men engage. The men appear to be heavy drinkers by conventional standards and are usually referred to as alcoholics, or in slang terms as "bums," "drunks" or "winos." Generally they meet on the street, pool meager funds, send a member to a package store to buy an inexpensive bottle of fortified wine, share the bottle in some public place (e.g., alley, doorstep, park or street corner in rooming-house areas, urban slums or Skid Row quarter) and separate once the bottle is emptied.

Previous studies of bottle gangs on the West Coast[2] concluded that Skid Row is a way of life and that heavy drinkers there support an ethic of sharing and mutual aid, center their life around drinking and participate in drinking groups which regulate conduct by rules and sanctions.

Setting and Methods

In Maple City,[3] institutions and establishments catering to homeless men are scattered in various pockets around the center of the city. All are within walking distances, rather than concentrated as in a typical Skid Row. Lodging houses, rooming houses, second-hand clothing stores, restaurants and taverns catering to the homeless, missions and shelters radiate from the center of the city. Important public places for the local and transient homeless are the King Street Mission and a grassy common in the center of the city called the Big Green. The Yankee State commission on alcoholism established a halfway house for chronic drunkenness offenders in Maple City. Unable to obtain quarters elsewhere, the commission leased facilities in the King Street Mission, calling its pilot project Shelter House,[4] and asked me to study the facility and its effectiveness, its clientele, and their way of life. In the course of the study, data on bottle gangs became available. Residents of Shelter House spoke of these drinking groups and of their own past experiences in them. As familiarity with the local homeless scene increased, direct observation on several bottle gangs and participation in a few became possible. Thus, the present study relies heavily on anthropological methods of field work. Most of the data come from informants, direct observation and participation, in that order.

the Bottle Gang

The setting assumed for the portrait to follow is the Big Green in Maple City during mild weather, in midafternoon. The Green is within easy walking distance of the King Street Mission, several package stores, rooming houses, an unemployment agency, a police station and important street-corner hangouts. There are six stages in the bottle-gang cycle: salutation, negotiation, procurement, consumption, affirmation and dispersal.

1. *Salutation.* Potential bottle-gang participants meet and acknowledge each other on the various paths which crisscross the Green. They have worked together, drunk together at some time, or are known to common acquaintances. They sit on a bench, pass the time of day and share information about "the boys." After a brief exchange of news, they negotiate.

2. *Negotiation.* By now, each has read the signs that the other is "on the prowl" (searching for a drink). Typically, one begins the negotiation by saying that he has a certain amount of money that he is willing to contribute toward the purchase of a bottle of wine, for example: "I have 18 cents; how much are you holding?" The other, if interested, reports his holdings. Generally, they will be "short" the price of a bottle (a pint of wine generally retails for 50 cents). The initiator collects the money, announces how much more they need and leads them to others. The leader asks if they wish to "go in on a bottle." If they are still short, a brief excursion in panhandling will be necessary until the price is collected.

3. Procurement. When the little group has collected enough money ("made the price" or "scored"), the leader chooses one man to buy the bottle. Buying the bottle is called "making the run." The buyer, called "the runner," should be not too shabbily dressed, not acutely intoxicated, and dependable; that is, if given money, he can be trusted to return with a bottle. The rest of the gang sit on a bench and await his return.

4. Consumption. The runner returns with the bottle (usually muscatel wine) in a brown bag concealed inside his belt, under his jacket or in his back pocket, and gives it to the leader. The latter looks up and down the pathways of the Big Green, peels the plastic seal, uncaps the bottle, takes two short drinks, and passes it, still in the brown bag, to the runner. The runner takes two short drinks and passes the bottle to another man. When the bottle has made the full circle of the gang, the last to drink returns it to the leader, who pockets the bottle, still in the brown bag. After the first round, the men sit back on the bench, light up cigarettes and talk. All during the phases of consumption, each man looks up and down the walkways for police officers or outsiders who might jeopardize the activity. All drink surreptitiously.

5. Affirmation. The leader as donor-host sets style, tone and topics of talk. There is little talk on personal troubles, much on others' troubles. All make negative comments on outsiders; ex-Shelter-House men, in particular, criticize current members of Shelter House, as well as its resident staff. The theme is that members and staff alike are "a bunch of phonies," "not real drunks," and more than likely "psychos rather than alkies." All compliment the leader on how well or how fast he "promoted" bottle money, praise the runner for his speed, and compare and contrast, usually favorably, the ease and sociability of the present gang with others they have been in. The phrase "You're all right" is heard frequently. In addition, all claim that when they have it, they share with others, and that when it comes to "making the run," they can always be counted on to come back.

6. Dispersal. The leader decides when the next round takes place. Again the bottle circles through the small group, traveling the same route as before. Each takes the customary two drinks. In time, the bottle is emptied. With that, the gang is ready to disband. The man holding the empty bottle, still in its brown paper bag, disposes of it in a nearby trash container or puts it under the bench. The rest announce their plans and leave. Any or all are free to reactivate the cycle of bottle-drinking; if this is done, the gang remains intact. Sometimes one member will decide to "treat" the rest to a bottle. At other times the cycle will begin with negotiation and move on through to dispersal.

Rules and Functions

Tacit rules for each stage are as follows: *(1) Salutation:* never snub a "drinking man"; say "hello" to friends and acquaintances alike; always be ready to pass the time of day with an equal. *(2) Negotiation:* be as ready to offer a drink as you are to accept one; show your money and be willing to share it; buy or work your way into a bottle gang—don't chisel in. *(3) Procurement:* make the run quickly but not obviously; have faith in the runner—wait patiently and be discreet. *(4) Consumption:* let the leader split the seal and drink; wait your turn, then match his drinks; take two and pass the bottle; don't show the world you're drinking. *(5) Affirmation:* follow the leader in talk and action; praise him, the runner and your partners; criticize persons known to have broken gang rules. *(6) Dispersal:* "duck the empty"; say goodbye and go when the going's good.

Functions for each stage in the cycle are as follows: *(1) Salutation:* ready greetings cement past ties and open up chances of future ones; opening ceremonies signify inclusion in an in-group, thereby reducing pains of stigma. *(2) Negotiation:* negotiation assigns one's status as a suitable drinking companion and opens up a role in a face-to-face group, no matter how deviant, stigmatized or short-lived it may be; it makes it possible to tailor a small budget and a large need for alcoholic drinks to a wider number of drinking encounters throughout the day. *(3) Procurement:* the technique reduces the visibility of the bottle-gang's activities; awaiting the runner's return creates a drinking-centered drama. *(4) Consumption:* satisfies the needs for alcohol and drinking company; reduces the tension and anxiety of awaiting the runner's return. *(5) Affirmation:* ratifies one's identity as a person and one's solidarity with gang members in the immediate situation; signifies that each is a "good man" and a good drinking partner. *(6) Dispersal:* disposing of the empty bottle removes evidence and reduces risks of exposure; shows respect for decency and public order and signifies the gang is about to break up; signifies that all rights and duties are at an end. The contract has been fulfilled. All are, for the time being, free of each other's company.

Transitory or permanent in character and composed of transient or regular participants, the bottle gang seems ideally suited to the needs of indigent alcoholics. Participation stretches meager funds, so that men get the maximum amount of alcohol possible for their money. For instance, a 2-ounce "shot" of whisky in a bar costs 40 cents. For a fourth of that amount, contributed toward a group bottle, a man can get almost as much absolute alcohol, now in the form of wine.[5]

Participation increases the range of acquaintance, given the easy entry rules, and gives one status and membership in a group. The exchange is made possible by the display of elementary social skills. Some men, indeed, simply trade their company for drinks.

Finally, as all become more deeply involved in a drinking-centered existence, statuses and roles, beliefs and norms all revolve round this axis. In the process, the usual urban complexities change in meaning and shrink in scope. Now obvious social failures[6] can sustain a life which is to be understood in terms of the metaphors of deviant social drinking, with all of its rewards and punishments. Obtaining and maintaining a supply of drinks in accordance with a set of rules provides a schedule, a calendar, a routine and a morality all its own. The net effect of this life-style is to deny failure in the pursuit of drink in company.

Breaches and Sanctions

It would seem that such a well-designed social form as the bottle gang, so nicely suited to the conditions of life of the homeless alcoholic, should not produce many problems of social control. Given the fixity of its ritual, the limited skills required in the activity, and the few and simple roles in the interaction, there should be few strains. The brevity of the encounter, so nicely attuned to the Skid Row demand for noninvolvement, seems a guarantee of efficiency.

Yet this most elementary form of the deviant drinking life has more than its share of deviance and problems in social control. According to Shelter House informants, deviance rather than conformity characterizes most stages of the bottle-gang cycle. There appear to be frequent breaches of the rules at all of the six stages, with either erratic and unpredictable application of sanctions or actual failure to apply them. In addition to these failures to solve internal problems of control, there is the obvious failure to screen activities from other "drinking men" or from the police. In the first instance, the internal peace and flow of interaction in the gang is upset; in the second, the very life of the gang is suddenly aborted.

Some infractions of bottle-gang rules are also violations of wider social norms and would be subject to sanctioning by both gang members and agents of formal control. It is primarily such offenses as drinking in public, drunkenness, disorderly conduct or simple assault which bring legal sanctions. On occasion, but again erratically, a bottle-gang may sanction a member for any of these activities which appear to infringe its own rules.

Legal sanctions involve disrupting the group, with or without arresting any of the members. The sanctions which gang-members use fall into two categories. The person may be asked to stop what he is doing, a sanction applied by talking to or about (labeling) him, or he may be denied present or future access to the drinking company. In the latter case the group walks away from the offender or does not allow him to enter their company.

A brief catalogue of the infractions of bottle-gang rules, ideal sanctions and the frequency of their application follows:

1. Salutation breaches consist mainly of saying hello to a person as if he were known, when this is not really the case; as when both were in jail together but were never formally introduced. The sanction is exclusion but it is rarely applied.

2. Negotiation breaches are all instances of attempts at illicit entry into a bottle gang. This may involve inducing an obligation, trying to obtain repayment for a past obligation or partial evasion of entry rules. Some men hover in the vicinity, hoping to be invited to share the bottle; others simulate tremors. Some offer a drink from their own bottles, particularly when only a drop or two is left. Others insist on repayment for drinks owed them by one of the gang members. Finally, a person may contribute toward the bottle, yet not really put up as much money as he can afford. The ideal sanction, of course, is to exclude all of these men from sharing the current bottle; this is done, but almost at random. All are typed by the manner in which they sought entry and these labels become a part of their reputations. The generic term for all is "chiseler" or "moocher." Those who stand at the periphery of the drinking group are called "merchants," "lap dogs" or "waiters." One who feigns tremors, the signs of acute withdrawal symptoms, is called an "actor" and a man who contributes less than he might is a "hold-out artist." Labeling is the predictable sanction; exclusion is always more or less a matter of chance. If a member can persuade his gang to invite the person to whom he is obligated, he gains while they lose, because the person whom he paid off with the group's bottle has no obligation to repay the favor.

3. Procurement breaches include failure to return with the bottle, returning very slowly or returning with a bottle from which the runner has already drunk or has offered a few "pulls" to people to whom he owes drinks. Sometimes failure to return is due to accident, loss of memory or arrest by the police. In the latter case, as in giving drinks to persons not in the gang, the runner has violated cover-up rules. He has become socially visible, with consequences for the gang. Sometimes failure to return is by intent; the runner keeps the bottle for himself. In view of the difficulty of knowing what has really happened the gang

generally labels the man as untrustworthy; he is a "Dick Smith," a person who "went South with the bottle," a label meant to exclude him from future drinking encounters. Again, the label is more likely than the sanction to be applied by the current and future gang members.

4. A person breaches consumption rules by drinking too fast, too much or too obviously from the bottle. Here the gang can tell the person about his failings. Later he will get a label, but again there is a marked reluctance to apply actual sanctions. However, if his drinking is so blatant as to attract police attention, he is a little more likely to be excluded from subsequent gangs.

5. Affirmation violations include incorrect talk or actions. Some men talk out of turn or on the wrong subjects, become argumentative or set up as experts on uninteresting subjects. This earns them appropriate labels; again whether this will exclude them from subsequent gangs is problematic. Exclusion is a little more likely in cases of "acting up," either by fighting within the gang or by engaging in antics. Either behavior may attract the police or disrupt the gang, sometimes both. These men are all labeled as "performers," "wacks," "characters," "nuts," "psychos," or "jail bait" and will be avoided whenever possible.

6. Dispersal violations include calling attention to oneself or the activities of the gang, ostentation in hiding the empty bottle and illicit ways of continuing the drinking episode at the expense of another member. Some beg or "con" money from gang members for their own drinking. Others try to rob, steal or beat up members thought to have money. The more violent are labeled and their reputations become widely known. Exclusion is much more likely to be applied against these offenders.

Discussion

The East Coast bottle gang described herein seems characterized by simple rules and by extreme variability in both conformity and sanctions on deviance. Some plausible hypotheses for these variations in social control can be derived by contrasting these gangs with those on the West Coast described by Jackson and Connor[7] in Seattle, by Peterson and Maxwell[8] in Fresno, Stockton and Sacramento, and by Rooney[9] in Spokane. Each of the West Coast cities has a concentrated, well-defined Skid Row quarter, in contrast to Maple City.[10]

Apparent differences in both ecology and social organization may explain the variance. Ecology includes numbers, territory, resources and the deviance contract with authorities. Social organization encompasses types of drinking patterns and experiences in bottle gangs.

Ecology

1. *Numbers.* West Coast Skid Rows concentrate a relatively large number of men in close contact. Maple City bottle-gang drinkers, much fewer in number, are scattered around the city. With the same meager resources and strong desire to drink, West Coast Skid Row men have access to more potential gangs. As a result, they need to invest less, while participating in a greater number of gangs throughout the day. In Maple City the smaller number means poorer chances of "getting in on a bottle." The higher cost of joining the fewer gangs poses problems with a slender budget. This situation is more likely to encourage holding out, scheming, attempts to chisel into gangs and similar offenses.

2. *Territory.* With an established territory, the West Coast bottle-gang participant goes relatively unnoticed. The Maple City bottle-gang drinker's greater need to move about increases his exposure to police, citizens who may lodge complaints, and other men searching for a drink. Increased exposure, in particular, encourages illicit entry into bottle gangs.[11]

3. *Resources.* There are more resources on Skid Row than off it for bottle-gang participants. Panhandling, a way of getting money for a bottle, is less noticed and more tolerated than in other parts of the city and package stores and other liquor outlets are plentiful. By contrast, when a man "makes the run" in Maple City he enters enemy territory; his activity becomes visible to those he would prefer did not see it.

4. *The Deviance Contract.* Police are regarded as having a "contract" with Skid Row men. They agree to make predictable expeditions into the territory to arrest a certain agreed-upon number of violators of public order.[12] Hence, West Coast Skid Rows are subjected to less surveillance; its occurrence is known in advance, and this permits more relaxed and leisurely interaction in street-corner bottle gangs. In contrast, Maple City men must maintain constant vigilance in their activities; many claim to suffer from the "cop horrors." Surreptitious drinking, rapid gulping of drinks and tension in all members of the gang result. This concern with avoiding exposure to external controls weakens internal controls.

Social Organization

A city with a Skid Row has a way of life for homeless men.[13] A social organization with statuses and roles results from their manner of participating in the Skid Row culture. A homeless-alcoholic community exists in Maple City, but dispersion reduces the chance of maintaining those stable patterns of interaction which sustain a subculture. Thus, drinking patterns and experience with bottle gangs are two major factors affecting bottle-gang controls.

1. Drinking Patterns. The Skid Row social system of heavy drinkers is based on sifting out and sorting types of drinking pattern. As in any status system, the attempt is always to maintain status homogeneity. Maple City bottle drinkers have no such well-ordered social system; as a result, heterogeneity is more likely. The consequences for social control can be seen clearly in the case of drinking patterns. "Plateau drinkers," for instance, make ideal bottle-gang members, since they seek only to maintain a certain level of alcohol in the blood stream over the course of a day.[14] "Blitz drinkers," [15] on the other hand, drink as much as they can, as fast as possible, in order to get drunk and stay drunk. These men make the poorest bottle-gang participants, yet poverty and need drive them into bottle gangs. In Maple City, because of the greater difficulty in finding companions, there is a greater tendency to waive admission requirements; persons with bad reputations will be accepted in the bottle gang. This is less likely on the West Coast Skid Row scene.

2. Experience in Bottle Gangs. The evidence suggests that the more extensive experience in bottle gangs on the West Coast leads to more conformity in the member. In Maple City more extensive gang experience leads to greater deviance in the sense of violating gang rules. These differences are related to gang responses to deviant behavior. Both violations and punishments seem to be reversed between coasts: *(a)* Violations are less likely on the West Coast, but are more likely to be punished: Rules and sanctions are interdependent. *(b)* Violations are more likely to happen on the East Coast, but less likely to be punished: Rules and sanctions are relatively independent.

More experienced bottle-gang drinkers in both areas are aware of these relationships between breaches and sanctions and act upon the knowledge to maintain the status quo. But they do so in different ways. Seasoned West Coast bottle-gang drinkers take conformity for granted and thus need less frequently to state the rules, sentiments and sanctions of bottle-gang drinking. Because of the unpredictable relations between rules and sanctions in Maple City bottle gangs, seasoned participants talk at great length about gang rules, affirm the rules and the sentiments attaching to them and continually point to the sanctions for failure to observe them. They continually accuse others of infractions, simultaneously proclaiming their own loyalty and dependability. The net effect is to provide all participants, particularly the newcomer, with an illusory sense of a social order replete with definite rules and sanctions. Experienced members can thus gain the conformity of others while themselves secretly deviating. With increased experience, the gang member's suspicion and distrust are aroused by the knowledge that many violators go unpunished; he sees that nonconformity is much more frequently rewarded than conformity. He finds that his own self-interest lies more and more in nonconformity and begins to expect more violations by his partners, thus triggering more talk about the rules, the need for loyalty to them and for punishing violators.

When the need to drink increases inversely with the resources for getting drinks, as happens frequently in this impoverished setting, sanctions become a luxury. Because past violators may become current donor-hosts or even treat one to a desperately needed drink, bottle-gang drinkers must be tolerant of behavior which deviates from their norms. Because of their need and poverty most of them do not feel able to apply sanctions against offenders. Such control as may come about can be only of a symbolic character. The incessant talk about how others have breached the rules is, on occasion, a plea that the same behavior will not happen in the immediate drinking group.

That control in East Coast bottle gangs rests more on talking about rules and sanctions than in taking action on either suggests that any deviant subculture is only as good as the organizational conditions which surround it. Bottle-gang drinking in Maple City, because of the tenuous organizational conditions surrounding its homeless men, is more precarious and less internally controlled than it is on the Skid Rows of the West Coast.

Notes

[1] Howard S. Becker, *Outsiders* (New York: The Free Press, 1963); and Albert K. Cohen, *Delinquent Boys* (New York: The Free Press, 1955).

[2] Joan K. Jackson and Ralph Connor, "The Skid Road Alcoholic," *Quarterly Journal of Studies on Alcohol* 14 (September 1953): 468-86; W. Jack Peterson and Milton A. Maxwell, "The Skid Road 'Wino'," *Social Problems* 5 (Spring 1958): 308-16; and James F. Rooney, "Group Processes among Skid Row Winos: A Reevaluation of the Undersocialization Hypothesis," *Quarterly Journal of Studies on Alcohol* 22 (September 1961): 444-60.

[3] The names of all places referred to in this study are fictitious.

[4] Earl Rubington, "Grady 'Breaks Out': A Case Study of an Alcoholic's Relapse," *Social Problems* 11 (Spring 1964): 372-80; and his "Organizational Strains and Key Roles," *Administrative Science Quarterly* 9 (March 1965): 350-69.

[5] The cost of absolute alcohol in wine is cheaper than in distilled spirits. "Many winos in . . . Washington buy apple wine . . . containing 20 to 22 percent alcohol. In 1955, it could be purchased for 55 cents a pint in almost any tavern. The cheapest 80-proof whiskey, on the other hand, sold for $2.36 a pint. In other words, in wine an ounce of absolute alcohol cost only 17 cents as compared to 37 cents an ounce in whiskey. The differential is even greater in some cities at the present time, with cheap wine retailing at 50 cents a pint and Puerto Rican wine at 35 cents in certain Eastern cities." Peterson and Maxwell, "The Skid Road 'Wino'."

[6] For analyses of drinking as an adaptation to failure, see Howard George Bain, "A Sociological Analysis of the Chicago Skid-Row Lifeway" (M. A. thesis, University of Chicago, 1950); Robert Straus, "Alcohol and the Homeless Man," *Quarterly Journal of Studies on Alcohol* 7 (December 1946): 360-404; and David J. Pittman and C. Wayne Gordon, *The Revolving Door* (New Haven, Conn.: Yale Center of Alcohol Studies, 1958).

[7] Jackson and Connor, "The Skid Road Alcoholic."

[8] Peterson and Maxwell, "The Skid Road 'Wino'."

[9] Rooney, "Group Processes Among Skid Row Winos."

[10] The 1960 population of Maple City was 152,048, and the 1950 population of Seattle was 467,591, Fresno 133,929, Sacramento 191,667, Spokane 181,608, and Stockton 86,321. Lack of published studies precludes comparisons with bottle gangs on concentrated, well-defined Skid Rows in large or middle-sized East Coast cities or of bottle gangs in middle-sized West Coast cities without clearly defined Skid Rows.

[11] Howard M. Bahr, "The Gradual Disappearance of Skid Row," *Social Problems* 15 (Summer 1967): 41-45.

[12] Among Skid Row men, there is a widespread belief that police have a "quota" of arrests they must make in a given week. See Gus Oki, "How the Chronic Drunkenness Offender Views the Police, the Courts, and Jail," *Addictions* 11 (Summer 1964): 9-18.

[13] Samuel E. Wallace, *Skid Row as a Way of Life* (Totowa, N. J.: Bedminster Press, 1965).

[14] Robert Straus and Raymond G. McCarthy, "Nonaddictive Pathological Drinking Patterns of Homeless Men," *Quarterly Journal of Studies on Alcohol* 12 (December 1951): 601-11.

[15] Richard J. Kingham, "Alcoholism and the Reinforcement Theory of Learning," *Quarterly Journal of Studies on Alcohol* 19 (June 1958): 320-30.

Chapter VIII

the Changing Skid Row Scene

Skid Row stands in our society as the most dramatic moral symbol of a general failure of socialization and of a particular failure to learn moderate drinking customs. Its survival constitutes a stark social-control message for all to see, smell, hear and read about—this is what may happen to those who fail to learn or to abide by accepted drinking norms. Far out of proportion to the actual number of Skid Row territories or Skid Row persons, the words themselves evoke for most people a sense of degradation, hopelessness and denial of human aspirations.

The concern over the obviously damaging consequences of most forms of prolonged uncontrolled drinking produced a moral symbol. But the symbol probably encouraged more people to continue their own inappropriate drinking conduct than it helped others either to abstain from or curtail such drinking. As the symbol became starker and simpler, it also became falser to the social reality it sought to depict for resident and stranger alike.

Now that both Skid Row and the conditions that gave rise to it seem to be gradually disappearing, it may be well to give some attention to its broader meaning—for the world of alcohol problems in particular, for the intricate relations between deviant behavior and social control in general. Ac-

Reprinted from the *Quarterly Journal of Studies on Alcohol* 32 (March 1971): 123-35 by permission of the publisher.

cordingly, I will deal here with the effects of Skid Row symbolism on social reality, the realities of the Skid Row social system, the changes taking place in that system, and the consequences of those changes for alcoholics and their would-be helpers, both on and off Skid Row.

Moral Symbolism and Social Reality

If conduct is to be influenced, a moral conception of it must be formed and disseminated. Language, the set of symbols by means of which people communicate with one another, affords such a conception. Linguistic symbols both organize and affect social relations. They describe as well as prescribe conduct and, perhaps more important, they also evaluate it. They tell persons not only what to do and why and how, but also what to think and feel and how to act with persons who have breached moral norms. Only scientific language aspires to an ethical neutrality. All other languages, everyday speech, colloquialisms, slang, jargon, argots, are replete with terms that are not morally neutral. Many of these terms give a bad name to persons, objects or activities considered unworthy. And these terms of moral symbolism suggest the work that language can do on behalf of controlling deviant behavior.

Two definitions of Skid Row from two dictionaries, one of slang, the other of underworld lingo, afford pertinent examples:

> "*skid row* Any old, dilapidated street or section of a town containing very cheap bars, eating places, and flop houses where the permanently unemployed, vagrants, beggars, petty criminals, derelicts, degenerates, and, mainly unemployed, alcoholics hang out" (1).
>
> "*skid row* The Bowery in New York City; any similar street or avenue in other regions of the country where the dregs of humanity tend to gather" (2).

Both of these definitions are ostensibly descriptive and evaluative. That is, they give the reader some idea of what a Skid Row is and what the compilers of the dictionary (and probably most readers) think about Skid Row. In so doing, of course, the two definitions contain a hidden prescription for would-be conformists and deviants alike; they attest to the fact that language, as a social instrument, can be put to many uses, some of which are in opposition to the writer's or speaker's stated or implicit intentions.

It is clear that equating Skid Row as the territory for inappropriate drinking of all kinds and as the home of "drunken bums" and "alcoholic derelicts" has produced social-control results quite opposite to those intended by persons who employ such terms. The evidence suggests that the moral symbolism of Skid Row has actually steered inappropriate drinkers there, and at the same time it has provided camouflage for millions of problem drinkers in the United States during the past 50 years. Thus, the moral symbolism of Skid Row achieved reverse effects on the social control of deviant drinking behavior.

These results are not hard to explain. Most persons drunk in public view were generally found in or near Skid Row. Since drunkenness has long been identified as the key sign of alcoholism and since public drunkenness is found most often in and around Skid Row, a false equation of behavior (drunkenness) with setting (Skid Row) came to equal the inappropriate drinking condition (alcoholism). This false syllogism provided cover for "hidden" alcoholics, confusion for moderate drinkers, moral superiority for abstainers, and a rationale for at least some Skid Row alcoholics.

Perhaps most important of all, the Skid Row symbol became the major obstacle to the progress of the alcoholism movement. For today, just as 50 years ago, most alcoholics are hidden rather than overt, and all but a small fraction of the nation's alcoholics do not live on Skid Row. Consequently, denial, the major defense of the alcoholic, actually finds a powerful ally in the Skid Row symbol. The alcoholic can say to himself and to others who may be troubled by his drinking, "I have a job, a home, a family, so how can I be an alcoholic?" Or, "Since I don't live on Skid Row, how can you call me an alcoholic?" Or, "Since you have never seen me drunk on the streets, what makes you think I'm an alcoholic?"

By calling attention to the behavior and linking it with a specific setting, the Skid Row symbol has deflected attention from countless millions of developing problem drinkers. The growing strength of the alcoholism movement, the rise of Alcoholics Anonymous and the dissemination of research findings have finally begun to make it possible to separate the behavior from the setting and to make it clear that alcoholism is complex, not simple. But the Skid Row symbol made denial possible, discouraged recognition and delayed entrance into treatment and still continues to do so. Born in extremis, the symbol of Skid Row alcoholism made it possible for the innumerable varieties of alcoholics to pursue their deviant drinking careers in private desperation.

the Skid Row Social System

The Skid Row symbol is based on the false premise that it represents alcoholism. Since Skid Row is a social system, it cannot be caught up and understood through a falsely premised though significant moral symbol. It must be understood in systemic terms, rather than judged solely on the basis of some of its more obvious, more visible participants.

Skid Row is the special urban territory that has been set aside for certain varieties of unattached men. As the society changes, demands for certain kinds of work increase. The persons who emerge to perform this work require a host of special goods and services. The fact that these particular men perform these kinds of work and consume these goods and services renders them liable to disrepute and social rejection. This combination of irregular or unskilled work and low standards of consumption creates a problem of presumptive, if not real, deviance, which participation in Skid Row subculture is designed to solve.

1. *Work.* Various frontiers, particularly in agriculture, transportation and communication, have required casual laborers. And men with meager skills and few social ties sprang up to take the risks, to market their labors in unusual times, places and circumstances. Such men cut timber, cleared forests, built railroads and harvested crops. Mainly men who somehow did not fit into conventional primary groups, who found the bonds of conventional social life too restraining or were simply seeking adventure, took these jobs.

2. *Services and Facilities.* The special character and calendar of their work, their freedom from familial restraints and their relatively low income but large numbers created a market for goods and services. Their very numbers made it possible to provide them with cheap services. Thus Anderson reported that in 1929 a man could live on West Madison Street in Chicago for less than a dollar a day (3). Numerous entrepreneurs, moral, recreational, social and economic, appeared to provide this army of unattached casual workers with food, clothing, shelter, work, recreation, and religious, health and welfare services. The styles of companionship, recreation, entertainment and housing were all tailored to meager budgets, simple tastes and limited social skills. The main quarter for localizing and providing these services was generally adjacent to the central business district, an area of low rent but high land value. By 1900 most American cities had districts catering to several types of homeless men; one by one the special names of such districts all changed to one, Skid Row (4).

3. *Deviance.* The kinds of work the men engaged in, the territory in which they had their being, and their general style of life all singled them out as different from the ordinary, which implied disrepute and doubts about their legitimacy and adequacy as human beings. They faced, then, the general problems which presumed, if not actual, deviance creates.

Thus, a cadre of persons of given social types, confronting a special situation (homelessness) entered a specific territory (Skid Row), there to live their lives and cope with its exigencies in accordance with a set of shared definitions (Skid Row subculture).

4. *Drinking and Abstinence.* A specific moral symbolism is attached to both drinking and abstinence on Skid Row. Compliance with and deviance from the moral rules of heavy drinking form the basis of the Skid Row status order (5). The realities of abstinence, heavy social drinking and alcoholism constitute the basis of three different social segments on Skid Row, each of which practices ceremonial avoidance from the others and each of which has its own status hierarchy. Three sample surveys of Skid Row populations in three large cities using different sampling methods, interviews and interviewers, arrive more or less at the same conclusions about the proportions of abstainers, moderate drinkers and alcoholics, and about the way of life there, confirming the qualitative observations of a number of field workers (3—12).

The surveys in Chicago (13), Minneapolis (14) and Philadelphia (15) all report that about one-third of the Skid Row residents are abstainers, one-third are moderate drinkers (by Skid Row standards) and only a third are alcoholics. In addition, these surveys, together with the results of several Skid Row field studies, all tend to agree on two general conclusions: *(a)* Movement in the system is either down or out, but never up; and *(b)* status honor is inversely proportional to suffering and degradation.

The longer a drinker remains in the system, the more likely that his status will drop. Abstainers, by contrast, can maintain their status. Aged pensioners can rank fairly high, depending on the kind of housing their pensions will buy; indigent pensioners, by contrast, can only claim high moral but lower social status, particularly if their meager resources force them into contact with portions of the drinking segment in this community of deviants. Similarly, fraternization among the various kinds of heavy drinkers can only lead to a lessening of Skid Row status. Emergencies, indigency, exposure to social control (such as jail sentences and the like) enforce contact with men in the rung below. In time, with increased poverty, lessened ability or inclination to work, and increasing adaptation to alcohol, early conventional socialization gives way to the demands of adult deviant socialization. When that happens, under conditions of cross-rank contact, tastes change and with them techniques. And, as some men begin to accept the cheapest wine and later, out of necessity, nonbeverage alcohol, socialization downward has become a fact. The results are short-term effectiveness at the price of long-term incompetence for exhibiting and supporting a conventional style of life.

Anderson (3), reporting on Chicago's Skid Row in its heyday, documented the fact that hoboes ultimately became tramps and that tramps, in turn, ultimately became "bums." Not quite 10 years later, when Skid Rows across the country at the height of the depression were filled with close to 4 million unemployed homeless men, Sutherland and Locke reported similar findings (16). Continued association on Skid Row, particularly in the shelters built to assist the growing numbers of homeless men, unfitted large numbers of them for conventional work habits by a process called "shelterization." And some two generations later, Bogue (13), in his study of the same Skid Row, again showed how morale and standards drop and apathy grows as contact with Skid Row increases. The latter findings, however, depend rather heavily on the discovery of two significant kinds of change in Skid Rows in general: A shrinking population, composed more and more of older Whites and younger Negroes.

Social Change on Skid Row

By 1900, as Wallace (4) has pointed out, homelessness had both its place and its culture in the Skid Row territories of most middle-sized and large American cities. Now, however, another trend has become clear: what the economy had wrought, it could also unmake. As the industrial and agricultural frontier faded, the market for the kinds of casual labor Skid Row men have been supplying has declined. On the west coast there still exists a need for migratory agricultural workers; this need, however, is now being met by Puerto Ricans and Mexicans. As one moves nearer the east coast, the signs of steady population decline on all Skid Rows become clear.

In addition to the decreased needs for migratory, seasonal and casual labor, the emergence of the affluent society has produced a wide variety of health and welfare services which provide a floor against a possible descent into Skid Row. Extreme fluctuations in the business cycle seem either less likely to occur or less likely to precipitate again a massive emigration to American Skid Rows. Temporary fluctuations still send some marginal laborers to the Skid Row areas, but their numbers are also declining.

Bogue (13) has reported the steady decline in most Skid Rows in the 41 cities he studied. Data gathered on New York's Bowery at several points in time document the gradual passing of Skid Row. Around 1900, the Bowery population had grown to an estimated 15,000. By 1919, admittedly a depression year, the number had risen to 75,000. By 1949, it had once again leveled off to 15,000. But since that time the number of men actually counted has dropped off sharply each year; the most recent count, in 1966, yielded an astonishing low of 5406. If the trend continues, the prediction is that the population will only be 300 by 1971 (17).

In a matter of a few years, these trends, together with advancing urban renewal and the conversion of lodging houses and cubicle hotels to more profitable uses, should cause some well-known Skid Rows to disappear. The first significant social change, then, is the gradual disappearance of Skid Row. This does not mean that homelessness itself will disappear. On the contrary, there are reasons for thinking that homelessness may remain constant, if not actually increase. It does mean, however, that the territory for the traditional style of homelessness will have gone out of existence.

Internal changes in the composition of most Skid Rows are also responses to a changing economy, the results of improved health and welfare services, and the internal migration of Negroes. The changes in the composition of this population have also altered the characteristics of the three vertical segments, abstainers, moderate drinkers and alcoholics, that constitute Skid Row populations. As is true off Skid Row, the White population is considerably older than the Negro population. On Skid Row this skewed age distribution leads to a disintegration of such moral order and internal peace as most Skid Rows could claim.

Given the nature and character of this deviant community, it is not surprising that suspicion and distrust is spreading, particularly on the streets where bottle gangs have their short though eventful lives (10, 12, 18). Petty crime among the impoverished has always been the rule, but a balance was generally struck insofar as petty thievery was concerned. Particularly among men who slept in flophouses, having one's goods, money or bottle stolen is always a possibility; yet it is a risk all knowingly take. Such crime is petty, silent and anonymous. The "jackroller" steals from sleeping or intoxicated men (19) and a reciprocity in illicit exchange is assumed—a man expects that sometime somebody will steal from him, and he expects himself to be forced to steal at some point. A similar reversal of roles implies that, in accordance with simple Skid Row norms of sharing one's good fortune anonymously, a "live one" will "piece off" a "panhandler" today, only to become a "panhandler" himself tomorrow.

With the decline of several kinds of social types within each of the population segments, together with the increased numbers of older White men and younger Negro men, crime has increased, become uglier and more violent, in addition to retaining its basic pettiness. The young tend to gang up and prey upon the older White pensioners. Such muggings, formerly accomplished at night and in alleys, now take place more and more in broad daylight, in open streets and with more brutal violence.

It is a moot point whether there is more violence on Skid Row than formerly or whether the amount is about the same but simply that the decreasing numbers of men on the street make crime more obvious and visible. What is not moot is that two kinds of ironies are working themselves out on Skid Row. The first of these, manifest in some institutions of social control such as jails and mental hospitals, is that Negroes are assuming control over the situation by reason of their increasing numbers and their unwillingness to accept White domination as docilely as in the past. The result is a "Crow Jim" atmosphere, where the lower caste seeks to do unto the higher caste as it was done unto earlier by the latter.

The second irony is that, with the marked population decline on Skid Row, alcoholics, once in the minority but assumed to be in the majority, are now becoming the predominant social type. These two ironies, themselves the expressions of change in social life, give rise to a set of consequences. Some of these can already be observed; others can only be inferred. Yet in both instances they suggest the likelihood and significance of generalizations on problems in the social control of deviance when conflicts in the very definition of that deviance keep pace with the disappearance of an accepted place for its expression.

the Consequences

In the past, routes into Skid Row territories were taken by three social types, though in different and changing proportions over the years. These types were *workers, victims,* and *seekers.* Workers were men who predominantly engaged in migratory, seasonal or casual labor. Victims came into Skid Row because of natural disasters, wars, economic catastrophe or family break-up. Seekers entered Skid Row to avoid detection while engaging in such deviant pursuits as petty crime, prostitution, homosexuality, drug addiction or alcoholism.

Each of these social types, if they drank at all, ultimately became involved in different kinds of drinking patterns. In time, some of them went on to become alcoholics, albeit in a variety of species. Thus, the casual, seasonal or migratory workers banded together at work and at play in the sort of drinking culture that increases the chances of habituation over a long period of time. Hence, it is most likely that the plateau drinkers or delta alcoholics are most often found in the ranks of the workers (20, 21). In either case, their drinking can be described as situational alcoholism.

By contrast, victims, by virtue of events which rudely disrupt the routine of their daily life, turn in defense to explosive kinds of drinking, as if in retaliation for the suffering which they have experienced. In time, this style gives rise to the behavior of the periodic alcoholic, or Jellinek's epsilon type (21). This species of reactive alcoholism occurs much later in the life cycle and more often among married men (22).

Finally, the seekers, the most conflicted of men, are running from and to their own alcoholism simultaneously. These men correspond to Knight's essential alcoholics (22), persons whose adolescent socialization produced the kinds of conflicts that compulsive drinking alone seemed most likely to solve. Married as well as unmarried men are found equally in this cadre and they constitute the gamma alcoholics, the predominant American variety of alcoholic according to Jellinek (21).

With the changes in the numbers, routes into and composition of Skid Row populations, it may be inferred that seekers will come to predominate among the declining numbers of younger Whites who seek admission to the Skid Row social system. In turn, the increasing numbers of younger Negroes who constitute a cadre of internal casual workers are, similarly, likely recruits into situational alcoholism or plateau drinking.

The relative proportions of types of alcoholics, if this theory is correct, will vary with the changing proportions of types of men who ultimately gain access to and become accustomed to life in the Skid Row territory. It may now be possible to suggest the consequences of these population changes for both homeless alcoholics and agents of control, both on and off Skid Row.

For homeless alcoholics on Skid Row the consequences would appear to be some of the following: There will be, as already noted, a smaller population. But as the number of men decreases, the number and variety of personal problems of one kind or another for each man will increase. Unlike many of the Skid Row habitués of the past, more and more of the residents will be multiple-problem persons. And Dunham's prediction (7), of high rates of mental illness of all kinds and varieties, will likely be confirmed. One study already completed seems to confirm this assumption (23).

The older-White-younger-Negro relationship reverses the traditional patterns of racial exploitation. With the breakdown of the Skid Row moral order, rates of violent crimes, such as muggings and the like, are probably occurring at greater frequency both within as well as between both racial groups. The dissolution of this once relatively viable deviant subculture seems to be making the stereotyped label of Skid Row life finally true.

For agents of social control working on Skid Row, the following consequences seem most likely: Whether police officers, social workers, or others, agents will be making contact with fewer "clients." By virtue of the changes, however, the fewer clients will be manifesting a greater variety of troubles for the control agents to deal with. In turn this will produce lower rates of success, however defined. And, paradoxically, newcomers to the conception of alcoholism as an illness will most rapidly become the most case-hardened, the most apathetic, as their high hopes for "success" are immediately disappointed.

For homeless alcoholics off Skid Row, these consequences seem more than likely: Whites, when able, will seek to leave the territory for rooming-house areas or other congenial urban pockets; still others will avoid the Skid Row alternative. In either instance, dispersion rather than concentration will lead to an increase in solitary deviance and a corresponding decrease in social deviance; both of these are joint results of the expected decline in participation in Skid Row subculture. Deprived of the social supports of deviant groups, these alcoholics will be less protected against conventional ideas. Thus, some of them will not only appear sicker, but will also believe themselves to be sicker. In turn, away from the stigma of Skid Row, they will be more likely to look for help and more likely both to get and profit from it. Similarly, again because of the gradual disappearance of Skid Row and some of its typical services, it will be increasingly harder for them to "make it" or to "get by" as homeless men. If so, then a new kind of urban frontier may be developing in which there will be an increasing market for the services of well-trained health and welfare workers. Should this prove true, then the belated extension of health and welfare services to multiple-problem homeless men may actually succeed only in socializing many of them into dependent careers. Many of them will be going through a whole series of revolving doors in an increasing number of agencies, now on a permanent rather than a temporary basis as formerly.

For agents of control off Skid Row, these are some of the expected consequences: Homeless alcoholics, particularly those who participate in "bottle gangs," have a notorious tendency to "group up," to seek out one another for company and for social drinks. Should they, as seems most likely, follow their usual practices in urban non-Skid Row pockets, they will invite a negative reaction from most agents of social control and re-create the very stigma they were better able to manage while on Skid Row. An increased number of homeless alcoholics on the streets in new areas is more likely to be defined as "crime in the streets" rather than "illness in the streets." The social-control response, accordingly, will be punitive rather than therapeutic, despite the increasing rhetoric on using nonpunitive means to rehabilitate alcoholics. On the other hand, if public drunkenness is widely dispersed on city streets and is more often a solitary rather than a group occurrence, the movement to extend detoxification facilities will both grow and prosper. This will introduce a number of men into the circuit of new and old agencies seeking to assist homeless alcoholics and may well lead to increased tolerance for deviant behavior on the part of control agents. If they have heretofore had little or no contact with homeless alcoholics and with apathetic and cynical control agents, they may regard relapse as a medical rather than criminal event.

These consequences of changes in Skid Row imply a broad set of generalizations about deviant behavior and its control. They suggest a paradox—when persons adjudged deviant band together in accordance with a set of shared definitions to deal with their situation in a socially licensed territory, it is actually easier to control their activities despite the punitive moral conceptions of them held by both the general public and agents of control. And this seems to be so since to a relatively great extent they are permitted to regulate their own activities, however poorly. By contrast, when such deviants are deprived of their territory, the possibilities of controlling their activities, whether by punitive or therapeutic means, become more difficult, despite the developing tolerance and permissiveness of control agents and the seemingly increased willingness of such deviants to accept social controls when brought against them by legitimate society.

References

1. Wentworth, Harold, and Flexner, Stuart Berg. *Dictionary of American Slang*. New York: Crowell, 1960, p. 481.
2. Goldin, Hyman E.; O'Leary, Frank; and Lipsius, Morris. *Dictionary of American Underworld Lingo*. New York: Twayne, pp. 195-96.
3. Anderson, Nels. *The Hobo*. Chicago: The University of Chicago Press, 1929.

4. Wallace, Samuel E. *Skid Row as a Way of Life.* Totowa, N.J.: Bedminster Press, 1965.
5. Rubington, Earl. " 'Failure' as a Heavy Drinker: The Case of the Chronic Drunkenness Offender on Skid Row." In *Society, Culture, and Drinking Patterns,* edited by David J. Pittman and Charles R. Snyder. New York: John Wiley, 1962, pp. 146-53.
6. Bain, Howard George. "A Sociological Analysis of the Chicago Skid-Row Lifeway." Master's thesis, University of Chicago, 1950.
7. Dunham, H. Warren. *Homeless Men and Their Habitats.* Detroit, Mich.: Wayne State University, 1953.
8. Jackson, Joan K., and Conner, Ralph. "The Skid Road Alcoholic." *Quarterly Journal of Studies on Alcohol* 14 (September 1953): 468-86.
9. Lovald, Keith A. "From Hobohemia to Skid Row. The Changing Community of the Homeless Man." Ph. D. dissertation, University of Minnesota, 1960.
10. Peterson, W. Jack, and Maxwell, Milton A. "The Skid Road 'Wino'." *Social Problems* 5 (Spring 1958): 308-16.
11. Pittman, David J., and Gordon, C. Wayne. *Revolving Door.* New Haven, Conn.: Yale Center of Alcohol Studies, 1958.
12. Rooney, James F. "Group Processes among Skid Row Winos: A Reevaluation of the Undersocialization Hypothesis." *Quarterly Journal of Studies on Alcohol* 22 (September 1961): 444-60.
13. Bogue, Donald T. *Skid Row in American Cities.* Chicago: The University of Chicago Press, 1963.
14. Caplow, Theodore; Lovald, Keith A.; and Wallace, Samuel E. *A General Report on the Problem of Relocating the Population of the Lower Loop Redevelopment Area.* Minneapolis, Minn.: Minneapolis Redevelopment Authority, 1958.
15. *The Men on Skid Row. A Study of Philadelphia's Homeless Man Population.* Philadelphia, Pa.: Temple University, Department of Psychiatry, 1960.
16. Sutherland, Edwin H., and Locke, Harvey J. *Twenty Thousand Homeless Men.* Philadelphia, Pa.: Lippincott, 1936.
17. Bahr, Howard M. "The Gradual Disappearance of Skid Row." *Social Problems* 15 (Summer 1967): 41-45.
18. Rubington, Earl. "The Bottle Gang." *Quarterly Journal of Studies on Alcohol* 29 (December 1968): 943-55.
19. Shaw, Clifford R. *The Jack-Roller. A Delinquent Boy's Own Story.* Chicago: The University of Chicago Press, 1930.
20. Straus, Robert, and McCarthy, Raymond G. "Nonaddictive Pathological Drinking of Homeless Men." *Quarterly Journal of Studies on Alcohol* 12 (December 1951): 601-11.
21. Jellinek, E. M. *The Disease Concept of Alcoholism.* Highland Park, N.J.: Hillhouse Press, 1960.
22. Knight, Robert P. "The Psychodynamics of Chronic Alcoholism." *Journal of Nervous and Mental Disease* 86 (November 1937): 538-48.
23. Spitzer, Robert L.; Cohen, George; Miller, J. David; and Endicott, Jean. "The Psychiatric Status of 100 Men on Skid Row." *International Journal of Social Psychiatry* 15 (Summer 1969): 230-34.

Chapter IX
the "Revolving Door" Game

To play the "revolving door" game we need some players—public drunkards, police officers, municipal judges, and jailers—and a few playgrounds—the street, the lockup, the court, and the jail.

What is the object of this game and by what rules is it played? Has the game changed much in recent years? If so, is it because of changes in players or playgrounds, or both?

We shall first describe the players—their equipment, their styles and their playgrounds—and a typical game; then we shall examine some recent changes in playing styles.

the Players

The game is started when an unknown percentage of citizens primarily male and usually poorly dressed, appear drunk in public. Some assert that they do not belong in the game because they only seemed to be drunk when in fact they were sober, or that they got into the game accidentally by being in the company of those who really were drunk. (Thus we have perhaps one difficulty in the game—the number of unwilling players.) Willingly or not, "they all go when the wagon comes," as is said when they are put into the game

Reprinted from *Crime and Delinquency* 12 (October 1966): 332-38, by permission of the publisher.

by our next player, a blue-coated man called a "police officer." Officers take action (sometimes called "making a pinch") when they see persons who appear drunk in public.

Third we need a smaller number of players who are called judges. A day or so after the game has gotten under way, a police officer brings the public drunkards before a judge and says he found these men intoxicated in public. The judge usually takes the officer's word (he does not do this so frequently when playing in other games with them), and most of the time he makes arrangements for the drunkards, now quite sober, to meet the fourth player, the jailer.

The jailer takes control of the principal players for short periods of time, usually decided by the judge, and then sets them free. Shortly thereafter, many of the principal players enter the game again by going out "to make the price of a jug," as they put it. Soon afterward, they appear drunk in public again and thus another game is started.

Equipment and Playgrounds

The drunkards, the men who start the revolving door, need little equipment; in fact, the less equipment they have—such things as manners, morals, money, clothing, housing, jobs, etc.—the better they are at playing the game. But without a jug they cannot play; the jug is basic equipment. The best place to play is "on the street" a euphemism for "Skid Row."

Officers need whistles, blue coats, night sticks, and vehicles to transport the drunken players to the lock-up, where they must stay before they go to talk with (or, rather, listen to) His Honor the next morning in court. The court's most important equipment is a black robe, a high bench, and many low seats. Finally, there is the jail, usually an old building that does not meet any fire or health standards, has stout and interesting grillwork at its windows, and can always make room for one more. Many players disagree among themselves about the food, housing, and working conditions in the place called the jail.

Rules and Object of the Game

Originally, "making trouble" seems to have been the object of the game, and, of course, the trouble was made by those who played the part of drunkard. Appearing drunk in public, whether in the vertical or the prone position, is called a "misdemeanor" in the books officers and judges consult when in doubt. Sometimes, those who are drunk hit people, usually others in the street, and make loud noises; sometimes they take objects out of five-and-ten cent stores without paying. All these actions are called "making trouble." The other three players—the officer, the judge, and the jailer—dispense something they call "medicine." After "making trouble," the public drunkard is supposed to "take his medicine"—usually the time he spends in the place called jail. If he goes quietly and takes his medicine like a good boy, he is considered an excellent player by the other three players. If he resists and tries to spit out the medicine, he is not a very good player and sometimes it becomes necessary to prod him into the spirit of the game.

Originally, the object was to see how long one could keep playing. A strange feature of this game, however, in contrast with others, is that the skill and durability demonstrated in playing it do not bring increasing fame and fortune to the player. The reverse is the case. The longer he stays in the game, the less social honor he receives. The seasoned professional, in fact, is subject to increasing contempt or ridicule because of his expertise. Understandably, he sometimes falls to criticizing the other players. Thus, there is not too much friendly feeling, not even a spirit of rivalry. This lack of solidarity, coupled with public distaste, has brought about some changes in the game. We will now examine some of these changes in players, rules, playgrounds, and equipment.

a Change in the Rules

Three groups of spoilsports—an organization called Alcoholics Anonymous, scientists who have been studying the contents of the jug, and public health officials—would like to change the rules in this game a little bit at least. They have been arguing for some time now that those who so often appear drunk in public are unwilling players (unwilling because they cannot control their intake of alcohol) and shouldn't be in this game at all. The more they play the game, the more tired the players become, yet somehow they can't stop. But now the spoilsports are suggesting ways to give the players a rest.

Aside from these suggested revisions of the rules, there have been some interesting changes in the four players themselves.

In addition to being more and more often labeled as "alcoholics" (a new term for their part in the game), drunkards are different in some important ways from those who played the part a generation or two ago. Then, if they dropped out of school, there were crops to harvest and odd jobs they could do and trains to ride. Their society, less affluent and also less harsh in its view of these players, who lived on its margins, was also (perhaps as a consequence) less interested in helping and changing them. More and more of today's drunkards are coming out of broken families and seem to be sick or unable to cope with a complex world. They are satisfied just to get by, which means having a little left over for drinking. No one knows whether there are more of them than there were one or two generations ago; some students of the game say that there are actually fewer but that they are much more visible because of their tendency, as they approach middle age, to congregate on the street in the Skid Row quarter.

There have also been a number of changes in those who play police officer. The ethnic composition of many police forces is changing as new groups are entering police work in order to advance in social status; the Irish have moved over to make room for young Italians, particularly in the northeastern states. The younger patrolmen have a new and sometimes harsher view of the drunken players and tend to look askance at inebriety in ways the old Irish patrolman just could not. And where the latter might look the other way or even take the man home (and thus *out* of the game), the young newcomer takes the person found drunk in public *into* the game by bringing him to the lockup. Some students of the game say, like one Canadian public drunkard: "It's the young cops that are bad. I think they get a bonus if they get their quota." Others resent the young policemen even more strongly and call them "rag-pickers" or "dog catchers," particularly if they make use of a truck while playing.

Some municipal judges want to get out of the game entirely. Judge John Murtagh, of New York City, says no one should be arrested for public drunkenness. This explains why one of the largest playgrounds of them all had no arrests for public intoxication and 56,051 for disorderly conduct in 1965. Except when the Bowery had to be cleaned up for the World's Fair, most of the players in that huge city were happy playing other games. But in the nation's capital the judges became quite concerned a few years ago about the costs of this game. They found that to arrest, try, sentence, and incarcerate over and over again the steady players who form a faithful "hard core" cost the spectators, who are called "taxpayers," $2 million a year. (Nevertheless, after March 31, 1966, when the United States District Court of Appeals for the District of Columbia Circuit ruled in the *Easter* case that "chronic alcoholism is a defense to a charge of public intoxication and, therefore, is not a crime," many D.C. municipal judges continued to play "revolving door" in the usual manner.)

Finally, even the jailers are showing some signs of change. As their buildings become more decrepit while the number of drunken players increases, they wonder whether they need to have so many players assigned to them. (In Washington, their problem is not caused by an increase in the number of players but by the judges' view that the players need a longer time to take their medicine in the workhouse and the house of correction—playgrounds which are often substituted for jails in some places.)

Additional Changes in Playgrounds

Before listing some new players who have come into the game to change its rules and its object, we will discuss some changes in playgrounds which seem to have altered the manner in which the "revolving door" game is being played.

Some important changes are taking place in Skid Rows in various parts of the country, and the game assumes a different form along with some of these changes. To begin with, many of these playgrounds are disappearing before the "wrecker's ball," a basic piece of equipment in a relatively new but exciting game called "urban renewal." Some persons believe that this new game will eliminate the "revolving door" game simply because there will no longer be a playground. Events in such arenas as Boston, Detroit, and Washington indicate that this is not a correct assumption. By the time the dust had settled on the old playground, three small new ones had emerged elsewhere in the city. All the players remained constant; only the playground had changed. One might say that now the 6th rather than the 1st precinct had the franchise.

Students of these playgrounds find that, contrary to current spectator opinion, only one-third of the residents are bona-fide "alcoholics." Indeed, one-third of them are abstainers (a rate of abstention higher than the general population) and thus can never get into the "revolving door" game.

Again, despite incorrect spectator opinion, big troubles called "crimes" are relatively infrequent on Skid Row playgrounds. Aside from public drunkenness, vagrancy, panhandling, and disorderly conduct, little of note takes place on Skid Row. But to the spectators passing by in a car it may appear that every crime in the book is being committed—thus the mistaken impression.

But now with the changing welfare scene, the advancing age of older players, and the influx of some young ones called "hawks," the fairly orderly Skid Rows are becoming places of violence. The "hawks" wait for the elderly men to cash their pension checks in bars and taverns on the first of the month and then mug them; stabbings and murders do appear to be on the increase. Thus, a once orderly (within limits) Skid Row area has now become internally disorganized—a sign of changes in the larger playground called "society."

Enter: Some New Players

In earlier years, the "revolving door" game went on relatively peacefully. The orderly traffic and the stylized and routine performances of the players attested to the power that cultural traditions have in shaping the conduct of men. Drunkenness in public, arrest, trial, sentence, incarceration, and freedom to start once again all went evenly, undisturbed, according to the rules. Once the spoilsports we have noted above come on the scene, the "revolving door" game begins to lose what little fun there was left in it. Of course, as noted earlier, it is a very special kind of game in which fun is the diminishing return all players receive. All players could have gone on this way until the spoilsports came along. Now all is changing.

Some police officers in some cities like St. Louis now take all persons found drunk in public to a municipal hospital first. There a set of unwilling new players, called "residents" and "interns," look over the principal players to see what injuries they have and whether they are suffering from illnesses which would make further play dangerous for them. Only 10 per cent get into the hospital for something called alcoholism and related problems, and the local AA's would like to raise the ante. The police, however, feel much better since, in the past, an occasional dead body would be found in the lock-up and this would take much of the already declining fun out of their game. Over the years the police have come to feel that, in this as in any other game, it is always better if dead bodies are found in hospitals. Unfortunately, one student of the Chicago Skid Row playground has found that one dead body a day turns up in that area. Since this is a death rate higher than that of the so-called underdeveloped nations, a new set of players, called "doctors" and "welfare workers," are becoming a little concerned.

Now some police officers have become rather serious and walk a Skid Row beat, as in Rochester, and try to ticket some of the serious players (increasingly being called "alcoholics") into clinics. An even stranger thing took place a few years ago in Seattle. There some police officers sought to take players out of the game by putting them in a jail farm where recovered alcoholics did some coaching on how to stay out of swinging doors as well as revolving doors. The result was that a large percentage of these men got out of the game after they left the farm. Unfortunately, rumor has it that a high ranking police officer did not relish the loss of so many "revolving door" players, so he canceled the jail farm program. In that city, one presumes, the game is now played as well as it is anywhere else in the country.

A small hidden group of police officers who often were pulled into this door by other officers because of their inability to control their drinking, in public or private, somehow manage to retain their employment and to become members of the spoilsport group known as Alcoholics Anonymous. Many of these men, on their own, seem to be able to take a seasoned professional out of the game after much hard work. They seem to get a lot of pleasure in doing so—much more apparently than the little fun they were getting increasingly less of while playing "revolving door" themselves.

Of course, there have been a few judges who have had similar experiences, the most famous being Judge Ray Harrison, of Des Moines. In addition to his long years of experience on the legal side of the bench passing sentences out to the drunken players, Judge Harrison took a lot of them off to acquaint himself with all the other players and playgrounds. He became, in the new language, an alcoholic, got himself arrested many times for being drunk in public, faced the judge, and went to jail over and over again. By some mischance, he too fell into the hands of Alcoholics Anonymous. Now he runs a game of his own, called the "court honor class," where persons arrested for public intoxication attend weekly meetings. Over one hundred formerly good "revolving door' players are now in Judge Harrison's game, and the Des Moines "r.d." has suffered a 30 per cent cut in traffic.

Judge William H. Burnett, in Denver, though not an alcoholic, improved on Harrison's record in his own game of "court honor class." His court's attendance of old pros is as high as Harrison's, but he claims to have cut the revolving door traffic by 60 per cent.

In other courtrooms around the country, many judges make use of a new player called a "probation officer"—all in accord with increasing the fun by reducing the traffic flow. This new specialist schemes with the judge and others on how to put the player not into the jail but somewhere else. And if the probation officer has considerable personal experience with the wrong side of the door, he too can put his knowledge to good use in his new role as turncoat.

The earlier tradition among judges in playing "revolving door" was that those charged with public drunkenness needed harsh medicine, since they would not voluntarily get out of the game. A new kind of medicine, called "treatment," worked for people if they took it up voluntarily. Few judges bothered to ask a man to try it; they merely sentenced him to take the medicine called "punishment." Now, more and more, judges sentence men to treatment, including commitments to mental hospitals or assignment on probation to an alcoholism treatment clinic, an AA group, or a psychiatric clinic. Students of the game note that some variety seems to have been introduced into the proceedings.

"Medicine" in jail is now composed of unknown parts of punishment, custody, and treatment. Jails and reformatories and houses of correction have group therapy programs, AA meetings, individual counseling, and aftercare release programs with correctional counselors, institutional parole officers, and social workers. Through increasingly eclectic methods, the jailer seeks to get others to cut down his supply of revolving door players.

Effects of Change on the Game Itself

Like so many other aspects of changing society, certain features of the game seem to have undergone substantial modification. In some respects, however, only some of the names of the players have been changed while the basic rules and object of the game remain the same. It is too soon to tell, but students of the game are wondering just what has happened to the old "revolving door." Is it still the same; has it changed in name only; or have there been some real changes in the game itself? You can answer yes to all three questions and be correct, depending on the specific playground, players, rules, and equipment referred to. We have noted some places where some inroads on the old game seem to have been made.

One reservation, however, is necessary in future work or play in this game. First, changing the names of the players may be incorrect: many people who are excellent "revolving door" players are not alcoholics. And judges, psychiatrists, and police officers are not social workers.

Very likely the biggest changes in this game, possibly ending it completely, will come about when people decide once and for all whether the drunken player is sick, criminal, both, or neither. But there is no doubt that if being found drunk in public were not a misdemeanor, this ancient municipal game would disappear overnight.

Part Four

Personal Change

Chapter X

Relapse and the Chronic Drunkenness Offender

This chapter reviews experience with relapse in a new program for chronic drunkenness offenders. Programs which attempt to change men who have been drinking heavily for over fifteen years cannot hope for great effectiveness by ordinary standards. Yet the program under review has attained a fair degree of success by standards adapted to the realities of the chronic drunkenness offender problem. Shelter House,[1] a pilot facility of the Yankee State Commission on Alcoholism established in Maple City almost five years ago, owes its effectiveness to paradox. For Shelter House puts the negatively valued traits of dependency and recidivism to good organizational uses.

Meeting the Release Problem

Yankee State's typical offender depends upon alcohol, social agencies and other offenders to solve his problems of social and economic support. With advancing age, reliance on all three increases. After 45, most men in this deviant pattern of social life, finding it difficult to change, accept their fate. With increased reliance on alcohol, they often get drunk in

Reprinted from the *Connecticut Review on Alcoholism* 12 (November 1960): 9-12 by permission of the publisher.

public view. As arrests and jail sentences mount, they become known as "repeaters." Relapses become part of their way of life; agency help only sustains them between relapses.

The "release problem," which offenders typically face on discharge from jail or hospital, reveals one source of economic and social waste. Effects of treatment or punishment vanish rapidly in the face of the offender's release crisis. Unlike most high-status problem drinkers, he is alone, without social or economic support. Jobless, homeless, he can turn to few groups for help. Without food, shelter or a job before nightfall, he rejoins a drinking group.

The evidence seems fairly clear that offenders have only a dilemma, no choice, at release. If the only groups open are drinking groups, these are the groups to which they return. These groups require heavy drinking. Social or solitary drinkers, men with social or technical skills—each meets the release problem a little differently, but achieves the same negative results. Both rejoin drinking groups to meet their needs for social and economic support, only to wind up intoxicated once again. Release, nine times out of ten, under these conditions means relapse for the chronic drunkenness offender.

If membership in one group quickens drinking, membership in another kind can slow it down. The "delaying action" in the present state of knowledge is the best strategy against inebriety. In the case of the chronic drunkenness offender, delay can come about through membership in a sober group. A break in the pattern of increasing relapse may ensue if they can join a sober group immediately after their release.

Stop-gaps offering this choice at the time of release go by the name of halfway houses. Places of social and economic support, they are intended as turning-points in offender careers. Some offenders, by means of halfway house "therapy," will transfer their dependence on alcohol to the house, its norms, its people. In this way, they can reverse the direction of a life headed for increased dependence, misery, ultimate degradation.

Shelter House— "the Program" and How It Works

In February of 1956 the Yankee State Commission on Alcoholism opened its own pilot halfway house called Shelter House in Maple City. Action by the Yankee State legislature established Shelter House as a facility for the purpose of studying, treating and caring for selected samples of chronic drunkenness offenders. In common with other halfway houses, Shelter House started and continues on an exploratory basis; during its period of operation, there have been numerous changes in policies. And, in response to anticipated future developments, both internal and external, other changes will most likely take place.

Both staff and members of Shelter House refer to it as "the program." The informal, almost amorphous "therapy" which goes on daily within its walls is referred to as "getting the program." Despite many policy changes, two ideas continue as the core of the program. Distilled from the wisdom of all past and present self-help movements among problem drinkers, major emphasis is on "sticking with" a group of people who have alcohol problems and who are trying to stay sober. And, because of the homeless and jobless circumstances of most offenders, Shelter House, unlike Alcoholics Anonymous and most other treatment resources, provides shelter and opportunities for gainful employment. In the constant interplay between changing uses of its social and economic supports, some men "get the program," while others do not.

Shelter House is a semi-protective environment in which demands on members are kept to a minimum. All are asked to abide by a simple set of rules, most outstanding and important of which is staying sober just one day at a time. A group of 24 members live voluntarily under the supervision of a staff of five counselors all of whom are members of Alcoholics Anonymous. The members obtain outside employment as soon as they can, live at Shelter House, and pay three dollars a day in "dues" after the first week which is free. They eat two meals a day, breakfast and dinner, in their special dining quarters, and occupy a 10-bed dormitory on the third floor and 14 private rooms on the second floor. Men "graduate" from the dormitory to the private rooms as openings occur.

The nature of the "therapy," as noted above, is most informal. After the initial interview, a physician examines each new member and prescribes medication as needed. After a brief period of "restriction," the men go in search of work. Two evenings a week, they attend a meeting—one for the entire membership held on Monday nights in which "gripes" are solicited, heard and discussed—the other for a regularly assigned group of eight men and a counselor in which all aspects of problem drinking come in for discussion and analysis.

The very informality of "the program" appears to be a source of strength. Although there are only two regularly scheduled meetings a week, the bulk of a member's time at Shelter House is spent in public and private discussions with counselors and fellow-members. In many respects, the "program" resembles a kind of permanent, unstructured group therapy. During all of these discussions, membership and counselors exchange ideas, attitudes, exert diverse influences upon each other. Needless to say, all discussions center around alcohol problems and conditions which make for relapse.

Close contact under casual conditions makes for an atmosphere in which friendships may form and flourish. Moreover, because of the range of opportunities for intimate talks with counselors, intensive interpersonal relations between counselors and members frequently develop. These relationships seem quite comparable to those transactions which go on between psychiatrist and patient and are, many times, productive of real and lasting personality changes in some members.

Completion of the program is the major goal which the staff sets for the membership, to which the members, in turn, aspire. Formerly of three-months' duration, the program is now six months. Irrespective of its terminus, however, all concur, counselors and members alike, that if a man is to get anything at all from the program, if something is "to rub off on him," then he must complete the program, stay the limit.

Considering the past record of offenders in suddenly severing their memberships in groups, sticking to groups and rules presents a severe challenge. Thus, the program, on its face, gives every appearance of being an endurance contest. Members join Shelter House, agree to renounce alcohol during the period of membership, to abide by Shelter House's simple code of conduct. The abstinence norm, the source of all their past difficulties, in Shelter House creates conditions where social learning may take place. All problem drinkers have had periods of sobriety. Most of these "dry" periods were actual endurance contests, sacrificial rituals, tests or self-imposed punishments. During these periods, tensions cumulated, for the drinker was "dry" not "sober." Ultimately, he resolved these mounting tensions in the usual manner. However, in Shelter House, an opportunity exists for a man to go from the "dry" state to the "sober" state, a most difficult period of adjustment for most problem drinkers. Membership in a group who share common alcohol problems may increase the chances of a successful transition despite the many challenges which membership in groups have posed for most offenders.

In the "dry" state, most problem drinkers re-experience the kinds of personal discomfort for which only drinking gave relief. Once inner distress becomes unbearable, they "break out," and relapse into uncontrolled drinking. In the "sober" state, the problem drinker experiences as much personal discomfort, often a great deal more; the difference lies in acceptance of the proposition that drinking will only add to, rather than subtract from, the burden of discomfort. Social as well as problem drinkers have been quite aware of this sensible idea for years. Yet until it became a truly personal idea, its repetition never prevented relapse among problem drinkers.

Despite its easy atmosphere, a halfway house is not immune from those tensions which make for personal discomfort. Men who feel tension sooner than others are aware when it rises from within, from Shelter House incidents, from the outside world. They mount, when members, now "dry" for only a short period of time, suddenly desire to reverse the pattern of a lifetime overnight. Men, for example, who seek to regain status with wife and family expose themselves to rebuff. Unless they accede to cumulative group pressures, from counselors, members or both, to "take it easy," to "go slow," they will relapse in the face of these status crises. For the first time, many members actually find themselves in the company of men who seem to understand their own feelings and experiences. Under these conditions, a form of "on-the-spot" therapy, designed to nip tensions in the bud, makes it possible for some men to go from the "dry" state to the "sober" state. Sober periods which problem drinkers experience in isolation from their fellows rarely permit this type of social learning. Conditions in either jails, hospitals or welfare agencies are likewise unsuited to maximizing the influences which the group can have upon its members to remain abstinent.

Types of Effectiveness

Shelter House is a disruptive influence on the network of triple dependency in which most offenders become involved. Its purpose is that of the delaying action; to remake offenders overnight is out of the question. It succeeds and is effective to the degree that it interrupts the "revolving door," that it extends periods between relapses. As a wedge between the drawing power of alcohol, drinking men and the support of agencies, Shelter House succeeds to the extent that it maintains a grasp upon its membership.

Consequently, the several types of effectiveness which have come out of Shelter House experience depend upon duration of membership. Recruitment and retention of clients are the problems of all types of treatment organizations; to change men it is first necessary to break their old ties to groups and their norms, then to bind them to the new group and its norms. Recruiting the membership and then holding it in the group constitute the two major problems of Shelter House.

Since its opening, more than 600 admissions have gone through the Shelter House program. About half that number are first admissions. The remainder are "repeaters," who comprise a group of over a hundred men who have tried the program two times and a small number, around thirty, who have tried it three times, the maximum number permitted. The three major sources of admissions (all voluntary) have been and continue to be the Green Hills Hospital, the Maple City State Jail, and self-referrals. The remainder of admissions come from a variety of sources, such as the state hospitals, Alcoholism Division clinics, Alcoholics Anonymous, King Street Mission, court officers, clergy, etc.

Criteria for admission are minimal. Beyond a wish to gain sobriety by the methods of the "program," a man must qualify as an offender and state resident. If a man has had three or more arrests for drunkenness in the past five years, is between 30 and 55, and employable, he is eligible for membership in Shelter House.

The facts noted above specify the conditions of entry; there are, in addition, four principal modes of departure from the program. Reasons for separation from the program are designated as follows: A-according to plan; B-with notice; C-without notice; and D-disciplinary action. As with all treatment programs, there are preferred as well as undesirable conditions of exit. The rate of relapse, naturally, is quite high; perhaps as much as 60 percent of all admissions revert to drinking and fail to complete the program. Obviously, these constitute undesirable conditions of departure. On the other hand, since the major criterion of effectiveness is in sheer "sticking to the program," those who remain for the full six months are separated "according to plan." These are the select group of preferred discharges. And, as with halfway houses around the country, members who "complete the program" (or "the course" as some have called it) are considered "graduates" and occupy honorific status.

Most of these men, of course, have done more than just endure a six months period without drinking. That, by itself, is no mean accomplishment, as counselors and members all will agree. For to date the "according to plan" discharge rate stands at 13 percent, sharp testimony to the difficulties of attaining "graduate" status, yet these results are comparable to those attained in other halfway houses where accurate records are kept.

Follow-up data indicate, however, that "graduates" navigate best in the new and difficult post-Shelter House waters if they continue to "stick to the program," or embrace Alcoholics Anonymous, for relapse is an ever present threat. Those graduates who do not develop group supports for the post-Shelter House period relapse much sooner. Slightly more than half of the Shelter House's graduates have moved into private rooms in the King Street Mission. These men have remained physically close to the program. Yet most of them have stayed sober longer than those who ventured immediately into the outside world. Of those graduates who sought private rooms outside, only those who joined Alcoholics Anonymous or took an active part in the Alumni Club, a group composed of Shelter House graduates, were able to extend the period of sobriety they had first established for themselves as Shelter House members.

Positive examples, however, are more numerous. For, in addition to renouncing the homeless alcoholic way of life, many show signs of increasing respectability. The evidence, of course, is the acquisition of material goods, feelings of enhanced self-respect, and, in several instances, wives and children. Others assumed jobs of considerable responsibility; most notable in this connection is the fact that two of the current staff of counselors are graduates of the Shelter House program themselves.

Irrespective of ultimate relapse, graduates are enormously important, far beyond their numbers in both social and economic spheres. Their influence on fellow-offenders and current and other graduates is much stronger than personnel in jails, hospitals, and agencies. For they are positive proof that it can be done; despite all the evidences to the contrary, the wishes for sobriety are strong in most offenders. When one of their own makes it, morale rises. In a field already swamped with paradox, another is the instance of affiliation with Alcoholics Anonymous which occurs with some graduates. Day-to-day contact with counselors has broken down in some cases the almost universal, intense antagonism which offenders feel towards Alcoholics Anonymous. So far as these graduates have any influence in their former circle of drinking acquaintances, their example only serves to further break down barriers. When the news of a graduate's success spreads over the "grapevine," many of his friends seek admission to the program.

Economically, the "recoveries" of some graduates are frankly astounding. Reclaiming these men constitutes an enormous saving in dollars and cents to their community. When one considers the number of times that some of them have been in jail, alcoholism clinics, state mental hospitals, their complete reversal of form to self-supporting, sober citizens is amazing.

Graduates, then, stand at the pinnacle of effectiveness. They regain the most for themselves, are in a position to make contributions again as self-supporting citizens, remove themselves from the category of social and economic liability. Their effectiveness follows from completion of the program. The success of many other men can be ranked just below graduates—again on the criteria of length of stay in the program, days worked, money earned and dues paid to the state, days out of jail, hospitals, agencies—and most important, days sober in company with other men trying to achieve the same goal. These lengthy memberships, though they may end in relapse, constitute attempts to live without alcohol in a new kind of environment.

Conversion of Relapse to Therapeutic Advantage

In a certain sense, Shelter House has taken some clients who have been "failures" from the viewpoint of other treatment programs and made "successes" of them. It has done so, apparently, by capitalizing on the very defects of the offender's qualities—his tendency to relapse, to become a "repeater." This characteristic, most noxious to treatment, correctional and welfare personnel, is turned to therapeutic advantage in Shelter House's program.

For "the program" evokes the very behavior which is a source of annoyance and a sign of failure to all other agencies. The staff seeks, by all the means at their disposal, to induce dependency on Shelter House, on themselves, on the membership. In so doing, they seek to make possible those conditions whereby members are willing to transfer dependence on alcohol either to a group of people or to a set of social norms, "the program." All staff measures point to getting members to "stick close to the program," to put Shelter House before job, family, any other social obligations. And, as men near the completion of the program, counselors continually exhort them on the necessity of maintaining some "follow-up." Embracing Alcoholics Anonymous, "staying close" to the Alumni Club, visiting Shelter House at every opportunity after graduation—the staff encourages one and all of these. At the same time, for men who "relapse," staff arranges hospitalization for them, encourages them to think of readmission into Shelter House for another try.

A result is that Shelter House has established its own "revolving door." The consequences of its "revolving door" however are quite the reverse from those other agencies where "repeaters" are considered to be failures. Not so, by any means in Shelter House; more often, they show real improvements. This is quite the opposite of what the "revolving door" means in other agencies.

For example, probably one-third of all "repeaters" in the state jail system account for about two-thirds of all drunkenness arrests. At Shelter House, one-third of all men admitted to the program comprise almost 60 percent of all admissions; and, as time goes by, the number will probably increase. The differences in "repeating" at Shelter House are twofold.

First, Shelter House's "repeaters," irrespective of ultimate reasons for separation, remain in Shelter House longer than do first admissions (median stay for first admissions is only 25 days, for repeaters at first admission it is 40 days, on second admission 35 days, on third admission 75 days). Secondly, the percentage of "according to plan" discharges among Shelter House repeaters is exactly twice that of first admissions. Thus, dependency and recidivism at Shelter House make distinct contributions to organizational effectiveness.

From this organizational paradox, two important conclusions seem to follow. Certain types of offenders are more apt to perform the Shelter House member's role more successfully than others. Shelter House is more successful in inducing independent responses in some, but not all of its members. The differences between these types of members, in part, arise out of their previous adaptation to the network of triple dependency. Among those Shelter House members who relied more in the past on treatments for alcoholism, there is not only the tendency to seek help, but more importantly, the tendency to accept it in the form Shelter House makes available. These men seem to have suffered more inner shame and punishment for their drinking, and have always sought a way out, irrespective of the frequency of relapse. By contrast the bulk of men who drop out of the program early (more than 40 percent of the "without notice" group leave the program within the first seven days) continue to cling to a picture of independence in the face of the adversities which attend alcoholism. These men have experienced greater external punishment for drinking, on the average having many more arrests and fewer past treatments for alcoholism. They have drunk, on the average, more heavily for a few more years than the successful graduate group; they have a high frequency of relapse which impels them to seek help. But the form in which the help arises soon antagonizes them. Then they decide they cannot abide even Shelter House's simple routine and want to try it "on their own." In some cases, these men have strong urges for sobriety, yet grave doubts of ever accomplishing it. They respond to sudden changes by rapid relapse; many rebel against the dependent relationship with staff by arguing that since they have jobs now they have "straightened out." Talk about drinking problems finally annoys them and they leave, most of the time by getting drunk.

In its permissive attitude towards relapse, Shelter House invites readmission. It draws its readmission mainly from a group who appear to have gained some profit from their original experience at Shelter House and who seek to extend it. While this group seems better fitted to gain from Shelter House's program at the outset, because of the innumerable difficulties which beset the average chronic drunkenness offender, even they experience relapse. And, it will be noted, so do "successful graduates." But since relapse and readmission do not appear to connote any sign of failure either on the part of staff or of members, the opportunities for making the second admission more productive seem to increase. In any case, it would seem that experience with "relapse" and with "repeaters" in Shelter House often leads to results quite opposite from what these terms ordinarily connote in other treatment settings.

Notes

[1] Names of all persons and places are fictitious.

Chapter XI

Grady "Breaks Out": a Case Study of an Alcoholic's Relapse

Treatment ideology states: for the alcoholic, prolonged abstinence without personality change is unlikely. Since alcoholism exists in a web of ambivalence, conflicts—social, cultural, and psychological—are endemic in relations alcoholics sustain with non-alcoholics and alcoholics alike. Consequently, when conflicts persist and cumulate, alcoholics who have not changed will dissolve all conflicts by drinking again.

We present here case materials which suggest that absence of personality change and presence of persistent and cumulating conflicts need not necessarily lead to resumption of drinking. Our materials imply that some relapses may be viewed as aborted social relationships. These relationships, as are all relationships, are held together by a set of bonds. If these bonds—the "unwritten contract" as it were—include rules and roles for resolving conflicts, abstinence may be prolonged without modification of personality. Under the terms of these relationships, one alcoholic role-partner will relapse if and only if the other party has breached the contract.

Since the data on which this study is based were collected in a rather unique setting, the generality of the findings is obviously restricted. The materials to be presented depict the changing and shifting pattern of relationships which one homeless alcoholic sustained with a number of other alcoholics

---

Reprinted from *Social Problems* 11 (Spring 1964): 372-80 by permission of The Society for the Study of Social Problems.

variously situated in and around a halfway house for chronic drunkenness offenders for a period of some two and a half years. Nevertheless, we feel that the conceptual scheme through which this case of prolonged abstinence and sudden relapse will be interpreted can be extended more widely.

Social Setting and Methods of Research

An east coast state commission on alcoholism established Shelter House [1] for the purpose of rehabilitating chronic drunkenness offenders. Shelter House pursues this goal by attempting to break offenders' ties to drinking and drinking groups. When its members conform with and then internalize abstinence norms, enduring periods of sobriety are likely. When sobriety occurs, staff and members alike speak of someone as "getting the program." Though few can specify how Shelter House works, all agree that a member "gets the program through association." A director and a staff of four, all recovered alcoholics and members of Alcoholics Anonymous, operate the program, simultaneously discharging administrative and rehabilitative duties. That staff are all recovered alcoholics is said to reduce communication barriers; that members are all chronic drunkenness offenders is said to increase sociability.

Compliance with a simple set of rules, particularly the abstinence norm, is taken by staff to mean that a member is "getting the program." While residents, members agree to refrain from drinking, attend mandatory counseling and group discussions on alcoholism, attend meals, observe curfew, obtain outside employment, pay $21 weekly for room and board, and perform housekeeping and maintenance details as assigned. Ninety days residence suffices for maximum benefit; members who "complete the course" are called "graduates" and are encouraged to maintain close contact with Shelter House and/or join Alcoholics Anonymous to prolong their sobriety.

Three aspects of social organization, sources of most of the conflicts which beset Shelter House staff and members alike, need to be borne in mind. First, Shelter House staff as state employees sought to impose AA norms in a residential treatment facility on recalcitrant clients; secondly, by leasing space within the King Street Mission, Shelter House was in conflict with the mission over rules and scarce resources, and in competition with a facility likewise devoted to the rehabilitation of homeless alcoholics; and third, location in the mission increased chances of contact with homeless alcoholics who were currently drinking.

Our case materials stem from a field study [2] of the social organization of Shelter House. A major concern of the study was the observation and classification of conflicts and analysis of the means by which different Shelter House persons dealt with these conflicts as their own situations changed over time. A crucial case bearing on conflicts, their resolution, and changes over time was that of Windy Grady. Grady came into Shelter House to regain his sobriety, completed the 90-day residential treatment program, and "graduated" into a private room in the King Street Mission. Since Shelter House leased space within the mission, Grady stayed in contact with the halfway house. During his post-Shelter House career Grady was a mission resident holding outside employment, then a resident though unemployed, and finally both mission resident and employee. After almost ten months as night watchman and some 29 months since his last drinking episode, Grady "broke out." [3]

In view of the fact that Grady evinced none of the personality change that conduces to prolonged abstinence, how was it possible for him to stay sober as long as he did? And, when he finally did relapse, what social conditions made continued abstinence for him in the King Street Mission-Shelter House milieu no longer tenable? To answer these questions, this study examines certain observed changes occurring over time in Grady's situation. Materials on his case can be ordered in a five-part chronology: his pre-Shelter House role as chronic drunkenness offender, his career as member, and the three phases of mission residency culminating in relapse. We turn now to this chronology.

the "Loner" Role: Grady as Chronic Drunkenness Offender

Prior to entering Shelter House, Grady was a well-known though not necessarily well-liked member of Maple City's homeless alcoholic community. He was well-acquainted with both bottle gang and tavern norms, yet conducted himself primarily as a "loner." He had many acquaintances and few friends in this community; nevertheless, because he observed appropriate decorum, he never lacked for drinks when in need.[4] For example, while working as a truck driver, he stopped regularly at a local tavern where he customarily stood several rounds of drinks for the house, thus ensuring himself of reciprocity. Both garrulous and domineering, Grady claimed to have been on all the major Skid Rows throughout the country and to have drunk more than most people. A bona fide offender, Maple City police listed his name in their special "red book" of men who had compiled more than fifty arrests for public drunkenness. The fact that he had a son on the local police force did not endear Grady to his fellow-offenders.

Grady had been a Maple City resident all his life, had married and raised a large family. Then he separated from his wife and began drinking heavily. After several years of heavy drinking and homelessness, he contracted tuberculosis. He spent 29 months in a tuberculosis sanatorium only to resume drinking after discharge. Some time later, a physician at the Maple City out-patient alcoholism clinic referred him to Shelter House. Out of respect for this physician, Grady, now an alcoholic in his early fifties, investigated the halfway house located inside the heavily stigmatized King Street Mission and decided to affiliate.

the "Company Man" Role: Grady as Shelter House Member

Grady explicitly rejected the illness conception of alcoholism; in his own words, "alcoholism is no more than a falsified (sic) habit." Unlike others, he had drunk because he wanted to, not because he needed to. And like most offenders who entered Shelter House, he disdained Alcoholics Anonymous and thought anyone who "told his story" at an AA meeting was shameless, "phony," or both. Dissatisfied with the effects of his own drinking, however, he had resolved to regain his self-respect and to show "some people" that he could do it. Compliance with the Shelter House regimen seemed a sensible way of attaining these goals.

Though Grady was a member of the same heavily stigmatized social category as his fellow Shelter House residents, sociability was not thereby promoted. Though Shelter House staff were all recovered alcoholics, barriers to communication persisted. Grady came to dislike many of his fellow members when they failed either to comply with Shelter House rules or come to his assistance. He performed assigned details regularly without complaint, unlike most Shelter House members, and attended all group discussions as required. Though he enjoyed some of these discussions, he never revealed any of his "personal business" at these meetings or to his counselor, Ralph Gray. He disapproved of all staff counselors, particularly Gray. Grady deferred to only two persons in the building, James Sterling, Shelter House's director, and Bill James, the King Street Mission's director, himself a member of Alcoholics Anonymous, personal friend and sponsor of Sterling in AA.

In short, Grady had assumed the role of "company man"[5] soon after his admission to Shelter House. His commitment, however, was to Sterling and Sterling's organization, Shelter House, rather than to the moral beliefs and practices implicit in Shelter House norms. Though loyal to Shelter House, abstinence held different meanings for him than it did for the counseling staff.

Grady's work history while a Shelter House member had three phases: during the early part of his membership he worked at "spot jobs" (day labor), for the middle period he drew unemployment compensation, and during the last third of his membership, he worked for Security Service, guarding a local firearms plant. Significantly, when a counselor on duty had suggested he take a dishwashing job, he refused, saying "you don't send a doctor to do a butcher's job." In addition, he was the first member of the halfway house to request and receive seconds during an evening meal.

the "Graduate" Role: Grady as Mission Resident

When the investigator first became acquainted with Grady, he was a "graduate," occupying a private room in the mission, maintaining contact with Shelter House staff and members as well as mission staff and members. Grady continued to work nights as a guard for Security Service and spent much of his leisure time in the Shelter House sector of the mission. Sterling had given him permission to make use of all Shelter House facilities. Grady drank coffee in the Shelter House dining room and, again with Sterling's permission, filled his thermos jug with its coffee every day before leaving for work. Because numerous homeless alcoholics had begun frequenting the dining room, Sterling set down a rule that "outsiders" would not be permitted to use these facilities. "Outsiders," often ex-Shelter House members, drank coffee, ate Shelter

House lunches, visited, and solicited staff and members alike for funds. When Ralph Gray, Grady's former counselor, sought to enforce this rule, Grady told him flatly that Sterling had said that Grady could use any and all Shelter House facilities whenever he wished. Some time later, when Charlie Bragg, a Shelter House member, criticized Grady for drinking Shelter House coffee and eating its food, Grady informed Bragg that he had Sterling's permission.

About this same time, Grady overslept one afternoon and arrived late for work. His foreman, knowing he was an alcoholic, accused him of drinking. Grady became incensed at this accusation and only James' efforts at peacemaking forestalled a rupture. James arranged Grady's transfer to another plant and Sterling himself helped Grady move his belongings to the new plant. At the new plant, Grady became friendly with its president and spoke often of his association with him.

By now, Grady had become an articulate critic of the "bums," his favorite term for most Shelter House members and those transients who used the mission dormitory. Though a past master of the art of "ripping up the back"—derogatory comments made about a person soon after he leaves a small gathering[6]—he was still able to participate in conversation and coffee-drinking with Shelter House staff and members, acting the well-informed and dominating person whenever possible, save in the presence of either James or Sterling. "Bums," according to Grady, "are no good to themselves, and no good to anyone else." He saw them as selfish, jealous, and anxious to drag everyone down to their own level. Most of them had come into Shelter House for what they could get out of it rather than to "straighten out" as he had done. Though Grady thought of Shelter House as a "wonderful place," he revealed little of the personality change which ideology sees as requisite for continued abstinence. In AA terms, Grady was "dry," but not "sober." A characteristic indicator of this state is intolerance of "drunks." Other than not drinking, he was the same man he had always been.

the "Transitional" Role: Grady as Unemployed Mission resident

After eight months as guard, Grady quit and drew unemployment compensation. He had already amassed a fairly large bank account, obtained a wardrobe, and bought a car which he parked across the street from the mission. The car stood there as a symbol to Maple City's homeless alcoholics that Grady was "doin' good." On several occasions, Grady had taken the investigator to his room to display his wardrobe, radio and other properties, to report how he had reestablished credit with downtown merchants, and to contrast himself with the "bums." While unemployed, he ran errands for James, Sterling, and some Shelter House counselors. He continued to use the Shelter House facilities but now made some attempts to make himself useful. He made coffee in the morning for Shelter House and cleaned the tables in the dining room after coffee-drinking sessions.

He celebrated his "anniversary"[7] marking one year's sobriety during this period with five other Shelter House graduates in the Alumni Club. The conduct of its members only confirmed his negative opinions of the "bums." However, since only twelve per cent of Shelter House members had ever become graduates, Grady was an important person in this setting. And since only a handful of these graduates were able to extend their sobriety after separation from Shelter House, Grady became a cynosure in the Shelter House-King Street Mission milieu.

the "Reformed Drunk" Role: Grady as Mission Employee

When the mission's night watchman got drunk, James fired him and offered the post to Grady. Grady accepted and announced his appointment proudly to the investigator in the Alumni Club quarters, saying that he was now to be "night superintendent"[8] of the building. Besides supervising transients in the dormitory at night, Grady mopped mission offices, checked doors, answered phones, and watched the building. In addition, Grady was responsible for keeping noise levels down in the Shelter House lounge and in the Alumni Club while religious services were taking place upstairs in the mission's chapel. Performing these latter duties required the exercise of authority over Shelter House counselors and members.

Grady had made a few overtures towards reconciliation with assorted members of his family. Most of these overtures had ended in rebuff from his point of view. Shelter House had done more for his reformation than his "own people," he felt. When, mid-way during his career as night watchman, Sterling retired as director of Shelter House, Grady felt even more isolated. These changing events together with his own response to them gained for Grady the reputation of "reformed drunk"[9] not only in Shelter House but throughout the entire Maple City homeless alcoholic community. He was brusque in handling transients, many of whom had known him before, in jail or "on the street." Many sought preferential treatment from him because of past associations; he denied all requests vigorously. On King Street, he changed his policy refusing money to the ubiquitous panhandlers. While he was working to become known as a "tough giver," members of the homeless alcoholic community he had left were saying that if Grady ever "broke out" he would never be allowed to share in a group bottle again.

the Trash Bucket Incident: Breach of the Unwritten Contract

A series of seemingly trivial disputes had begun soon after Grady assumed the night watchman's post. As his circle of relations shifted, strains mounted and conflicts rose. As a mission employee, Grady was now entitled to free room and board. He now ate with mission personnel in their sector of the kitchen and drank coffee from the Mission's urn, rather than from the Shelter House urn. Sharing access to Mission facilities made possible the first dispute. For example, soon after Grady had become night watchman, James had to settle an argument between Grady and another mission employee over which TV program would be seen in the mission's lounge. A little later, Grady usurped James' space in the cramped mission parking lot; when James reproved him, Grady asked where he was supposed to park his car. James advised Grady to park his car across the street in the municipal parking lot and said the mission would foot the bill. Soon afterwards, there were two brushes with Charles Goodwin, a Shelter House counselor. Both times, Goodwin sought to park his car in the mission lot early in the morning. To park, Grady would first have to unlock the alley gate for him; Grady refused both times since he was eating at the time. Though he offered his keys to Goodwin, the counselor insisted that Grady open the gate for him personally. Finally, Herlihy, the assistant director of the Mission, advocated a more benign policy in the handling of transients. He wanted Grady to give transients more time for showering and to provide them with clean towels. Grady saw Herlihy as infringing his rights as night watchman and felt that all these disputes were signs of "friction."

In all these disputes, Grady approached James, protesting the indignities in his situation as he viewed them. James always listened patiently, advised tolerance, then rewarded him with a small raise. Implicit in these patterned encounters was the threat of Grady's quitting. This pattern of resolving disputes continued for ten months until the trash bucket incident. One evening, Herlihy reminded Grady to empty the trash bucket. Grady refused angrily and conveyed his annoyance and intentions of quitting in a note to the associate director of the mission, Mrs. O'Brien. James saw the note and said: "Well, if he wants to, let him. Maybe it'll teach him a lesson." The following day, Grady got drunk, after 29 months of abstinence.

Folk and Scientific Interpretation of Relapse

Though little systematic study of relapse exists, folk and scientific interpretations abound. Alcoholics themselves, their associates, employers, clinicians and researchers alike all seek to endow relapses with some meaning. Their interpretations usually fall into one of the following five classes.

1. *"Researching":* When an alcoholic, after a period of abstinence, resumes drinking with the intent of experiencing the pleasant, cathartic effects of alcohol, this is called "researching." Whether the alcoholic seeks to avoid the unpleasant consequences of heavy drinking or disregards them entirely, most persons view his resumption of drinking as an attempt "to drink normally."

2. *"Alcoholic Psychology":* In this, the most popular view of relapse, resumption of drinking is a predictable occurrence, depending for its regularity on some widely accepted notions of alcoholic personality. Given their low frustration tolerance and high need to reduce anxiety almost immediately, alcoholics, in this view, resort to alcohol at the first sight of stress.

3. *"Strains of Sobriety":* Use of alcohol as a means of coping with intolerable withdrawal distress explains this class of relapses. In the short run, alcoholics handle both psychic and physiological tensions brought on by withdrawal by resuming drinking.[10] In their own words, "what makes you sick, makes you well." And, in the long run, a life without alcohol has no meaning for many alcoholics.

4. *"Pattern of Sobriety":* Jackson Smith[11] and his colleagues have described what they call the "pattern of sobriety." Relapse, according to

them, is a predictable aspect of a regular abstinence-relapse cycle. Family members, associates, employers, and clinicians recognize the typical signs which precede a drinking bout; in some instances, the alcoholic himself may be aware of the pattern. In this pattern, the alcoholic builds up interaction credits for his renunciation of alcohol. All role-partners are aware of the sacrifice he is making; periodic indulgence is granted, given the gravity of the sacrifice he has made. The stability of the abstinence-relapse cycle in many instances is quite marked and the pattern persists over a period of years.

5. *"Strains of Society"*: In this, the most popular sociological view, alcoholics relapse when felt difficulties in meeting role obligations mount and cumulate. When conflict in norms and roles reach the breaking point, the alcoholic evades social norms, withdraws, and dissolves all conflicts by drinking again.

Both Shelter House and the King Street Mission were settings in which relapse was a frequent occurrence. Shelter House staff and membership alike, for instance, had little difficulty in assigning particular relapses to one of these five interpretive classes. Implicit in all of these interpretations was the notion that without personality change, abstinence could not be prolonged. Yet Grady's relapse, occurring in a setting in which relapses were generally accounted for in the above terms, poses problems for these accepted interpretations.

Counselors, Shelter House members and King Street Mission staff were all agreed on two major points. It was quite clear that Grady had undergone little if any personality change; if anything, abstinence had made his heart grow harder. At the same time, all informants had placed his relapse in the "strains of society" class, though few had given consideration to the key questions. Social strains had existed from the moment Grady had entered Shelter House and had only grown in a cumulative spiral culminating in his relapse after 29 months. Given his personality as viewed by most others, Grady was an excellent candidate for relapse, a man who ought to have succumbed to mounting cross-pressures long before his ultimate relapse. To know why Grady finally "broke out," it becomes important to find out what kept him sober over a long and stressful period. In understanding his case, we may come to a better grasp of why men in similar circumstances actually relapsed a lot sooner than he did.

Grady's relapse is rightfully classified as falling in the "strains of society" category. But his is a special instance of this category. For like all homeless alcoholics who had become members of Shelter House, social strains were unavoidable, changing and cumulative.[12] If we view the process of social rehabilitation as part of a social game, the question of rules becomes paramount. Grady, in common with his fellow chronic drunkenness offenders, faced a set of cumulative social strains. Unlike most of them, however, he had recourse to an umpire who decided all disputes arising in this game in his favor. Alcoholics in the process of rehabilitation who undergo personality change have less need of umpires in resolving conflicts; those who undergo no personality change very likely will confront as many if not more conflicts and strains. Without an intermediary, the probability is high that resumption of drinking will take place when these strains are deemed illegitimate. Yet Grady, in the anomic situation of the marginal ex-alcoholic, was able to remain sober in the face of mounting strains primarily because of an intermediary who managed social disputes for him.

Interpretation of Grady's Relapse

Grady's situation reflects, on the one hand, some of the problems implicit in paternalistic mission culture and, on the other, the problems of marginality for recovered homeless alcoholics, particularly those who had been "loners" on Skid Row. Because sobriety, Shelter House's paramount objective, was a scarce commodity, Grady had actually become a "big fish in a little pond." Since Grady symbolized success, both James and Sterling indulged him. Both men had adapted the AA sponsor-protege model [13] to their relations with Grady. Primarily, these efforts were in behalf of shoring up and maintaining Grady's sobriety.

As more and more doors to the conventional community closed, Grady came to rely more upon his contacts with these two men as signs of his official redemption. He had cut himself off from any possible social rewards from other homeless alcoholics; as he put it, "living with the bums" had taught him a lesson. Praise from them had no meaning for him whatsoever while efforts which both James and Sterling made on his behalf justified his existence. After Sterling retired as director of Shelter House, only James was left to him as a source of self-respect. Grady's redemption, however, as a person of some moral worth rested solely on those concrete efforts which James made on his behalf and, in a social world fraught with conflicts, these efforts consisted primarily in the resolution of conflicts.

Once Sterling had retired and Grady had become night watchman, strains mounted and cumulated in a vicious circle. Being forced to work with and associate with persons he considered his moral inferiors, being placed in situations which required him to antagonize rather than please clients, only forced home the discrepancy between Grady's self-concept and social reality. Just as alcoholics turn repeatedly to drinking when similar discrepancies prove unbearable, Grady turned to James for resolution of all disputes arising out of these discrepancies, and James, bound to this relation as benefactor and sponsor, never failed him until the trash bucket incident. At that point, when he failed to manage the dispute in the expected manner, Grady's social world collapsed for him. James' sudden refusal to arbitrate breached the premises of their unwritten contract. In the words of one informant, Grady had left himself with no "out" and had no alternative save to get drunk. James' failure to arbitrate sundered the bonds of this relationship.

Summary and Conclusion

Treatment ideology, whether of the professional or Alcoholics Anonymous variety, implies that prolonged abstinence without personality change is unlikely. Nevertheless, countless alcoholics both in and out of Alcoholics Anonymous have obtained their sobriety without personality change.[14] The question arises: how is sobriety possible without the personality change which treatment ideology deems indispensable?

Grady's case sheds light on this important question. Those social settings in which alcoholics seek to practice abstinence can be characterized by degree of social strain and by presence or absence of umpires. Given low strain and personality change, abstinence seems rather likely. Without personality change, abstinence seems likely only under two social conditions: when strains are minimal, or when strains are maximal and umpires are present. Grady's case exemplifies the second condition most clearly.

Notes

[1] Names of all persons and places referred to in this paper are fictitious.

[2] The study was carried out by means of participant-observation. During its course, the investigator assumed all of the roles in field work which Ray Gold describes in his valuable paper, "Roles in Sociological Field Observation," *Social Forces* 36 (March 1958): 217-23.

[3] Skid Row argot for relapse.

[4] For studies of drinking ritual among homeless alcoholics, see Joan K. Jackson and Ralph Connor, "The Skid Road Alcoholic," *Quarterly Journal of Studies on Alcohol* 14 (September 1953): 468-86; W. Jack Peterson and Milton A. Maxwell, "The Skid Road 'Wino'," *Social Problems* 5 (Spring 1958): 308-16; and James F. Rooney, "Group Processes among Skid Row Winos. A Reevaluation of the Undersocialization Hypothesis," *Quarterly Journal of Studies on Alcohol* 22 (September 1961): 444-60.

[5] A "company man" contacts staff frequently and supports their values while restricting contacts with fellow-members and rejecting their values. For a detailed discussion of the other roles by which members coped with Shelter House conflicts (e.g., "regular guy," "mixer," and "loner"), see Earl Rubington, "The Reformed Drunk," unpublished paper.

[6] For a systematic analysis of comparable phenomena see Erving Goffman, "The Treatment of the Absent," *The Presentation of Self in Everyday Life* (New York: Doubleday Anchor Books, 1959), 170-75.

[7] Many AA groups have ceremonies marking years of abstinence.

[8] Most mission personnel had always referred to Grady's new post as the "night man." The Skid Row term for the post was "crumb boss," so named because the person had charge of delousing operations. The Shelter House cook, who was praying along with a lot of other people that Grady would get drunk, sarcastically labeled him the "security officer."

[9] Shelter House staff and members, King Street Mission personnel, and members of Maple City's homeless alcoholic community all agree that a "reformed drunk" received help in regaining his sobriety and later claims to have "sobered up on his own," is intolerant of drink, drinkers, and drunkenness, refuses help to fellow-alcoholics and, upon relapsing, runs for help to the very people whom he snubbed when sober. For a fuller discussion of this social type, see Rubington, "The Reformed Drunk."

[10] Lindesmith has defined a drug addict as a person who knows that relief from withdrawal distress can only come from another dose of the drug itself. See Alfred R. Lindesmith, *Opiate Addiction* (Bloomington, Ind.: Principia Press, 1947). For a systematic application of these ideas to alcohol addiction, see Robert F. Bales, "The Fixation Factor in Alcohol Addiction: An Hypothesis Derived from a Comparative Study of Irish and Jewish Social Norms" (Ph.D. diss., Harvard University, 1944).

[11] Jackson A. Smith, Howard Herrick, and Lester H. Rudy, "Patterns of Sobriety in the Alcoholic," *Diseases of the Nervous System* 21 (November 1960): 622-25.

[12] For a discussion of social strains facing heroin addicts comparable to those confronting Shelter House members, see Marsh Ray, "The Cycle of Abstinence and Relapse among Heroin Addicts," *Social Problems* 9 (Fall 1961): 132-40.

[13] For an excellent discussion of this model, see Freed Bales, "Types of Social Structure as Factors in 'Cures' for Alcohol Addiction," *Applied Anthropology* 1 (April-June 1942): 1-13.

[14] Bales, "Types of Social Structure," argues that Alcoholics Anonymous is not so much an organizational vehicle for personality change as a set of relationships by which alcoholics can continue to act as they always have without the need for drinking.

Chapter XII

Organizational Strains and Key Roles

Four conditions seem both necessary and sufficient to produce displacement of goals[1] in bureaucratic help organizations: great size, extensive status barriers, a prolix set of rules, and a highly impersonal social climate. When these conditions are emergent, the organization works more often to the advantage of its experts than to that of its clients; when these conditions are fully developed, the organization very frequently works to the clients' disadvantage.

Awareness of this contradiction between treatment culture and bureaucratic structure has prompted some changes in structure in new help organizations as well as revisions in older help organizations. The terms "milieu therapy," "social therapy," and "therapeutic community"[2] are examples of such changes in the structure of mental hospitals. Similar changes have spread to organizations seeking to change behavior of prisoners, drug addicts, juvenile delinquents, parolees, alcoholics, and so forth.[3] These changes, in part the result of a social movement whose own organizational history has yet to be written, reflect a strong interest in de-emphasizing bureaucratization.

Under conditions of debureaucratization in the case of established help organizations (or nonbureaucratization in the case of innovation), the organization becomes client centered,

---

Reprinted from *Administrative Science Quarterly* 9 (March 1965): 350-69 by permission of the publisher.

thereby increasing its therapeutic effectiveness. For example, reduction in size increases contacts between experts and their clients; reduction in status between experts and clients increases chances of communication; reduction of prolixity in rules decreases complexity in social interaction; and, finally, a more friendly social climate makes it more likely that expert-client interaction will have benign effects. This reduction in bureaucratization of the help organization cuts down contradictions between treatment culture and bureaucratic structure.

Shelter House,[4] a halfway house [5] for chronic drunkenness offenders, seems simple in structure and well-designed for social rehabilitation: it is small, informal, with simple rules and minimal status differences between counselors and members.

In practice, Shelter House does not escape contradictions, however. Despite optimal conditions, strains on counselors and members exist because of the demands that the social structure makes on the members. A structure of negotiated intimacy requires that role partners play changing, diffuse, and multiple roles with the same role partners. As a result the nonbureaucratized structure at Shelter House does not eliminate strains; rather, it changes the structural sources and increases the complexity of the strains.

This paper [6] deals with problems that counselors face in Shelter House. It discusses *(a)* strains on counselors, *(b)* key roles as coping mechanisms, and *(c)* their interactional consequences. A major concern is to show how the key roles of counselors, evolved to reduce strain with members, induce strain between counselors. Ordinarily complex help organizations induce strain and evoke adjustive mechanisms by personnel in closest contact with clients; these mechanisms induce solidarity with colleagues, and antagonism toward clients. At Shelter House, however, under its close-knit conditions of interaction, the adjustive mechanisms, designated here as key roles, produce solidarity with clients and antagonism towards colleagues.

Setting of Shelter House

Chronic drunkenness offenders make little use of established alcoholism treatment agencies. Those few who do cannot consolidate treatment gains because of acute problems upon release. On discharge from clinics, state hospitals, and jails, offenders are cut off from groups which might sustain sobriety. Drinking groups alone accept them, but on condition they drink. To bridge this gap between the institutions and the community, the Yankee State commission on alcoholism set up Shelter House, a pilot project that explores rehabilitation potentials of transitional facilities for offenders.

Culture[7]

Shelter House beliefs, values, and norms center on relations between sobriety and association. Counselors and members believe sobriety comes from association with men who are sober and who want to stay sober. "Getting the program," the major goal of Shelter House, stems from association. Conformity with rules ensures continued association and improves chances of sobriety. Rules include abstinence, gainful employment, mandatory attendance at group meetings and counseling sessions, performance of assigned housekeeping and kitchen details, observing curfew, and payment of dues.

Organization

Four counselors and a director, all recovered alcoholics and members of Alcoholics Anonymous, make up the staff. Clients, called "members," live in Shelter House, which at full capacity has twenty-four members. A commission physician examines incoming members and is on call in case of illness. A commission psychiatrist sees occasional members in individual psychotherapy and attends weekly staff meetings to discuss the problems of members, and, when necessary, of staff. Social workers at the Maple City Alcoholism Clinic do case work with members from time to time. The secretary to the Shelter House director is the only nonalcoholic who has more contact with the staff. Counselors and members believe that "Only an alcoholic can understand the alcoholic." Shelter House objectifies that belief and makes close contact between alcoholics the means of social reintegration.

Achievement of Shelter House goals requires maintenance of this contact. Discharges possible from Shelter House depend heavily on the duration and nature of staff-member contact as follows: *(a)* "According to plan," when a member completes the program successfully;[8] *(b)* "With notice," when a member severs contact amicably some time prior to a maximum stay; *(c)* "Without notice," when a member severs contact before completion without staff consent and knowledge;[9] *(d)* "Disciplinary discharge," when the staff severs contact with a member prior to completion because of an infraction of rules, usually drunkenness. Frequent disciplinary discharges and a median stay of thirty days make duration of membership singularly important for counselors.

Space

Shelter House leases space and facilities in Maple City's King Street Mission. The lease separates most Mission activities and personnel and some Shelter House activities and personnel. The director's office, which serves also as meeting room, is at the rear of the first floor and is called "the back office." A glassed-in front office, on one side of the mission's entrance and looking out on King Street, serves as headquarters for the counselor on duty and is called the "fishbowl." Shelter House bisected the mission's kitchen, set up its own equipment, and hired a catering staff. It also trisected the mission's cafeteria, erected temporary partitions, and put in seven tables to make a dining room. Across the hall is the TV room which serves as a lounge and as a meeting room for the Monday night meeting.[10]

A third-floor dormitory adjoins the mission's spacious transient dormitory and houses ten Shelter House newcomers. These men become eligible for private rooms as they become available. Fifteen cubicles are on the second floor overlooking King Street. Until recently, the director lived in a room next to the dormitory. Over the eight years of its existence, seventeen men have served as counselor or director; twelve of these men lived in private rooms in the mission.

Ecology

King Street, despite urban renewal, continues as an important thoroughfare and habitat for Maple City's homeless men. A YMCA, a Goodwill Industries, a Salvation Army, an inexpensive down-town hotel, occasional rooming houses, package stores, and bars line it for several blocks. The mission caters to homeless men at its central location on King Street.

Shelter House culture prizes abstinence. Space and ecology set limits on its pursuit. Social organization, however, decides how counselors and members seek abstinence and what problems arise in its pursuit.

Complexities of the Counselor's Position

The expectations are that as contacts mount, members emulate counselors, adopting their attitudes on abstinence and then their actions. A model of the socialization process would be: contact—communication—consensus—conformity. The nonbureaucratic structure facilitates the process. Small size increases chances of contact, reduced status differences enhance possibilities of communication, informality induces consensus, and simple rules maximize conformity. The formula behind the model implies that Shelter House social relations simplify pursuit of abstinence. Like Alcoholics Anonymous, Shelter House strives to "keep it simple."

In practice, complexities in the counselor's situation nullify the formula. The complexity of social relations increases with the number of role partners and changes in interaction. Shelter House adds a third dimension to complexity; namely, that counselors deal with the same members in four different capacities. The official job description of counselors lists both managerial and advisory duties; the unofficial description includes duties as an alcoholic and as a companion. Thus, each counselor has duties as manager, advisor, alcoholic, and companion. A tour of duty starts at noon and ends the next day at noon; then another counselor comes on duty. Counselors work alone for one day, have three days off, then return to duty again.

Manager

During a tour, counselors perform numerous managerial duties. For example, counselors supervise breakfast, rouse late sleepers, eat breakfast, then take up their position in the fishbowl. Here, they answer telephone calls and write down messages for staff and members alike. They process employers' requests for help, acting as brokers between them and Shelter House members. And, throughout the day, they are in charge of the door.

The King Street Mission has two door bells, one for the mission, the other for Shelter House. Counselors answer the door for members and visitors of all kinds; ex-members, members of Alcoholics Anonymous, tradesmen and delivery men, mailmen, persons seeking information about or admission to the mission, commission employees, members of the alcoholic community, and others.

In addition, counselors record observations in the "log." Here they report quality and quantity of food, member's earnings and hours worked, messages, and observations on members. They also record appearances of prospects, ex-members, and visitors. While "on the desk," they collect dues from members and issue receipts. If members volunteer no information on where they worked, for how long, and at what daily rate, counselors must ask them. If members do not pay dues unasked, counselors must request payment.[11]

In addition, counselors supervise housekeeping and kitchen chores. Each day they make up a detail roster which rotates members' names by task and day. Counselors then supervise these details, check performance, and assign new members to special cleaning and repair tasks. Besides initiating these interactions, counselors, of course, enforce all Shelter House rules.

Advisor

Counselors conduct intake interviews with Shelter House prospects. When interviewing, they record responses on an intake form which becomes part of the man's case folder if he is admitted. In "taking a man's intake," counselors establish if he meets admission requirements (i.e., between 20 and 55, state resident, employable, no obvious psychopathies, at least three arrests per annum for public drunkenness, and desire to remain sober). The counselor, also during intake, obtains a brief drinking history, which allows him and other counselors to "get a line on the man's drinking problem" and to find out whether he is a bona fide alcoholic.

Once admitted, members are assigned to one of the four counselors. Assigned counselors must be available for impromptu counseling as well as for periodic mandatory interviews. Counselors write progress reports and termination reports as well. Termination reports include comments by counselors on all discharges regardless of type, capsule case histories, performance as Shelter House member, and prognosis for sobriety.

In addition to individual counseling, counselors conduct two kinds of group meetings. One is the "special group" meeting which meets with its assigned cadre of members one night a week in the back office. The counselor on duty chairs these meetings, which resemble "closed group" meetings of Alcoholics Anonymous. In the "Monday night meeting," Shelter House meets as a collectivity in the basement lounge. The counselor on duty that night, together with the director (if present), conducts this meeting. Counselor and director, at this time, talk a great deal about drinking, and the need to change attitudes and values. They also invite discussion of Shelter House problems.

Impromptu conversations between counselors and members can and do become counseling sessions in the fishbowl when there is privacy, or over coffee in the dining room. Occasionally, both repair to nearby restaurants for continued discussion. Less frequently, married counselors invite members home to dinner.

In their advisory capacity, counselors seek to influence members on abstinence, the main objective.

Companion

Counselors have those duties which accrue to all who act as participants in informal social interaction.[12] Here persons who discharge these duties are called "companions." The organizational structure increases chances of companionship between counselors and members in two ways: *(1)* the counselors are on duty twenty-four hours; *(2)* most counselors live as well as work in Shelter House. Counselors on duty as well as off-duty counselors who live in the mission eat meals in the dining room at Shelter House. In addition, coffee time goes on throughout the day at the round table in the dining room.[13] Thus, mealtimes and coffee time make possible frequent contact between counselors and members, under circumstances that produce intimacy.

Shelter House, then, encourages informal contacts, which other helping organizations discourage, either directly or indirectly. As a result, the expert-client relationship is different and the reduced social distance makes cross-status friendships possible. Some counselors even become "buddies" of members.

Alcoholic

Counselors, though recovered, are still members of the alcoholic community. Though loosely organized particularly when members are not drinking, this community has its own subculture.[14] Members of the alcoholic community share a common perspective, the joint result of involvement with drinking and reactions of others to their drinking behavior. Membership in this community also imposes some rather broad social obligations. In the alcoholic community, one "drunk" is expected to help another "drunk." The burden of proof is on help givers rather than help seekers, and help includes a wide range of goods and services.

Occasions arise when counselors are asked to put their duties as alcoholics above all others, and frequently enough, counselors honor these obligations unasked. Common bonds with alcoholics extend beyond current Shelter House members to active participants in the alcoholic community who ring the doorbell throughout the day seeking food, shelter, money, coffee, company, medical assistance, and so on. As members of Alcoholics Anonymous, counselors "carry the message" to visitors. As fellow alcoholics, they feel bound to give whatever aid and comfort they can, even if the person with whom they are dealing at the moment does not appear a very likely candidate for sobriety. "Piecing off" men who ask for money for drink is the most frequent way of discharging one's obligations to other alcoholics. And when dealing with Shelter House members, the most frequent way of discharging obligations as members of Alcoholics Anonymous is by "planting the seed" (proselytizing).

To a certain extent, counselors have problems because Shelter House is a new kind of organization, seeking difficult goals with resistive clients. But the major sources of their problems are structural, for the division of labor requires a counselor to discharge duties as manager, advisor, companion, and alcoholic with the same person. Thus, division of labor causes strains which counselors must cope with during their daily tour of duty.

Persistent Dilemmas of Counselors

Each set of duties sets up a dilemma with regard to successful discharge of at least one other set of duties. To be successful in performing one set of these duties is to risk failure in the performance of another set. All counselors face the following dilemmas.

Counselor's Dilemma as Manager

Authority jeopardizes the rapport essential for gaining a member's trust for advice and counsel. When counselors enforce Shelter House rules, they risk being called (behind their backs) "hacks" or "screws." Thus, counselors who "push the drunk" gain short-term conformity to Shelter House rules at the expense of its major concern, changes in behavior and attitudes regarding abstinence; for members are unlikely to become intimate with persons who order them about.

Moreover, the counselors' work requires them to police fellow alcoholics, actions quite incompatible with their duties as alcoholics. For example, drinking requires immediate expulsion. Counselors must detect breaches of abstinence and sanction rule breakers,[15] but such detective work impedes the development of mutual trust. And discharging a member for drinking exposes the counselor to the charge of lacking compassion for his fellow alcoholic. As one counselor put it, "If I throw him out, where can he go?"

Finally, good managers make poor table companions. In other settings, those who give and those who receive commands usually remain apart during informal interaction. But Shelter House mealtimes and coffee times give counselors and members access to each others' company. A counselor who manages well can expect greater reserve, if not actual hostility, when he crosses ranks and joins members for meals or coffee.

Counselor's Dilemma as Advisor

The dilemma here is that of the friendly expert. To foster closer contact, counselors indulge members and tolerate some violations of rules, but these concessions tend to discredit their authority as managers. Moreover, by becoming too friendly counselors risk becoming too emotionally involved and losing detachment. Then members can manipulate the fund of good will counselors [16] worked so hard to build up.

Appearing "too close" invites charges of favoritism and inconsistency in enforcement. If a counselor makes a concession to one of the men assigned to him, then other Shelter House members may ask for similar consideration once such concessions become public knowledge. If counselors get intimate enough, some members will make disclosures to the counselors that they later regret. With regret, these members abort further contacts with their counselors.

Counselor's Dilemma as Companion

To gain friendship a counselor must give up some of his commitment to his duties as manager and advisor. As informal contacts between counselor and member increase, deference gives way to friendly sentiments. With these imperceptible shifts in interaction members may take liberties with the counselors, who may become aware of the imposition too late to call a halt.

To ingratiate themselves with members, counselors draw on their own past suffering through alcoholism. But a disclosure made by a counselor as a testament of the closeness of the relationship can reduce his influence, particularly if the member admitted to the confidence regards the disclosure as a sign of weakness rather than of strength.

Counselor's Dilemma as Alcoholic

If counselors attend to their duties as alcoholics, other duties suffer by default. For example, counselors may not ask for dues or press members to go out and look for work. Or they may not press certain forms of work on members for fear they may get drunk because they consider such employment as demeaning. In doing this, they discharge their duties as alcoholics at the expense of managerial ones. For Shelter House must show some kind of economic improvement in its members if it is to survive.

Again, if a counselor acknowledges his obligations as alcoholic, he does so at the expense of his duty as advisor. Indulgences granted to induce rapport may be taken as signs of weakness by members. Whenever a member "cons" a counselor, he damages his influence as advisor. Admission of a common alcoholic brotherhood, at least in Shelter House, is not an unmixed blessing for counselors.

The conflicting duties of counselors induce strain and present them with the dilemmas noted. If a counselor discharges one set of duties, he may neglect another set. Yet he must act even though in a position where conformity to one set of norms entails non-conformity with another set.

Key Roles as Solutions to Dilemmas

Despite turnover, four major solutions arose to the persistent dilemmas. Though personnel came and went, these solutions remained as constant as the dilemmas they were designed to resolve, so that they are treated here as roles. The solutions consist of selecting one set of duties and making it the *key role.*[17] This key role then becomes the basic adaptive mechanism to the strains that members put on counselors. This does not mean that counselors neglect their other duties, but rather that in observed instances, the key role was more often the way out of the dilemma. The four key roles which emerged as systematic responses to strains are controller, confidante, crony, and convert.[18]

Controller

The controller has an instrumental orientation towards Shelter House members that dominates in the performance of his various duties. He acts to improve the efficiency of members as sober alcoholics.

Nysol, who worked six months as Shelter House counselor, is an excellent example of a controller. Repeatedly, he noted that he was not "in any popularity contest with the other counselors." His concern was in "straightening out" Shelter House members. Since these men had lived disorderly lives for years, order and discipline were requisite for a return to adult life in the general community. Thus, when supervising members, Nysol stressed rules and their importance. As advisor, he devised a series of nine formal "indoctrinations" for new members; in these indoctrinations, the assigned counselor discussed topics from an outline. As table companion, he lectured and stressed order. Finally, as alcoholic, he constantly compared his past inefficiencies with his present self-control. In all situations, Nysol emphasized order, routine, discipline, and control of the interaction on behalf of members' sobriety.

Confidante

The confidante has an expressive orientation towards members. He acts to maintain their expressiveness as sober alcoholics. The confidante stresses feelings and emotions. He wants members to gain a better understanding of themselves and their drinking problems. In advisory situations, he wants to know how members feel; in time, he hopes they will become curious about their own feelings. He wants them to see the connections between drinking and feeling states. Feelings pervade a confidante's management; when acting as manager, a confidante wonders how members feel about taking orders.

The confidante desires first that members be comfortable while Shelter House residents and that they come to like the counselors. Unless these conditions are met, he sees little chance of effecting changes in actions, attitudes, and values. The management of members, then, imposes considerable hardship on him.

Confidantes are at home as companions. While talking with and listening to members around the dinner or coffee table, they indulge their curiosity about members' reactions to events, situations and people. When necessary, they can be supportive.

Finally, when honoring obligations as alcoholics, they report how past misuse of alcohol made them feel and how other people treated them because of alcoholism.

Crony

The crony has an expressive orientation towards himself as the major object in all role performances. He acts to maintain his own expressiveness as a sober alcoholic.

Cronies see their job as "creating friendly feeling" in Shelter House. When friendly feeling exists, they are certain they are doing well. Given this orientation, cronies seek to induce friendly feeling. In no situation, if they can avoid it, will they attempt a course of action that may evoke hard feelings. As supervisors, for example, they put orders in the form of favors requested of members. And when completing intake interviews or acting as advisors, they feel a certain embarrassment. They are reluctant to probe members' feelings, to assess probable motives for actions. And cronies assume that if members raise no questions, they have no complaints.

Cronies are more apt to engage members in informal interaction that extends beyond eating meals and drinking coffee with members. Some have played cards after hours with members, others have gone bowling or to movies. Recently one counselor took several members horseback riding. When doing their duty by other alcoholics, cronies induce friendly feeling. More so than other counselors, when cronies report on past alcoholic escapades, they draw no moral lessons for their listeners.

Convert

The convert has an instrumental orientation towards himself, main object of concern in interaction. He acts to maintain his own efficiency as a sober alcoholic. Being a recovered alcoholic is the convert's main concern in the performance of his various duties. This role is open to all counselors rather easily, since all are members of Alcoholics Anonymous. Yet not all counselors place as much emphasis on Alcoholics Anonymous in their dealings with members as does the convert.

For some counselors, Alcoholics Anonymous has been the difference between life and death, a fact which they cannot let themselves or others forget. The fear of forgetting imparts a compulsive quality to their relations, which affects all interactions whether as supervisor, advisor, companion, or alcoholic. In all situations the convert stresses his own recovery through application of principles of Alcoholics Anonymous.

When supervising members, the convert injects Alcoholics Anonymous folk wisdom into all actions. And when advising members, he plays the role of sponsor to their role as protegé in a style typical of Alcoholics Anonymous members;[19] all consultations between counselors and members are "Twelfth Step Calls," in the convert's eyes. Similarly, at meals or over coffee or when honoring broad-based obligations as alcoholic, the convert interprets present conduct of others in the light of his own past conduct. In doing so, he continually dramatizes what he had been until he joined Alcoholics Anonymous.

By these four key roles, counselors cope with the strain of contact with members. But these roles, useful for reducing strains when dealing with Shelter House members, serve to induce strains between counselors.

Counselor Roles and Interactional Consequences

Key Roles and Social Solidarity

Although key roles make contacts between the counselor on duty and members fairly smooth, they create problems in the interaction of counselors with each other. When changing shifts, counselors may pass on unresolved problems to their replacement.

Cronies, for example, frequently fail to record information in the log. These lapses exasperate controllers who require order and routine as a condition of successful role performance. In addition, failure to collect data for the log embarrasses the director, who draws much of his material for monthly reports from this source. Records are essential, though cronies find them a nuisance.

This frequent difficulty only bemuses confidantes who believe that feelings always have priority over facts and figures. Confidantes find the controllers' insistence on order and efficiency very distressing and lose few chances to mock them as compulsive, impersonal, or sticklers for detail. And two confidantes, in a special interpretation of confidentiality rules, told the director they were not writing down everything members told them in their case folders. Where cronies often fail to report facts and figures, confidantes fail to report important feelings. Confidantes feel strongly that controllers' actions smack of regimentation or institutionalism, and believe emphasis on rules defeats the goals of Shelter House. As one confidante was fond of repeating, "You can't make rules for the alcoholic."

But the confidante's concern with spontaneity and adapting to individual members ("playing it by ear") runs contrary to the convert's commitment to Alcoholics Anonymous principles of recovery. The convert sees the confidante's flexibility violating Alcoholics Anonymous tenets. Should a convert learn that a confidante is holding a member's bankbook for safekeeping, he will shake his head critically and remark: "You carry the message, not the drunk."

Controllers, in turn, point out that confidantes really want to be "one of the boys" and to be loved by all the members. Hence, when confidantes argue for a policy of flexibility or permissiveness, controllers cry laxity. Nysol, for example, aware that policy varied with each counselor's tour of duty, argued for consistency, insisting that "we all play from the same sheet of music." These efforts to establish a more consistent policy and enforcement of that policy won for Nysol the dislike of Sterling, then director, and Bright, the senior counselor. Ultimately, Nysol had to resign. His case typifies frequent disagreements between counselors; first, because controllers who suggest more orderly procedures ultimately lose out, and secondly, because all counselors accept frequent staff disagreements as part of the job.

Stafford Bright, a counselor for three years before he served as director for an additional two years, repeatedly said, "We never have any problems with members, only with staff." [20] All counselors accepted Bright's proposition as empirically true of Shelter House staff relations; all saw these problems as inevitable, mostly because of "personality differences."

But, in fact, the source of the antagonism was more structural than psychological.

In traditional bureaucratic helping organizations, staff members make common cause with colleagues in defending themselves against encroachments by clients. Coping mechanisms make colleagues solidary with one another, antagonistic towards clients. Shelter House reverses this situation. Despite dual affinities of common staff position and Alcoholics Anonymous membership, solidarity among counselors is weak. Counselors play each other off in order to maintain their own key role adjustments with members. In other organizations, staff personnel play clients against each other.

Key roles, fairly effective in handling members, create strains between counselors because each counselor is part of a triangle. One side of the triangle consists of relations with fellow counselors. Relations with members are more apt to set a counselor against other counselors because counselors have proportionately greater contact with members than with counselors.[21] In addition, contacts with other counselors are also intermittent, uneven in tone, with equals, productive of problems, and less amenable to control.

The other side of the triangle consists of contacts with members. Contacts with members, unlike counselors, are constant and increasing as the day wears on. Moreover, "the door" brings the counselor on duty into contact with an even greater number of persons, most of whom are members of the alcoholic community. The persons with whom the counselor deals so frequently are like customers. And since he has to deal with them more frequently than with counselors, their wishes are of some importance to him. In addition, his main task is to give help, to "sober them up." Once he works out his own key role for dealing with members, he is more apt to experience problems with other counselors who elect key roles which clash with his. Additionally, professional jealousy enters when some counselors accuse more affluent ones of trying to "buy the men" by loans or outright gifts of money. The critic points out that in contrast, he does not have to "buy the men," since he wins their respect solely on the basis of his sound advice and the manner in which he conducts himself as counselor.

Types of Negotiations

Early negotiations between counselors and members deal with social rewards; later ones, with withholding of punishments. In early negotiations, counselors offer rewards of close contact and indulgence. For example, ex-member and self-styled "con artist," Jimmy Newlie, described actions of two counselors as follows: "Both these guys are in the 'con' here. They want to see new faces so they can carry on their own style of 'con.' First, they have to protect their jobs; then, they 'con' you into liking them by taking you to AA meetings, offering you cigarettes, lending you or giving you a shirt, doing you favors, lending you a coat, telling you to come see them if you have any problems, and taking an interest in you."

Later negotiations between counselors and members deal with negative sanctions. Generally speaking, it is to the counselor's interest not to be put in the position of enforcing any Shelter House rule, if he can help it. No counselor, for example, regardless of key role, wants to terminate a member for drunkenness if he can avoid it.[22] Nor does he want to press members for dues money, or for performance of assigned details, or for failure to attend the mandatory meetings, if he can avoid it. Selective inattention to various violations of Shelter House norms by counselors becomes a form of tacit negotiation. Not inflicting punishment becomes a kind of reward that counselors can dispense.[23]

Tacit negotiations on the use of sanctions establishes rules. The following instance of a counselor's violation of tacit rules shows their import. A member, Stanley, spent a weekend in Bear City, mostly in tavern drinking. He returned to Shelter House on Sunday night, was helped into bed by several members, and got up the next morning and went to work as usual. Two days later, Goodwin came on duty. Somehow he had either guessed or learned that Stanley had broken the no-drinking rule ("one drink and you're out"). That evening after work he asked Stanley when he returned from his job if he had been drinking. Stanley admitted that he had been drinking over the weekend, whereupon, Goodwin terminated him on the spot. When members heard of Goodwin's action, they became indignant. Goodwin had not *seen* Stanley drinking nor had he seen him with the "signs of drink on him." Furthermore, Stanley was sober when Goodwin put the question to him. Thus, Goodwin's action, to these members, appeared officious and retroactive. The tacit negotiation which Goodwin had apparently violated was punishing an infraction he had not himself seen. Where Goodwin selectively attended an infraction he could not have personal knowledge of, other counselors selectively did not attend to infractions of which they could and did have personal knowledge.

Summary and Conclusions

Shelter House social structure is more complex than it appears. Counselors sort the various claims made on them by members. Since some claims negate others, counselors cannot discharge all duties satisfactorily. Each meets the dilemma by evolving a key role for interactions with members. Counselors become controllers, confidantes, cronies, or converts.

But these roles strain relations with colleagues, for nonbureaucratization puts counselors in a weak bargaining position with members. Beyond ambiguous friendship with members or laxity in enforcement of rules, counselors have little to offer members. Members are in a somewhat better position since they are free to go at any time; and, once employed, "pay their own way" and need not feel dependent. In addition, since counselors seek psychological changes, member compliance is essential. But counselors cannot coerce members into this compliance; they can only manipulate.

For interpersonal relations to cause psychological change, counselors require a social structure that enhances manipulation. Then counselors can trade laxity in enforcement or friendship in return for a member's sobriety. These relations, however, place them in competition with one another, since they employ key roles which conflict. As a result, counselors have two faces; the grim visage for one another, the smile for members. In both cases, social structure sets the conditions for the faces they present to colleagues and members.

Notes

[1] For a theoretical discussion of displacement of goals, see Robert K. Merton, *Social Theory and Social Structure* (Glencoe, Ill.: The Free Press, 1957), pp. 199-201. For one application in research, see Thomas J. Scheff, "Differential Displacement of Treatment Goals in a Mental Hospital," *Administrative Science Quarterly* 7 (September 1962): 208-17.

[2] For an early statement of how to debureaucratize the mental hospital, see Maxwell Jones, *The Therapeutic Community* (New York: Basic Books, 1953); for a study of a therapeutic community, see Robert N. Rapoport, *Community as Doctor* (London: Tavistock Publications, 1959).

[3] A description of the social structure of a new help organization for drug addicts is found in Lewis Yablonsky, "The Anticriminal Society; Synanon," *Federal Probation* 26 (September 1962): 50-57.

[4] The names of all persons and places are fictitious.

[5] For survey data on characteristics of halfway houses, see Edward Blacker and David Kantor, "Half-Way Houses for Problem Drinkers," *Federal Probation* 24 (June 1960): 18-23.

[6] Revised version of a paper presented at the Research Sociologists' Conference on Alcohol Problems, Southern Illinois University, May 1, 1964.

[7] This report is based on a long-term field study of Shelter House. The study began with the opening of Shelter House in 1956; data collection, almost exclusively by participant observation, ceased in 1962.

[8] Originally 90 days, the maximum stay increased to 120 days, then six months, and finally became indefinite. At present, the maximum stay is six months.

[9] Counselors term these discharges "AWOLS."

[10] The mission donated a rear basement storage room to ex-members of Shelter House. Here they set up quarters for the Alumni Club, offering facilities for recreation, sociability, and asylum. A few months ago, the mission repossessed these quarters and the Alumni Club was discontinued.

[11] Data on hours worked, earnings, and dues are submitted in the commission's annual report. These economic data are treated as signs of reduction in social deviance and return to regularity. Without this evidence of economic improvement, it is unlikely that Shelter House could have continued to exist as long as it has. Yankee State legislators, for example, were so impressed with the first financial report that they voted additional sums for the commission to set up Shelter Houses in other cities.

[12] For a systematic analysis of behavior that most sociologists would regard as either unstructured or informal, see Erving Goffman, *Behavior in Public Places* (New York: The Free Press, 1963).

[13] Some members refer to the dining room as "the coffee shop." Coffee is free; yet the standard invitation to share coffee is for one person to ask another if he can "buy" him a coffee.

[14] For norms of homeless alcoholics, see Joan K. Jackson and Ralph Connor, "The Skid Road Alcoholic," *Quarterly Journal of Studies on Alcohol* 14 (September 1953): 468-86; W. Jack Peterson and Milton A. Maxwell, "The Skid Road 'Wino'," *Social Problems* 5 (Spring 1958) 308-16; and James F. Rooney, "Group Processes among Skid Row Winos: A Reevaluation of the Undersocialization Hypothesis," *Quarterly Journal of Studies on Alcohol* 22 (September 1961): 444-60.

[15] Members label counselors preoccupied with violations of the no-drinking rule as "snifters." Counselors gain this title when they appear to be sniffing the air while admitting a member at the front door.

[16] For a study of the relations between distance and detachment, see Charles Kadushin, "Status Differences between Clients and Professionals," *American Journal of Sociology* 67 (March 1962): 517-31.

[17] Frederick L. Bates develops this concept in his useful article, "Position, Role, and Status: A Reformulation of Concepts," *Social Forces* 34 (May 1956): 313-21.

[18] These are ideal, not social types. The terms are the writer's, not the counselors' nor the members; yet few counselors or members would have trouble assigning particular counselors to one of these role descriptions.

[19] For analyses of this pattern, see Irving Peter Gellman, *The Sober Alcoholic* (New Haven, Conn.: College and University Press, 1964); and Freed Bales, "Types of Social Structure as Factors in 'Cures' for Alcohol Addiction," *Applied Anthropology* 1 (April-June 1942): 1-13.

[20] A supervisor of a treatment-oriented prison camp echoed Bright when he said, "Well, strangely enough the biggest problem I've had is not with the inmates but with people that work for you." Oscar Grusky reports this comment in his "Role Conflict in Organization," *Administrative Science Quarterly* 3 (March 1959): 452-72.

[21] Here, Shelter House differs from other help organizations not so much in expert-client ratios as in rates of expert-client contact. For example, in a hospital for patients incapable of improvement, custodial-ward staff had higher rates of staff-staff contact than staff-patient contact. See Rose Laub Coser, "Alienation and the Social Structure: Case Analysis of a Hospital," in *The Hospital in Modern Society*, ed. Eliot Freidson (New York: The Free Press, 1963), pp. 244-45.

[22] To decrease ill-feeling attaching to the terminator, counselors now inform all members that decision to terminate was made by the entire staff and not just the counselor on duty.

[23] When persons with power to inflict negative sanctions say to those under their supervision, "Don't let me see you do it," they license deviance. For negotiations of this kind between prisoners and guards, see Gresham Sykes, "The Corruption of Authority and Rehabilitation," *Social Forces* 34 (March 1956): 257-65.

Part Five

Organizational Change

Chapter XIII

the Halfway House for the Alcoholic

Members of Alcoholics Anonymous, students of alcohol problems, and public health workers have all combined to make the movement for alcoholic rehabilitation a success. Their leaders, programs, objectives, and techniques for helping alcoholics to recover have all worked where other institutions persisting in established ways have failed. The broad social movement for alcoholism rehabilitation is now a going concern, having met the first test of getting results.

Movements arise when the existing social organization produces mounting dissatisfaction because of its failure to solve the presenting problem. In interposing its own workable solution to the persistent difficulty, the movement becomes socially organized in its own right. The second test of a social movement can be phrased in the question, Will success spoil the movement? When the movement becomes a going concern, maintaining organizational routine sometimes becomes more important than the movement's original goals.[1] The movement is then in real danger of becoming a member of the Establishment, if not an Establishment in its own right. Friendly critics of Alcoholics Anonymous, for example, decry its increasing tendencies toward formalization and reduction of sponsor-protégé relationships.[2]

The emergence, development, organization, and changes

Reprinted from *Mental Hygiene* 51 (October 1967): 552-60 by permission of the publisher.

in the idea of a halfway house for the rehabilitation of homeless alcoholics can be understood best as a social movement. And at this very moment, the idea of a halfway house as a social movement seems rather insecurely poised halfway between meeting the first test of a movement, namely, getting results, and the second test, coping with its own organizational problems.

The present chapter analyzes this submovement at this critical juncture, halfway between obtaining results and solving the organizational problem.

the Situation of the Homeless Alcoholic

In categorizing the alcoholic, one can focus on his acts, his attributes as an actor, his situation, and the consequences of his actions for himself and others. All of these are most relevant, though the weight to be attached to any one of them will no doubt vary from time to time. But most critical is the social definition of the alcoholic and the alcoholic's definition of himself in response to that social definition.

The homeless alcoholic, then, is a person who has no regular membership in a family unit of whatever kind, is socially isolated, is usually jobless, and suffers more injuries than he causes through excessive drinking. What complicates this definition is that the person to whom it is being affixed may not agree with any or all of its particulars. Similarly, people who come into frequent contact with the person may or may not agree. The fact of the matter is that both will use whatever parts of the definition are convenient for them at that time, in that place, and in that situation.

For example, it may be convenient for the person so defined to claim that he is homeless if he seeks shelter, or to ask for work if he sees himself as jobless. Similarly, it may also be convenient for him to claim that he is an alcoholic if his self-inflicted injuries are more than he can handle. But, also, it may be convenient for him to claim that he is socially isolated when he is in search of drinking company. Much will depend on his situation and with whom he is talking at the moment.

The alcoholic's situation is most crucial in the formulation of both social and self definitions; for, inevitably, no one ever meets him when he exhibits the pure essence of homeless alcoholism. Everybody—well-wishers, rehabilitators, neutrals, or evil-doers—always meets him in a particular situation. The inability to define his situation correctly and to produce an adequate response to it is the basis for the persistent institutional failure that ultimately gave rise to the halfway house movement. And the simple, obvious fact is that the situation in which anyone, particularly those who are official agents of social control, confronts a homeless alcoholic is always one of transition.

It might be well to see him as the "man between." When drunk, he is between a state of social awareness and unconsciousness. On the street, sober, he is frequently on his way from jail, hospital, mission, or clinic to a job, a "flop," a drinking group, or a solitary bottle. He may often claim that he is short only the price of a drink; supply his want, and he is off to the nearest bar or package store. There are, however, other shortages that cannot be met so easily. And it is these shortages that guarantee that, unless they are met, he will be back to ask for the price of a drink again, that he will continue to be in transition simply because no person, group, or agency can perform successfully in the role of go-between.

Most agents of social control, official or unofficial, punishment-oriented or treatment-oriented, meet the homeless alcoholic in transition. And, for the most part, it is usually at the point of release from an official establishment, such as a mission, a jail, a hospital. Invariably, the first words out of the man's mouth are "I just got out of . . ." And the reason the man is destined to meet some agent of social control (and alcoholism counselors as well as police officers are here included as such agents) is because of some inability to cope with his acute release problem.

Upon release from an official establishment that has just finished housing, punishing, or treating him, the homeless alcoholic almost achieves pure essence. For now he is acutely homeless, socially isolated, jobless, and still very much the alcoholic regardless of how sober he seems to be at the particular moment. Given the fact that he generally lacks social skills for making contact with legitimate persons who uphold conventionality and has few technical skills to make any exchanges with them worth their while, he is thrust back upon meeting his transitional state in typical fashion—hunt up cronies, go in on a bottle, and while away the day in seeming nonchalance. Cronies answer the problem of social isolation; the bottle solves the problem of how he will define himself at that moment. Shelter for the night, the traditional "flop," even a job may all be obtained. But arrest and incarceration are soon to follow; and arrest for public intoxication activates the correctional cycle whose business is persistent institutional failure.[3]

the Social Background of Institutional Failure

A man who is homeless, socially isolated, usually jobless, and an alcoholic comes into frequent and increasing contact with agencies of social control. None, apparently, is able to assist the man in dealing with his transitional state so that he can permanently find a home, conventional associations, work, and sobriety. The simplest explanation, of course, is that the man really doesn't seek these values; or that he seeks them, but in the wrong times, places, and circumstances; or that he seeks them, yet is really unable to manage them if he does realize them. No doubt all this is true.

But truth has an interactional character, for it takes at least two people to sustain a given definition of the situation. Agents and agencies of social control find their work with homeless alcoholics much easier if they define them at face value. And, since these faces are frequently dirty and unshaven and show the ravages of drink, it is easier to say "once a drunk, always a drunk." Here counselor and client agree on a definition of the situation on which both of them can act, thereby creating the situation itself.

Obviously, the homeless alcoholic bears some responsibility for the failure of institutions to control him effectively. But these institutions, similarly, must bear an equal if not a greater responsibility for that failure. Study of the social conditions of this failure may suggest a set of conditions that might facilitate rehabilitation. Analysis of institutional failure may similarly suggest what gave rise to the halfway house as a social movement.

Social systems all have the dual task of defining and enforcing moral rule. Definition of, and instruction in, moral rule is called socialization. Enforcement of moral rule is called social control. Changes in complex modern society affect both socialization and social control and establish the conditions of institutional failure in rehabilitating homeless alcoholics. The words "bureaucratization," "industrialization," and "urbanization" sum up these far-reaching changes, which also make it possible, at the same time, for the halfway house movement to emerge.

1. *Industrialization.* First, a new social form for producing goods and services evolved. Industrialization consists of a special way of organizing the production of goods and services, making extensive use of machine tools. Agriculture, for example, today is highly industrialized, a rational business enterprise in its own right. One concomitant of industrialization

is the constant upgrading of the social and technical skills of workers who will use the new tools. The other is a decrease in the need for a large supply of unskilled labor. The hobo, who followed the crops as a migratory worker, has all but disappeared, supplanted by a much older, but equally unskilled, homeless man who lives all year in the Skid Row quarter, who tries to comply with the independent cultural tradition of the hobo in a social situation in which the dependent role actually makes better sense.[4]

2. *Urbanization.* Industrialization, in turn, only speeds up urbanization. More and more people now live in urban areas (for the first time, in 1960, the U.S. Census showed more Americans living in urban than in rural areas), and the trend continues unabated. Urbanization reduces the ability of the family to perform its socializing functions. There are now several social codes from which to choose, as well as more opportunities to disobey them without being caught. And, as all studies show, the frequency of regular drinking rises with the degree of urbanization. There are more stresses and strains in urban life, and therefore more chances that some people will seek relief from their acute personal and social discomforts in extensive drinking.

3. *Bureaucratization.* Institutions of socialization and social control, such as the school on the one hand, and the prison or mental hospital on the other, become increasingly bureaucratized. A new social form for the administration of persons who staff large, complex organizations and who are sometimes inmates in them emerges. Impersonality, specific rules, hierarchy, and specialization of tasks characterize bureaucracy.[5] But, other things being equal, bureaucratization in social control agencies, in turn, frequently means that organizational success often depends upon therapeutic or correctional failure.

Routine processing of the many inmates who come before agents of social control in these large, complex organizations becomes the rule. Pilgrim State Hospital in New York, for example, is a skyscraper of the sick. Here, over 15,000 mental patients live in what some call a "human warehouse." Impersonality, formal rules, hierarchy, and task specialization cause clients to become faceless, to lose individuality, to become numbers, and to accept the stereotyping with which the organization manages them. The result is that prisons and mental hospitals succeed as going concerns only to fail as corrective or rehabilitative enterprises.

These are the social conditions that spell institutional failure in the rehabilitation of homeless alcoholics. These are the selfsame features that spelled failure in the rehabilitation of non-homeless alcoholics and spawned the birth of Alcoholics Anonymous. The established ways, for instance, of defining alcoholics and of ignoring, avoiding, punishing, or even treating them for their highly stigmatized condition all contributed to the perpetuation rather than the alleviation of their acute personal problem. Faced with the persistent failure of persons, groups, and agencies to understand and cope with their dilemma, alcoholics had no recourse but to rally around the call of a leader. They banded together, met, formulated a program, set forth their objectives, and sought to change their situation. Their program worked, and Alcoholics Anonymous became a successful movement.[6]

There are ironies in the rehabilitation of alcoholics as a social movement. For the movement to prosper and grow, particularly so far as Alcoholics Anonymous are concerned, it must always seek out new clients. The members must "carry the message," they must seek out and make converts. For, in sobering up others, they themselves maintain a more secure grasp on sobriety, particularly in the early stages of A. A. affiliation. Yet for A. A. to be started and to gain adherents and a following, it was absolutely necessary to distinguish in the minds of recruits that one need not be a Skid Row bum to be an alcoholic. (Until that distinction is made—and there are probably millions of people today who are still unable to make that distinction—the "hidden" alcoholic continues to *(a)* deny his alcoholism or *(b)* affirm it publicly only in the privacy of Alcoholics Anonymous meetings.) Having succeeded in making this important distinction, the movement to rehabilitate alcoholics has now begun to turn more attention to the eyesore, the stereotype, the public drunk, to the homeless alcoholic himself. The movement can now seek out as clients those who were at one time most likely to endanger its own early beginnings.

Structural Principles of the Halfway House

The halfway house was born, then, out of institutional failure to cope with homelessness, social isolation, joblessness, and alcoholism. The man between, the homeless alcoholic, in a state of perpetual transition, required a social broker of some kind, an organizational go-between, if he were to negotiate the passage from deviance to conformity. A bureaucratic establishment could not fill this bill of rehabilitation. But how, one might ask, could a halfway house succeed where more organized, more powerful, bigger enterprises had ostensibly failed? Simply by turning the principles of organization of these enterprises upside down the halfway house has established the conditions of institutional success.

The new movement has spawned residential centers of many varieties: some are public, others are private; some are rural, others are urban; some are found in houses, others, in missions or in hospitals; some charge a lot, others charge nothing at all; some have limited lengths of stay, others, unlimited stays—and so on. The list is capable of indefinite expansion.[7]

This seemingly endless variety, however, should not suggest infinite complexity. Behind this apparent complexity and variety there is a certain simplicity, which all halfway houses share. Certain factors, common to all, constitute the structural principles of halfway houses. They are four in number; all, as should be readily apparent, are reactions to bureaucratic structures.

1. *Small size.* Large organizations make their clients feel like pebbles on the beach, or like cards, easily lost in the organizational shuffle. Once the clients come to feel that no one in the institution cares about their welfare, it is only a matter of time before they come to look upon themselves in exactly the same fashion. Eventually, being apathetic about themselves and their acute personal problems becomes for them a natural state of affairs. Thus they simply come to accept the large organization's definition of them.

No halfway house worthy of the name has more than 25 clients; some have only 10 or 15. In all of them there is an unmistakable trend toward smallness. Simply by reducing the number of clients, the halfway house makes it possible for the staff to get to know the client, and for the client to learn the getting-well role the staff would like him to assume in place of the deviant sick roles.[8]

2. *Simple rules.* A large book of innumerable rules, complete with precise specifications of tasks and of who can and cannot do what to, for, and with whom, betokens bureaucracy. Some predictable consequences are extreme specialization, formalized routines, and the sluggishness that people associate with the word "bureaucracy" when it is used in evaluative terms. As the world drives on and on toward complexity, halfway houses strive for simplicity and "human" scope.

One means of accomplishing this is to have a set of simple rules, understandable ones, and a small and consistent number at that. Thus, a typical halfway house will insist on strict abstinence, have a curfew, and require the payment of rent and the performance of gainful employment "on the outside" and certain housekeeping duties on the inside. It may or may not require attendance at certain kinds of group meetings, such as A. A. or group therapy. Beyond that, there are no further formal rules; and frequently these rules are never formalized, but are handed down by word of mouth and honored as practices rather than as precepts.

3. *Reduction of status differences.* Additional consequences of the bureaucratic process, arising from extreme specialization, are a set of powerful status differences between counselors and clients. Eventually, given other problems, counselors spend more time defending their social position than in helping their clients to get well. Size, numerous and complex rules, formal atmosphere, and marked status differences all conspire to cut down meaningful contact between counselors and clients. What little contact is left is often negative in sentiment and neutral in outcome, if not actually antitherapeutic. At the least, communication between counselor and client is non-existent or at outright cross-purposes.

Many halfway houses employ as staff counselors men who are recovered alcoholics, frequently members of Alcoholics Anonymous. Many of these men were formerly homeless alcoholics, well-versed in homelessness, social isolation, joblessness, and alcoholism. As "experts" their rank and experience are therefore not so far removed from those of the residents that meaningful communication cannot take place. In general, even when counselors in halfway houses are non-alcoholics, every effort is bent toward reducing status symbols that impede communication.

4. *Informality.* A large helping organization sustains an impersonal, matter-of-fact, social atmosphere. Formality, for the most part, describes its characteristic style of social interaction. Essentially, all participants are strangers. All deal with one another with but a fragment of their personalities, and usually that fragment is but the public behavior that their position in the organization calls for. The words "cold" and "distant" always come to mind when people describe their experiences in any of these vast social establishments. The lack of warmth and the social distance depend rather heavily on the personal fragmentation the large, complex organization actually requires if it is to function "successfully."

Again, in reaction to bureaucratic institutions, the unmistakable trend in all halfway houses is toward an informal, homelike atmosphere. Social arrangements reminiscent of a large, extended, and happy family seem to be the goal. Some are able to produce this atmosphere quite naturally by having staff and residents both eat and drink together. In addition to taking meals together, staff and residents drink a lot of coffee together throughout the day. Here it may be true that the customs of the bar and tavern milieu have infiltrated the halfway house "culture." Now, however, the customs in the milieu enforce the norm of sobriety rather than inebriety.

These structural principles are the basic premises of the halfway house as a social movement. Born of the institutional failures of the complex agencies of social control, they have been established so that the halfway house may yield institutional success. The shift has been from big house to small house.

The ideology of the halfway house, upon which it bases its hopes for success, can be summarized as follows: As size decreases, residents have more of a chance to get to know one another as complete individuals. As the rules shrink in size and increase in clarity, interaction may prove much easier, particularly for persons not especially noted for their interpersonal prowess. And, with easier interaction, consensus becomes more likely. As status differences between expert and client shrink, communication can proceed more easily, reach its mark, and take effect. Informality, in making for a homelike atmosphere, can induce a desire to remain a member of the group, to abide by the rules, and thus to be subject to increasingly positive influences to change behavior, the prime objective of the halfway house.[9]

the Halfway House Movement at Midpassage

The movement itself is in a state of transition at the same time that it labors on behalf of homeless alcoholics who would negotiate their return to conformity. If it is to negotiate its own trip from tentative origins to steady growth, it has to pass the two tests of a social movement, as noted earlier: it needs to get results and then to solve the organizational problems that confront all social movements. These questions of results and administration can be considered under the four rubrics that follow.

1. *Organization and society.* At present, relations between any halfway house and the larger society couldn't be better. "Halfway house" is a term to conjure with; under appropriate social conditions, one can even conjure up a building, a staff, and a budget simply by mentioning this magic term. Furthermore, the prestige and drawing power of the halfway house are not limited to alcoholic rehabilitation. Though halfway houses are hard to define, new ones appear almost daily in the world of treatment and corrections. There are, conservatively, about fifty halfway houses for returning mental patients, besides the untold and growing numbers for paroled prisoners and drug addicts.[10]

Coupled with this growing organizational prestige, strangely, is a lack of concern about measuring the results the halfway house is uniquely constructed to obtain. At present, though there are signs of change, the claims of success for halfway houses must be taken on faith. Much of the literature on them consists, broadly, of testimonials, endorsements, institutional advertising, or even, occasionally, outright bragging. Though there are now, by conservative estimates, at least a hundred halfway houses for alcoholics in this country, perhaps only three of them have ever given any attention to obtaining an independent assessment of their effectiveness. Here a word to the wise may suffice. Unless halfway houses give some thought to independent studies of their functioning, they are very likely to disappear from the rehabilitation scene as fast as they appeared.

Enthusiasm sustains motivation for workers in this area and for the public at large. But, if this is not quickly used to obtain systematic data on structure and functioning, types of clients, and measures of effectiveness, the public will be raising questions that those in the halfway house movement will be unprepared to answer. Without these systematic answers, the prestige of the halfway house will be found to rest solely on loud voices rather than verified knowledge.

2. *Relations among organizations.* Although the public relations of the halfway house movement are, in general, quite good, its relations with other agencies of social control, both within and outside the field of alcoholic rehabilitation, could stand a vast improvement. Many halfway houses open up without first seeing if there is a need for the services they seek to render, without consulting with other agencies servicing the homeless alcoholic population; and, once open, they blithely go their own way. Having found the one true message, they cannot waste time in listening to others, since the other agencies have been tarred with the brush of institutional failure.

This form of parochialism can fast wear out a welcome that may not have been the warmest to begin with. People in the halfway house movement have a splendid new idea, based on sound principles of rehabilitation of alcoholics. Nevertheless, they are Johnny-come-latelies to rehabilitation in general, and to rehabilitation of alcoholics in particular. Social welfare is rapidly becoming one of this country's largest industries. If halfway houses cannot learn the techniques of community organization and how to get along and co-operate with the entire network of social agencies, they will very quickly become the junk heap of alcoholic rehabilitation, performing for that network of agencies the same role as Skid Row performs for the average large American city.

3. *Internal relations.* All reactions, of course, invite, and usually get, their own reactions in turn. In quite properly reacting against the faults

of bureaucracy, halfway houses came into being as a defense against institutionalization. There are signs, however, that an excess of informality can have negative effects in two important areas, therapeutic policy and orderly administration.

(a) Therapeutic policy. In the halfway house, the house director is a key figure, perhaps the dominant one, the one setting the over-all stamp on the manner in which therapeutic policy is shaped and executed.[8] This concentration of power leaves room for personal feelings to play a large part, and makes it difficult to know if a simple rule in a supposedly simple organization is really a rule or not. Charismatic leaders of halfway houses may be the most effective leaders, but it is still hard to routinize charisma. Stability is an essential in any therapeutic policy, and homeless alcoholics, perhaps more than other social deviants, need more, rather than less, routine.

(b) Orderly administration. The staff in some halfway houses, other things being equal, would much prefer to be alcoholism counselors rather than administrators or overseers. Frequently, because of shortages, however, the staff often finds itself performing both roles. It is very hard to develop counseling rapport with a man whom you must also command, and sometimes even punish. Yet, in the solution of this role conflict (usually in favor of being a good counselor), orderly administration suffers.[11]

In addition, there are signs that house operations and fiscal management lack system. Naturally, everyone on the staff is most anxious to get on with the business of rehabilitating homeless alcoholics. Detail work is bothersome; in some state-operated halfway houses, it is seen as "red tape" or the "busy" work designed by administrators who don't truly understand the first things that come first in rehabilitating the homeless alcoholic. However, unless more attention is given to running the allegedly simple organization in accordance with sound methods of administration, the entire halfway house movement is in jeopardy.

4. *Counselor-client relations.* Counselors on halfway house staffs, particularly when they are recovered alcoholics, often victimize themselves, perhaps more often their clients, by their beliefs. Abstinence sometimes makes a staff heart grow harsher as contact with difficult clients increases. A natural defense is the use of typifications, or unkind categorical generalizations, about the resident alcoholics.

For instance, the alcoholic is widely known for his dependency. Halfway house ideology requires the staff to get clients to transfer dependency on alcohol to the halfway house, its staff, its rules, its residents, in some therapeutic combination thereof. Unless some care is exercised, staff members can find that they have actually created a dependency that they are not very anxious to break, for there is power in such relationships. Without the natural checks and balances that can operate against such relations in a somewhat larger organization, the staff may become manipulative without being therapeutic. When that comes about, it is sometimes difficult to distinguish the manipulator from the manipulated. Therefore, unless counselors on halfway house staffs become aware of the kinds of feelings that underlie these relationships, they are apt to extend the very dependency they seek to check.

Notes

[1] Robert Michels, *Political Parties* (New York: Collier Books, 1962).

[2] Milton A. Maxwell, "An Exploratory Study: Alcoholics Anonymous and Professional Relations," in *Selected Papers* Fifteenth Annual NAAAP Meetings (Washington, D.C.: North American Association of Alcoholism Programs, 1965), pp. 115-30.

[3] David J. Pittman and C. Wayne Gordon, *Revolving Door* (New Haven: Yale Center of Alcohol Studies, 1958).

[4] Nels Anderson, *Men on the Move* (Chicago: University of Chicago Press, 1940).

[5] Peter Blau, *Bureaucracy in Modern Society* (New York: Random House, 1956).

[6] *Alcoholics Anonymous* (New York: Works Publishing, Inc., 1945).

[7] Edward Blacker and David Kantor, "Half-Way Houses for Problem Drinkers," *Federal Probation* 24 (June 1960): 18-23.

[8] David Landy and Milton Greenblatt, *Halfway House* (Washington, D. C.: U. S. Department of Health, Education, and Welfare, 1965).

[9] Thomas B. Richards, "The Function of the Halfway House in the Rehabilitation of Male Alcoholics," in *Selected Papers*, Raymond L. Buckler School of Alcoholic Studies (Avon Park: Florida Alcoholic Rehabilitation Program, 1964), pp. 114-23.

[10] Robert G. Meiners, "A Halfway House for Parolees," *Federal Probation* 29 (June 1965): 47-52.

[11] Earl Rubington, "Organizational Strains and Key Roles," *Administrative Science Quarterly* 9 (March 1965): 350-69.

Chapter XIV

Legal Commitment and Hospital Behavior

Hospital patients, like heroes, are made, not born. Many people, including the patient himself, have spent much time and labor in training the patient for his difficult social role. Long before he ever sets foot in a hospital, the patient has heard things said and seen things done about hospitals and illnesses. By the time he enters the hospital, he has been prepared for a certain kind of experience.

Nine times out of ten, the patient's training and prior information have been incorrect in some very important respects. Then both he and the hospital staff have to set to work to *(a)* undo and correct the past errors, and *(b)* train him to perform as the hospital expects. Frequently the hospital's training is as bad as the patient's prior expectations. The conditions are then ripe for a mutually difficult and unsatisfactory experience for all concerned. Usually the result of this experience is that the patient is typed as a "recalcitrant patient." This is a very "bad name" to have for one's self in any hospital in general, and in tuberculosis santitaria in particular.

Just as frequently, the hospital's training is even better than the patient had anticipated. Then the results are mutually satisfying in the short run, though not necessarily in the long run. Patients who are typed as "good patients" have been

Reprinted from *Mental Hygiene* 53 (January 1969): 41-53 by permission of the publisher.

well trained and respond quickly to both treatment and hospital staff. Some patients in this category become *over*-trained. Illness becomes a way of life; they find a home in the hospital, and then make every effort to stay home.

In either case, both types of patient—the "recalcitrant patient" and the "good patient"—were trained to assume these hospital roles. On the one hand, they brought certain native talents and skills and ideas to these roles; on the other, the hospital routine and its staff assisted them in organizing these talents and skills into these two kinds of hospital roles. In advance of hospitalization, patients have little or erroneous knowledge and little power. After a number of hospitalizations, their knowledge increases, and sometimes so does their power. To the extent that they and the staff are willing that they share some of this power, to that extent can they all collaborate on achieving the hospital's stated goals of the restoration of health. To the extent that they are unwilling (either staff or patients or both), to that extent will they be in conflict, open or hidden, in seeking the stated goals of health.

In training patients for their hospital roles, then, it is a moot question whether the hospital and its staff want slowly to give knowledge and power to the patient in exchange for co-operative performance as a patient or whether they prefer to hold the lion's share of both knowledge and power. The hospital's policy in these matters affects the manner in which it trains its patients and how they respond to this in-service training in the full-time job of being a hospital patient. By the same token, the manner in which hospital staff members share knowledge and power among themselves determines morale among treatment personnel.

Frequently, of course, hospitals have very little control over the conditions under which patients come to them and the stock of information the newly admitted patient has on arrival. These are critical factors in determining whether or not the hospital succeeds in making patients out of the human raw material that has been brought to it for health processing.

The burden of my remarks here will stress the consequences of legal commitment on the hospital behavior of the tuberculous alcoholic. For example, the "recalcitrant patient" is the usual result of legal commitment. I want, first, to point out why that is the typical case and, second, to suggest some legal as well as medical ways of reducing the recruitment, selection, and training of "recalcitrant patients."

The case in point is, of course, the tuberculous alcoholic. To make the case, I shall first deal briefly with knowledge and power in hospitals. I shall then consider the social conditions of the model treatment relationship. Next, I shall show why tuberculosis, alcoholism, and mental illness point, in ascending order, to increased recalcitrance in treatment relationships, and how patients as well as hospital staffs try to come to terms with recalcitrance. Then I shall examine commitment laws in theory and in practice and the consequences these laws have for treatment relationships. And, finally, I shall try to suggest some factors that might mitigate recalcitrance as a social process in hospitals dealing with tuberculous alcoholics.

Knowledge and Power in the Hospital

By knowledge I here mean no more, but certainly no less, than a stock, of information about what is about to happen in the next social situation one steps into. By power I here mean no more, but certainly no less, than the ability to have something to say about whether or not what is about to happen actually does take place. Two examples, both from mental hospitals, will illustrate the point. One deals with patients, the other with staff or, more particularly, with mental hospital attendants. In both instances, however, a change in the knowledge of both patients and attendants affected their power to labor on behalf of, or in opposition to, hospital goals.

First, the case of the mental patients (1): Some years ago, at Worcester State Hospital, the staff became concerned about the mental state in which patients arrived and the results of their agitation, both for themselves and for hospital staff. For a variety of reasons not hard to imagine, patients, on arrival, were intensely fearful, anxiety-ridden, and markedly disturbed. In accordance with the laws of collective behavior, they communicated their fears and anxieties to the staff. The staff reflected the incoming patients' fears without reducing them, with the obvious result that these fears increased. In time, some staff members as well as patients became involved in reciprocal agitation since they were total strangers in a beginning relationship of mutual uncertainty and distrust.

To change this situation and, in effect, reduce the tension in the hospital atmosphere, two psychologists on the staff introduced a very simple procedure. Each patient, on arrival, was ushered into the admitting office and was given a letter from the superintendent to read. Regardless of their state on admission, all patients had a chance to read this letter from the superintendent, who welcomed them to the hospital in much the same way persons receive guests in their own homes. Next, the receiving staff person presented the patient with a set of expectations. These informed him that he was in a mental hospital, that he was a patient, how long he might be expected to stay, what the hospital's rules and regulations were, and just what he might expect of the hospital during his stay.

Since this was a before-and-after study, the psychologists had obtained measures of the agitation and its consequences for a six-month period before the institution of the new admission policy. They then collected similar data in the ensuing six months and showed, again as might be expected, a marked reduction in both patient and staff agitation.

The simple interpretation of these changes seems rather obvious. The hospital began training the patient for his hospital role immediately on admission. By increasing his stock of information about what was to happen, it actually reduced his power to wreck the intended happenings by spontaneous combativeness, withdrawal, or delaying tactics. At the same time, it increased his power to consent to these happenings, since he was now made, to some extent at least, a partner in them.

Second, the case of the mental hospital attendants (2): Some years back, in a Canadian mental hospital, psychiatrists in charge of the continued treatment of chronic schizophrenics became concerned with back ward atmosphere. Patients were combative with one another and attendants, broke furniture, and soiled linen through their incontinence. The psychiatrists sought to change this situation. They had no illusions about the recovery of these patients, most of whom had been in the hospital for ten or more years. They had hopes, however, of changing the ward atmosphere.

First, they recorded over a six-month period the amount of furniture-breakage and its cost, the frequency of combat between patients and between patients and attendants, and the ward laundry bill. Then, they instituted a round of ward staff meetings in which they sat down with nurses and ward attendants and discussed with them ward treatment policy and administration and solicited their views and opinions on these matters on a regular basis.

The consequences of these meetings were rather striking. To be sure, no patients recovered and were discharged. But the atmosphere of the ward shifted markedly. The attendants' morale rose sharply as they came to feel, for the first time, that they were a part of the hospital and had some knowledge of, and say about, what took place on the ward. Further, in the six-month period during which these meetings took place, the number of fights decreased considerably, and furniture and laundry bills were drastically reduced.

Here again we have a dramatic example of how shifts in knowledge and power affected the behavior of both hospital staff and patients. As the attendants' morale in the Canadian hospital rose, they conducted themselves in a different manner on the ward. The result, indirectly, was that they retrained the chronic patients on their back wards to conduct themselves differently as patients—hence the decline in fights, breakage, and soiling. In some ways the patients must have come to see that their own power to wreak havoc no longer needed to be exercised. The hospital had gotten the patients' message, somehow, and had changed the patients' knowledge and power to disrupt ward activities.

Both of these examples revealed rather nicely that a stock of information on orderly hospital procedure actually made it possible for staff and patients alike to contribute to an orderly rountine. And both also revealed that some sharing of knowledge and power made for predictable and more regular hospital process. In neither case did the sharing imply equality of status, but in both cases it did imply a common humanity.

Treatment as a Social Relationship

Whether a patient is "recalcitrant" or "good," he is always so in a certain social context. He can only be "recalcitrant" or "good" in relation to another staff figure. To say this is only to point out that treatment is but another of the many kinds of social relationships that men establish and sustain with one another. In the cases just cited, for instance, newly admitted patients in the Worcester State Hospital, knowing what to expect on admission, were able to assume the patient role that much better. Assuming a role means taking a given and usually expected part in a customary social relationship. But to take that part the person must also know the counterpart, what the other person can be expected or counted on to do. The self and the other, taken together, are the social context.

"It takes two to tango." Similarly, doctors and nurses without patients or patients without doctors and nurses are in no relationship to each other. A husband implies a wife, and vice versa; the same, obviously, is true for parents and children. The main point is that it is practically impossible to think of a social role without conceiving of its reciprocal, its counterpart. Thus, the recalcitrant patient requires someone to be recalcitrant with, just as the good patient requires someone with whom he can be good. It is perhaps not so obvious that some recalcitrant patients are actually good patients from the perspectives of some staff members whereas some good patients are recalcitrant from the viewpoint of other staff members. Furthermore, recalcitrant patients can, in time, become good patients, just as good patients can also, in time, become recalcitrant patients.

Whether or not health will be restored, then, depends quite heavily on how well people perform their assigned roles in the treatment relationship. If we think of the treatment relationship as having a career of its own over time, then the optimum conditions for such a relationship can be met if the ailing person and the helping agent take certain roles with one another in sequence (3). The optimum model may be illustrated thus:

Ailing person	*Helping agent*
1. Recognizes condition, admits need	1. Defines the situation
2. Decides to get rid of it	2. States the solution
3. Comes in freely for help	3. Motivates, supports admission
4. Complies with orders	4. Gives orders
5. Gets rid of condition	5. Certifies condition is gone

The optimum conditions for a successful treatment relationship occur when a helping agent defines the situation as troublesome and the ailing person recognizes the definition and admits the need for help. In the next step the agent points out the solutions available, and the ailing person decides to avail himself of help and get rid of the troublesome condition. The agent motivates and supports the ailing person as he moves into the situation of help, and the ailing person comes in freely of his own accord. Once the relationship has been established, the helping agent issues orders designed to solve the presenting problem; and the ailing person complies with these orders. Finally, the agent certifies that the condition is gone, and person and agent sever their relationship soon after certification.

This hypothetical model can account more or less well for most of the medical conditions that bring people to doctors. The person, for instance, says, "Ouch"; the doctor looks around for the source of pain and prescribes drugs or changes in actions; the person takes his medicine; the pain goes, and the patient is relieved. That, in a nutshell, is how the medical model is supposed to work. It does so for countless millions precisely because at each step in the sequence patients and doctors collaborate in the pursuit of health goals, and for countless millions the health of the ailing person is restored. With that, the treatment relationship comes to an end, to the mutual satisfaction of both parties to the relationship.

Unfortunately, the model does not always work out in accordance with these role expectations for all kinds of illnesses. When that happens there is a change in the relations between ailing person and helping agent. Then, either the treatment relationship has not been established in the first place, or maintained in the second. And, as is commonly known, even when establishment and maintenance take place according to custom, frequently health is not restored. In this last case, both parties to the relationship must adjust to an outcome at variance with their joint aspirations. For example, when the operation is successful, but the patient dies, the physician must make a reasonable accounting to himself and his colleagues as well as to the deceased patient's relatives.

Certain illnesses militate against the establishment, maintenance, and successful fruition of the conventionally conceived treatment relationship. Tuberculosis, alcoholism, and mental illness, in ascending order, are illnesses or processes that interfere with the traditional concept of how treatment relationships ought to work out over time. And the concept of how much time the relationship ought to consume is one very important aspect of the relationship from the viewpoint both of the ailing person and of the helping agent.

Treatment relationships in all three of these conditions are time consuming since they do extend over large portions of the patient's life-history. In fact, because tuberculosis, alcoholism, and mental illness have higher status than the ordinary common cold, they require great investments of time on the part of both helping agent and ailing persons. The very time perspective connected with the course of these illnesses deters many people from seeking out, let alone remaining in, the treatment relationship. It may be most unwise to deny the condition, but it is perfectly understandable why the prospective patient would want to do so.

In the case of tuberculosis, for instance, a person recognizes the condition once a doctor puts a name on it. He usually wishes to get rid of the disease. Going into a hospital for treatment, however, is not done as freely as all would like. Furthermore, because of the uncertainty of prognosis and the element of time involved, gaining and keeping compliance with orders (many of which seem quite irrational to patients) become harder. And, finally, the patient is never certified that he is rid of the condition. He must live with it, though the disease is in an arrested state.

In the case of alcoholism, the alcoholic is usually the last to admit his illness no matter how many doctors name it for him. Even when he admits rather than denies the illness, he is of two minds about it. He wants to stop drinking, and he also wants to continue. As has been stated, alcohol is his crutch, his curse, and his delight (4). He'll not give it up lightly, nor will he come into treatment freely. The extent of his compliance with orders will vary directly with the acuteness of his pain and distress; shortly after successful "drying-out," he may well forget how and why he came to the hospital in the first place. Finally, alcoholism, like tuberculosis, is a condition the patient never gets rid of, even if he complies with the doctor's orders. He must learn to live with his illness, and that is a full-time and sometimes very painful job.

In the case of mental illness, the patient usually does not recognize the condition, let alone admit it, and hence finds little that he would want to get rid of. He must be dragged into treatment, and is most unwilling to comply with orders whose meaning and intent are unclear to him, if not actually superfluous. Again, it is unlikely that anyone will certify that he has gotten rid of the condition. The best he can hope for is a "remission of symptoms."

All three of these illnesses therefore place marked strains on the usual treatment relationships. In addition, each of these illnesses carries a good deal of stigma and social punishment for persons said officially to suffer from them. That knowledge alone sometimes is sufficient for persons to insist that they do not have the illnesses even when helping agents have collected a preponderance of clinical evidence that they do.

Besides the stigma, there are a few other social and cultural factors that either delay the recognition of the illness or strengthen the denial. Social classes vary in the education they share and in the value they place on physical and mental health. They also vary in the amount of deviance by reason of mental or physical illnesses they will tolerate; in what continued ill-health can cost them in status, family, and work relations and in what they may gain from its continuance; and, finally, in the extent to which they agree with medical authorities on a number of factors—not only on definitions of health and its absence, but also on what to do to sustain and maintain health.

It seems clear that persons said to have any of these conditions would be most reluctant to enter treatment. Further, given their reluctant entry into treatment, it also seems quite clear that they would continue to be unwilling patients, in varying degrees. Consequently, the sociocultural conditions surrounding the definitions of these three illnesses seem to militate against the development of a working treatment relationship as this is customarily defined by helping agents and most ailing persons.

This is not to say that tuberculous patients, alcoholic patients, or mental patients have not entered treatment relationships, performed creditably in them, and, in the bargain, gotten well—far from it, many have. As we come to learn more about the dynamics of treatment relationships and how to arrest the clinical course of these illnesses, even greater numbers can profit. The reluctance to enter, to remain in, and to profit from treatment relationships depends heavily on a proper ratio of informal coercion and social support.

We know, for example, that higher-ranking persons, that is, persons of middle-class or higher social and educational backgrounds, with jobs and families, are much more apt to enter and sustain a relationship with an outpatient alcoholism treatment clinic than is the average Skid Row alcoholic (4). We know, further, that informally both the patient's wife and his employers have said "enter treatment" or else. Given this secret coercion and knowing what he stands to lose, the middle-class "hidden, but respectable" alcoholic enters treatment and, in the bargain, comes to realize a good deal of support from others for continuing his treatment. The average Skid Row alcoholic receives little informal coercion of the same order to engage in treatment; and, were he to do so, he could expect derision and little social support (frequently both, even from persons charged with treating and helping him).

As can be seen from these two contrasting examples, the motivation and the pressure, if not actual coercion, to bring the tuberculous, the alcoholic, the tuberculous alcoholic, and the mentally ill into treatment must come from without. For the reasons cited, the chances of the awareness of difficulty coming from within and the pressures to seek help coming from the same source are considerably reduced, again in ascending order—that is, other things being equal, a person is more apt to seek or accept help for tuberculosis than he would be for alcoholism (particularly since great numbers of people also deny that alcoholism is an illness); and, similarly, he is more apt to seek or accept help for alcoholism than he would be for mental illness. Hence, by a simple law of social life, if there is an absence of self-control that appears to threaten property, other people, or the person himself, then some system of social control must come into play to restrain the person from doing further harm. And that mechanism, of course, is legal commitment, operating, as it does, as part of the police power of the state.

the Theory, Practice, and Consequences of Legal Commitment

Given the understandable reluctance of persons suffering from stigmatized illnesses to enter treatment, some means must be available to force them to seek treatment, at best, or to prevent others from acquiring their ailments, at worst. The constitutionality of the police power to quarantine persons suffering from communicable and serious ailments, such as typhoid, smallpox, and tuberculosis, has been well established for a number of years. Hence, if an x-ray reveals a person to have the positive signs of tuberculosis, a court order remanding that person to a sanitarium can be obtained by a public health officer, almost immediately, should the allegedly tuberculous person seem the least bit reluctant to enter treatment. Similarly, all 50 states have laws for committing the mentally ill. Frequently, alcoholics are committed to state mental hospitals—for example, if they are suffering from any of the alcoholic psychoses—under such legal commitment. Each year a small percentage of first admissions to state hospitals are for alcoholic psychoses (perhaps some 10-15 per cent), and the vast majority of these are commitments under the heading of mental illness (5).

More recently, since the development of state alcoholism rehabilitation programs in the early fifties, laws have been enacted that make it possible to commit alcoholics for the treatment of their illnesses (6). These commitments, it turns out, can be either voluntary, e.g., the person signs himself into a state mental hospital, or involuntary, e.g., a group takes psychiatric action against him to have him commited against his will to a state mental hospital, there to receive treatment.

I shall present a short outline of the theory of legal commitment, how it works in practice, and the consequences of that practice for treatment relationships of alcoholics and tuberculous alcoholics.

The Theory of Legal Commitment

The theory behind the commitment of alcoholics is more or less identical with that underlying court orders quarantining persons with tuberculosis. Police power permits the state to quarantine a person with tuberculosis in a sanitarium, thereby both achieving his enforced isolation from others, to prevent contagion, and also ensuring the beginnings of medical treatment. Except for the manner of initial entry, voluntary and involuntary commitments share certain features so far as the theory of legal commitment goes. In addition, there are some practical similarities, namely, that certain involuntary commitments are actually arrived at by consent, whereas some voluntary commitments are "voluntary" in name only.

The principal features of commitments are a petition, the hearing, the presence or absence of the person and/or legal counsel, the duration of commitment, the place to which the person is committed, the characteristics of the treatment to be administered and received therein, the conditions of discharge, and the protection of civil rights or, more particularly, the rights of redress. Since the police power acts forcibly to bring a person into custody, attention must be directed to safeguarding the person's rights. Stripping a person of his freedom is an extremely serious business, and it is therefore important to guarantee that every effort is made to be certain that a decision to remove personal freedom is not taken lightly. Thus, the burden of proof is on the state to show that the person is a source of potential or actual harm to others and to himself and/or is actually unable to act for himself and his own best interests.

Generally, interested parties petition for a hearing. There is a great range of variation from state to state in who can make the initial petition. With only a few exceptions, the hearing is in a court. In one state, a county health commissioner hears the case; in two others, the head of the hospital himself listens to the petition. In some states, counsel is present; in others, sometimes absent. In some states, the person who is to be committed must be present at the hearing; in others, he need not be. Some states have emergency hearings; and the tendency is to make more and more use of these fast hearings, particularly when the situation seems to warrant immediate action.

Commitments can be for 30, 60, or 90 days or can be indefinite and left to the discretion of the hospital authorities. Most commitments are to state mental hospitals; the remainder are to the state alcoholism rehabilitation program, particularly if it has its own inpatient treatment facilities. The voluntarily committed person can, in some states, should he so wish, ask to sign himself out at any time. In most cases, however, there is a rather long delay before the hospital acts on his petition. In other states, however, he has no way of getting out once he has signed himself in.

Commitment in Practice

There appears to be a good deal of discrepancy between the theory of legal commitment and how it works out in actual daily practice. On the procedural side, legal safeguards are lacking in many instances. In the matter of treating the patient for his illness, there are, similarly, a number of discrepancies. The state, it seems, may be temporarily reducing potential harm to self and others, in addition to property, in the short run. However, doubts have been raised concerning the long-range treatment and changes in the subsequent behavior of the committed inebriate.

A number of studies in recent years have pointed to the illusion of due process in hearings on the commitment of the allegedly mentally ill. There is some impressionistic evidence suggesting that this is also true in hearings committing alcoholics to the state mental hospital. Since I have said "impressionistic" (although "by analogy" might have been a better expression), let me present such evidence as I have.

First, it has been shown in a few systematic studies that in "drunk courts" the average time spent by judges in listening to the pleas of offenders is around 45.0 seconds (7). One study of commitment hearings on the mentally ill in a Midwestern state indicated that the psychiatrists spent no more than ten minutes in deciding whether or not to commit the person to a hospital (8). In addition, in Philadelphia, where there are some 5,000 active cases of tuberculosis, only 63 a year are put into custody by court order (9). The evidence, such as it is, suggests that commitment for tuberculosis and/or alcoholism may well be similar to penal commitment for the crime of public intoxication—that is, only the homeless are arrested, tried, and sentenced for this crime. If all of this evidence is correct, then the state is actually not presuming innocence, but is rather, as many have suggested, presuming guilt in advance, in violation of the theory underlying legal commitment.

Turning to treatment, it is clear, once again, that a number of reasonable objections may be raised concerning the efficacy of the procedure. So far as there is treatment, according to some observers, it is primarily for "drying out." Beyond physical repair, no further attempt is made during the time the alcoholic is in the hospital to engage him in a more intensive kind of treatment relationship. Moreover, some legal commitments are very much like short-term jail sentences, being a maximum of either 15 or 30 days. Again, as numerous observers have pointed out with respect to jail commitments for chronic alcoholics, 15 or 30 days provide little time in which to do anything beyond restoring a degree of physical health.

Finally, there is no escaping the impression that the term "treatment" is really a disguise for an obvious punishment. If so, of course, then the entire procedure is manifestly illegal. In some commitments to a state mental hospital, little if anything is done for the alcoholic. Moreover, for many it is actually a form of cruel and unusual punishment, particularly if they are not segregated from mentally ill patients. In their haste to enforce public morals, some judicial bodies actually violate the law. For instance, in an important appeals court decision some years ago, it was declared unconstitutional to put a person with tuberculosis in a county jail to await treatment (10). In time, it may turn out to be just as illegal to do that with alcoholics. An ostensible commitment to a mental hospital for treatment in which treatment, in fact, does not take place, is a clear violation of the law.

The Consequences for Treatment Relationships

The consequences of commitment for the establishment and maintenance of treatment relationships of alcoholics with hospital staff or, in markedly similar circumstances, of tuberculous alcoholics with hospital or sanitarium staff are rather obvious. To begin with, in the case of certain commitments, as already indicated, there is no treatment for the person to enter into or be recalcitrant about. The absence of treatment is but another name for punishment. In addition, in the case of certain voluntary commitments, it is not uncommon, particularly if the person is a "repeater," to assign him to a ward for the criminally insane. Though told by all that he, an alcoholic, is suffering an illness, he learns through this assignment that it is actually criminal for him to have a relapse, despite the fact that the authorities say he is suffering from a chronic illness.

If, on the other hand, as is true for all tuberculosis hospitals and some state hospitals, a bona fide treatment relationship is available, then once again the circumstances of the admission only deepen the reluctance of the patient to participate in the treatment according to the staff's rules on how to play the hospital treatment game. In time, of course, after the patient has entered the hospital's "revolving door" system (all state hospitals and sanitaria have doors that revolve as frequently, if not more so, than those of the jail), he may develop a *modus vivendi* with staff members who come to know him. When this stage in patient socialization has been reached, however, we have the "good patient" role dedicated to ends other than good health. These well-trained patients comply with the hospital's rules without being at all committed to its treatment regimen and its goals.

This form of adjusting to coercive treatment is more subtle, of course, than assumption of the obvious role of "recalcitrant patient" into which commitment thrusts a person. The problem becomes particularly acute when the person is both tuberculous and alcoholic, for then both he and the staff recognize the signs of the tuberculous condition, but not necessarily those of the alcoholic one. Similarly, both patient and staff agree on getting rid of the tuberculous condition. Thus, when staff members become aware of the alcoholism, they see it as something that interferes with the hospital treatment of tuberculosis, and they react to it more or less as a horse in a stable reacts when he finds a fly on his back. When the patient begins to run bottles in or becomes a "bottle-carrier," the staff disciplines him for the action, rather than seeing it as both a way of coping with hospital confinement and an expression of alcoholism.

There is no question about the problems that alcoholism creates for the staff of the tuberculosis hospital. On the average, the rate of irregular discharge is around 15 percent for non-alcoholic patients; for the alcoholic tuberculous patient, the rate of irregular discharge rises to 60 percent (11). In addition, a high rate of relapse, particularly among homeless alcoholics, results from a return to the kind of social environment in which the tubercle bacillus is said to thrive, something very much akin to, if not actually, Skid Row itself. Hence, if many hospital staff members were to feel frustrated about all this, there would be none to blame them.

Alcoholics on locked or unlocked wards in the sanitarium are great management problems, perhaps a little more so than the run-of-the-mill tuberculous patient, who also requires a great deal of training by staff before he assumes the patient role correctly. The walkaway rate is always fairly high; generally speaking, it is higher among involuntary than voluntary patients. When, as in the case of the homeless alcoholic, who is more and more showing up in the declining number of patients in tuberculosis hospitals in the United States, one adds a difference in values, beliefs, and norms, it is clear that the enforcement of morals in the guise of public health flounders in the face of what seems massive, if not passive, recalcitrance.

On balance, it becomes rather clear why staff members and alcoholic patients in a tuberculosis hospital would have great difficulty entering into, and then sustaining, the treatment relationship. If, as is very often the case, one or both parties to the relationship are unaware of the dual illness, one source of difficulties develops (12). If, on the other hand, the staff is as ignorant about alcoholism as the patients are about tuberculosis, then an even more powerful source of difficulty becomes abundantly clear. If to all of this is added the fact that many patients suffering the dual illness are stereotyped and stigmatized as if they were criminals, are frequently jailed illegally, and are rarely told much of anything about what is going to happen to them and when, it is a wonder that any treatment can occur at all.

Now, in view of the gradual disappearance of tuberculosis in the general population, its marked prevalence among the homeless, the indigent, and the denizens of Skid Row, and the gradual decline of tuberculosis hospitals, the problems we have been considering are apt to get worse before they get better. Workhouses, poor-houses, county farms, and tuberculosis sanitaria are rapidly disappearing; meanwhile, the number of homeless alcoholics who suffer from tuberculosis seems to be rising in existing institutions. Given the increased visibility of multiple-problem, homeless men as Skid Row slowly breaks up and disappears, a wish to enforce public morals rather than to treat illnesses is likely to parallel the continuing frustration of expectations both legal and medical staff face with these highly skilled "recalcitrant patients." We should expect to find, along with greater concern among lawyers for the extension of civil rights to homeless alcoholics, as the *Driver* and *Easter* cases so rightly show, a similar and increasing plea for the use of punishment for those who fail to respond to treatment (13). This paradoxical state is practically upon us, if not already here.

Some of the reactions to the *Driver* and *Easter* cases in Washington, D. C., reveal the crisis in what some newsmen will probably call the "treatment gap." Briefly, both of these important appellate hearings make chronic alcoholism a defense against the crime of public intoxication. Consequently, a judge in Washington can no longer sentence a chronic drunkenness offender to prison if he is satisfied that the person is a bona fide alcoholic. To date some 2,000 offenders have been designated chronic alcoholics.

To implement the *Driver* and *Easter* rulings, judges committed alcoholics arrested for intoxication to the workhouse at Occoquan for a brief period of observation. Lawyers in the *Easter* case looked into this situation and found that the men were actually locked up while they were awaiting observation whereas prisoners were free to parade the workhouse grounds. They also found that the men waited an interminable time, in many cases longer than they would have if they had been sentenced to serve time for public intoxication. Only the aggressive efforts of these lawyers revealed the state of affairs in Washington (10).

All of this is tragic or comic, since a 1947 law requires that judges commit chronic alcoholics to a facility for diagnosis and observation in order to form a treatment plan. Yet, 20 years have passed, and in that time Congress has not seen fit to make the facilities available. Since there are few lawyers examining the situation in the rest of the country, we can be certain that a number of crimes are being committed daily under the guise of "treatment." Thus it is that alcoholism and tuberculosis, at least when housed in certain bodies, can really be called, after Pirandello, two illnesses in search of a treatment.

the Mitigation of Recalcitrance

The evidence suggests that it is pertinent to ask why there is not more recalcitrance in the treatment relationships between tuberculous alcoholics and the helping agents on the staff of the tuberculosis hospital. The sociocultural definition of the illnesses from the point of view of the sufferers, on the one hand, and the management problems the staff has, on the other, guarantee the present state of affairs; and, for the immediate future, there is little reason for the situation to improve.

There are, however, a few things that hospital staffs might do to mitigate, if not reduce, recalcitrance. I should like to make a few suggestions, all of which hinge on the view that the staff in tuberculosis hospitals is a partner in, if not co-producer of, recalcitrance. If, then, staff members reexamine their treatment roles, they may be able to devise ways and means of managing these pervasive problems a little better than they do at present.

So long, of course, as patients continue to enter the hospital by involuntary commitment, there is little the staff can do about the legal issues. If due process of law becomes more of a fact than a theory in legal commitment, then reluctance to enter treatment will diminish, though, of course, in this particular connection, only slightly. But if a sense of injustice does not attend the admission process, the staff has less resistance to fight against. Since that resistance is initially rather massive, help from any quarter is welcome.

Turning now to the matter of knowledge and power, if the staff shares appropriate and accurate information with the unwilling tuberculous alcoholic patient, it can begin to develop a relationship based on trust. Considering this patient's past experience with trust in other human beings, it is clear that his demands may seem inordinate. The truth is occasionally good medicine, particularly if staff members simply live up to their own statements. Unhappily, one of the most pleasant forms of intramural sport in tuberculosis hospitals (and probably in all institutions where a staff exists to "treat" patients) is observing the discrepancy between what the staff says and what it does (13). Patients cannot invest trust for long in a staff that makes promises, in an uncertain ward environment, that it later cannot make good.

So, if the staff tells the truth as often as it can and makes only those promises it can fulfill, it has begun to make some inroads on recalcitrance. If it can explain what is happening and can make it happen in accordance with the expectations it has induced, it can begin to produce and sustain an orderly hospital social world. If it can provide real data for all the sequences the patient role implies for each individual patient, it can produce trust, thereby reducing the additional grounds of recalcitrance.

Finally, if the staff can let the patients teach it what alcoholism is all about, just as it tries to teach the patients what tuberculosis is all

about, then a further condition of recalcitrance will have been considerably reduced. Here, the use of patients who have recovered from both illnesses (though "arrested" is probably the more accurate term) as brokers or middlemen between patients and staff would go far toward easing the breakdown of communication so many observers have commented on. Such a go-between would be of great importance in the case of the homeless alcoholic.

All of these steps could go far toward cutting down the role that moralizing and disciplining have in creating and sustaining patients' reluctance to continue treatment relationships. The staff can afford to be matter-of-fact about alcoholism as well as tuberculosis once it learns the facts, for then it can say to alcoholic patients, just as it tries to do with respect to tuberculosis, "Look, this is where you are and the kinds of troubles you have and can expect to have. When you make up your mind which way you want to go, come see us; and, if we can be of any help at all, then we will do what we can." To do this, of course, the staff must make it possible for the patient to ask for help that the staff can give. When this comes about, reciprocity returns to the treatment relationship. But until it does come about, we should expect recalcitrance, which is no more and no less than a form of negative reciprocity.

References

1. Dembo, Tamara, and Hanfmann, Eugenia. "The Patient's Psychological Situation Upon Admission to a Mental Hospital." *American Journal of Psychology* 47 (July 1935): 381-408.
2. Galioni, E. F.; Adams, F. H.; and Tallman, F. F. "Intensive Treatment of Back-Ward Patients." *American Journal of Psychiatry* 109 (February 1953): 576-83.
3. Parsons, Talcott. *The Social System.* Glencoe, Ill.: The Free Press, 1951, pp. 428-79.
4. Gerard, Donald L. and Saenger, Gerhart. *Out-Patient Treatment of Alcoholism.* Toronto: University of Toronto Press, 1966, pp. 185-91.
5. Moore, Robert A., and Buchanan, Thomas K. "State Hospitals and Alcoholism: A Nation-Wide Survey of Treatment Techniques and Results." *Quarterly Journal of Studies on Alcohol* 27 (September 1966): 459-68.
6. Curran, William J. "Civil Commitment of Alcoholics: A Legal Survey." In *The Legal Issues in Alcoholism and Alcohol Usage.* Boston, Mass.: Boston University Law-Medicine Institute, 1966, pp. 36-70.
7. Oki, Gus. "How the Chronic Drunkenness Offender Views the Police, the Courts and Jail." *Addictions* 11 (Summer 1964): 9-18.
8. Scheff, Thomas J. "The Societal Reaction to Deviance: Ascriptive Elements in the Psychiatric Screening of Mental Patients in a Midwestern State." *Social Problems* 11 (Summer 1964): 401-13.

9. Ottenberg, Donald J. "Experiences in Tuberculosis Control." In *The Alcoholic Tuberculous Patient and the Community.* Glenn Dale, Md.: Glenn Dale Hospital, 1959, pp. 68-78.
10. *District of Columbia* v. *William H. Strother,* 1966.
11. Tesch, Henry T. "Tuberculosis and Alcoholism." *Public Health News* 41 (January 1960): 1-4.
12. Jackson, Joan K. "A Social Science View." In *The Alcoholic Tuberculous Patient and the Community.* Glenn Dale, Md.: Glenn Dale Hospital, 1959, pp. 33-52.
13. Roth, Julius A. "Ritual and Magic in the Control of Contagion." *American Sociological Review* 22 (June 1957): 310-14.